The violent muse

Violence and the Artistic Imagination i̶ ̶ ̶ 1910–1939
Edited by Jana Howlett and Rod Mengham

The violent muse presents a comprehensiv̶ ̶ ̶ ̶ ̶ ̶ ̶ ̶ ̶ ̶ enon
of the aesthetics of sexual and political vi̶ ̶ ̶ ̶ ̶ ̶ ̶ ̶ ̶ ̶lture
of the early twentieth century. Presenting ̶ ̶ ̶ ̶ ̶ ̶ ̶ ̶ ̶cross
disciplines and an analysis of the sources o̶ ̶ ̶ ̶ ̶ ̶ al and
cultural context, this volume provides an unusually broad trea̶ ̶ ̶ ̶ ̶ eme of
violence during this turbulent period.

The major cultural movements and individuals of the early twentieth-century avant-garde are examined for their use of violence as inspiration in their artistic production. Themes explored include: violence and the body; machinery and technology; Vorticism; Dada; Italian Futurism; and Surrealism; violence in the avant-garde cinema; military defeat and the representation of war; the relationship of creativity and violence. Exploring the work of English, German, Italian, French, Spanish, and Russian painters and writers, including Georges Sorel, Wyndham Lewis, Paul Nash, Brecht, and Louis-Ferdinand Céline, the contributors provide an invaluable insight into the early twentieth-century European avant-garde.

This book will be of interest to lecturers and students in the fields of art history, cultural studies and modern languages.

Jana Howlett and Rod Mengham are both Lecturers at the University of Cambridge, Jana Howlett in the Faculty of Modern and Medieval Languages and Rod Mengham in the Faculty of English.

The violent muse

Violence and the artistic
imagination in Europe, 1910–1939

edited by
Jana Howlett and Rod Mengham

Manchester University Press
Manchester and New York

Distributed exclusively in the USA and Canada by St. Martin's Press

Published by Manchester University Press
Oxford Road, Manchester M13 9PL, UK
and Room 400, 175 Fifth Avenue, New York, NY 10010, USA

Distributed exclusively in the USA and Canada
by St. Martin's Press, Inc., 175 Fifth Avenue, New York,
NY 10010, USA

British Library Cataloguing-in-Publication Data
A catalogue record for this book is available from the British Library

Library of Congress Cataloging-in-Publication Data
The Violent muse : violence and the artistic imagination in Europe, 1910–1939
  / edited by Jana Howlett and Rod Mengham.
     p.   cm.
  Includes bibliographical references (p.) and index.
  ISBN 0–7190–3717–4 (hardback), — ISBN 0–7190–3718–2 (pbk.)
  1. Avant-garde (Aesthetics)—History—20th century.   2. Violence
in art.   3. Arts, Modern—20th century.   I. Howlett, Jana.
II. Mengham, Rod, 1953– .
NX650.V5V56   1994
700—dc20   93–28248
                                                                      CIP

ISBN 0 7190 3717 4 *hardback*
       0 7190 3718 2 *paperback*

Photoset in Linotron Sabon
by Northern Phototypesetting Co. Ltd., Bolton

Printed in Great Britain
by Redwood Books, Trowbridge, Wiltshire

Contents

Abbreviations

CP   Bertolt Brecht, *Collected Plays*, vols 1 –, translated by J. Willet and R. Mannheim (London, 1970 –)

GW   Bertolt Brecht, *Gesammelte Werke*, 20 vols (Frankfurt, 1967–82)

IRSL   *Istoriia russkoi sovetskoi literatury*, 4 vols (Moscow, 1967)

MC   *Mort à crédit*, in Louis-Ferdinand Céline, *Collected Works*, vol. 1 (Paris, 1981)

OC   Ramón del Valle-Inclàn, *Obras completas*, 2 vols, (Madrid, 1954)

RLA   *Russkii literaturnyi avangard: Materialy i issledovaniia*, ed. M. Marzaduri, D. Rizzi, M. Evzlin (Trento, 1990)

SW   Ernst Jünger, *Sämtliche Werke*, (Stuttgart, 1978–80)

T   Velimir Khlebnikov, *Tvoreniia* (Moscow, 1968)

V   *Voyage au bout de la nuit*, in Louis-Ferdinand Céline, *Collected Works*, vol. 1 (Paris, 1981)

VM   Vladimir Maiakovskii, *Sobranie sochinenii v 13 tomakh* (Moscow, 1955–57)

VK   Velimir Khlebnikov, *Sobranie sochinenii*, 4 vols (Munich, 1968–72)

Rod Mengham and Jana Howlett

Introduction

The essays in this book bring into focus a period when violence was apparent on an international scale not only in the destructiveness of war and the conflicts of social and political life, but also in the chosen strategies of avant-garde movements.

Fascination with sexual and political violence characterises the work of many European artists of this period. It also informs much of the theoretical activity of the groups or movements which these individuals participated in or defined themselves against.

The central question posed here is whether the rhetoric of violence in the literary and plastic arts reflects other, more palpable forms of aggression, or whether it issues from the internal logic of evolving art forms and the changing social role of art. Somewhere, in the area disclosed by a tension between these two possibilities, arises the further question of political affiliation, of whether the attractions of violence can be associated with a predominantly left-wing or right-wing orientation.

Our answers to these questions are complex and varied, but certain distinctive patterns do emerge. The essays by David Forgacs, Naomi Segal and Elizabeth Wright all show how a violence of reaction, overwhelmingly masculine, is provoked by fears of bodily contact with, and contamination by, the alien. The literature of Italian Futurism and anti-Semitic Nazism are linked in a discourse of anxiety about the regulation of bodily boundaries and the need for a distinct or purified identity. It is fascinating to compare David Forgacs's investigation of Fascism's surgical imagery, where violence is regarded as sanitary and sanitising, and victims are cast as patients, with Elizabeth Wright's analysis of Brecht's early plays where she identifies the role of aggressivity as a reaction to the threat of bodily disintegration.

Forgacs also explores the issue of the integrity of the corporate subject in the work of Georges Sorel, whose ideas were appropriated by Wyndham Lewis in a way which highlights the connection between artistic and political strategies. Mengham concentrates on the link between Sorel's attitude towards the *syndicat* and the State and Lewis's perception of the role of the avant-garde in a bourgeois society.

Forgacs stresses Sorel's conception of violence as a cohesive force: the imagining of violence creates a revolutionary collective identity in the proletariat. Howlett's essay shows writers's responses to a violence which was real, the violence of the Russian Civil War. This catastrophic conflict destroyed the bourgeois values assailed by the avant-garde, but it also expunged their freedom to experiment and take risks. Michael Minden's survey of German Expressionist writing records a similar anticipation of the uses of violence as a means of constructing a sense of community to overcome the isolation of the individual artist. As so often in the case studies discussed in this collection, initial enthusiasm for the apocalypse was transformed into pacifist rejection.

Some of our contributors stress a response to violence which exceeds the obligations and constraints of partisanship. Richard Cork observes that Paul Nash's landscapes painted both before and during the First World War provide a measure for the unnaturalness of trench warfare, and give the spectator a means of gauging the importance and scale of the issues involved. Alison Sinclair, in contrasting literary critiques of the Spanish Civil War with Goya's *Desastres*, Picasso's *Guernica*, and Wilfred Owen's grasp of frontline experience in the First World War, reaches a comparable position in drawing distinctions between the *parti-pris* and non-aligned comprehensions of military conflict. Intriguingly, this quality of 'total disgust', as Sinclair phrases it, is close to what broadens the compulsive treatments of aggression and hatred in the fiction of Céline, in Michael Tilby's account of his work.

The sequence of fascination with, confused involvement in, and final recoil from, the uses of violence is repeated within and across national cultures, political systems and artistic movements. But the transformation of attitudes is hardly unexpected in the case of artists whose stance and technique can be revealed as intrinsically ambivalent from the start. David Midgley is particularly concerned with the doubleness of response he finds inflected in different ways and in different proportions in the various *oeuvres* of Otto Dix, Ernst Jünger and Arnold Zweig. Tim Mathews contrasts the manic relish of the Italian and French Futurists and Simultaneists with the more complex and measured paradoxes of English Vorticism; in his analysis, it is the artistic deployment of machine imagery which marks involvement in a 'desperate and defensive battle' for the autonomy of art, and in this concern he touches on some of the fundamental tenets of avant-gardism: it is insisting on autonomy at the same time as it claims the right to provide a political direction for the culture as a whole. The historical passage of the avant-garde is characterised by the violence of its relations with a broader culture which it alternately wrenches itself away from, and then forces itself back upon. Even the key technique of the historical avant-gardes, montage, is motivated by the same reaching after the effects of violent juxtaposition. Katherine Hodgson's essay on Maiakovskii and Khlebnikov traces the political implications of an hyperbolical Futurism subject to technical exaggerations and distortions, succeeded by the apparent neutrality and control of Socialist Realism.

These essays stop, historically, at 1939, because the beginning of the Second World War coincided with the effective demise of the movements born out of the inter-war period. The movements and ideas discussed in the present book are interesting not only from a historical point of view but also as guides to the present, when Europe is once again destabilised by the demise of an empire and the realignment of political forces.

Moreover, the close relationship between violence and experimental art has not been weakened but strengthened in the last two decades, and many of the issues opened up in this book have resurfaced in debate, performance and text from the 1960s onwards.

Warfare has changed its character in the postmodern period and the relationship between violence and everyday life has shifted to accommodate the frequency and cultural significance of terrorism, with which the new avant-garde art has become, if anything, increasingly involved. The parallels between the activities of a terrorist cell and those of an artistic avant-garde should be approached cautiously. But developments in recent theory, in the work of Jean Baudrillard and Paul Virilio, have stressed the challenge to representation mounted by terrorism on the one hand, and what Guy Debord has called the 'society of the spectacle' on the other. In some ways, terrorist acts can appear exactly as senseless and indeterminate as the system they are designed to combat; present-day terrorism, argues Baudrillard, 'offers a homologue deep down, of the silence and inertia of the masses. . . . In its deadly and indiscriminate taking of hostages, terrorism strikes at precisely the most characteristic product of the whole system: the anonymous and perfectly undifferentiated individual, the term substitutable for any other'.[1]

Several recent artistic projects, in investigating the phenomenon of terrorism, have posed important questions about the relationship between history, representation and the avant-garde. Cheryl Bernstein makes the daring claim that the Symbionese Liberation Army (SLA), which captured Patty Hearst and apparently converted her to its cause, was, in fact, a group of postmodern performance artists. She cites the surrealistic character of the SLA's politics, its carefully timed releases of information and instructions geared to the most skilful manipulation of the mass media, its nice sense of irony in kidnapping the daughter of a media mogul, and the sophisticated ambiguities of its baffling communiqués. Bernstein proposes that the SLA was a highly self-conscious group of experimentalists who had chosen as their medium prime-time national network TV news. Intentionally or not, the SLA undoubtedly disclosed, in a very powerful way, the moral and political bankruptcy of all the available institutions of representation, which became virtually dominated by its own creation of its own story, its own spectacle, its occupation of 'all the available space' with a performance of revolutionary, and avant-garde, gratuitousness.

Gerhard Richter's sequence of paintings *18 Oktober 1977* commemorates the deaths – whether by suicide or murder will probably never be settled – of Andreas Baader, Gudrun Ensslin, and Jan-Carl Raspe, three prominent members of the terrorist Red Army Fraction, who died in Stammheim prison on the same day, 18 October 1977. The paintings consist of treatments of enlarged black and white press and police photographs, the photographs having been over-painted with black and white pigment. They were shown at the ICA in London in November 1989 and before that at galleries in Krefeld and Frankfurt-am-Main. Richter has said that he intends never to sell them. He does not want their value to be set at a price in the international art market, so that to some extent at least they will be able to remain in the context of avant-garde artistic practice, achieving some distance from the receiving apparatuses of the typical West European state. On the one hand, these paintings belie the conventional view of avant-garde art as having little to do with the depiction of a social historical reality, but on the other hand, in their insistence on painterly distortion they are registering their distance from that social reality *and* from the photographs on which they are based. In this situation, the viewer is left uncertain as to exactly what position to take up; by making the paintings adhere more or less to the forms given by the photographs, Richter is proposing that the autonomy of avant-garde art is an illusion, while at the same time his modifications of texture stress the constructed nature of the images found in the photographs.

The SLA and Gerhard Richter provide particularly salient examples of the continuing interconnections between political violence and avant-garde art; in the literary field, corresponding projects are especially numerous. Notable among them are Nanni Ballestrini's novel about the Brigate Rossi, *The Unseen*, Douglas Oliver's *The Diagram Poems* which feature the Tupamaros guerrillas, and Drew Milne's 'Nostalgia' which meditates on the phenomenon of the Angry Brigade. Violence has taken on different forms, but the Violent Muse is still as significant a presence in European culture as it was between 1910 and 1939.

David Forgacs

Fascism, violence and modernity

The discourse of Fascism is full of imagined acts of violence which heal and restore order where there had been a perceived state of disease and disorder. What is the significance of these imaginings? Why does Fascism represent aggression as a cutting out, making whole, administering the good death, turning victims into patients and patients into victims? How does this imaginary[2] relate to what it has become customary to call 'modernity'?

I shall explore some of the real effects and some manifestations of this imaginary. I take as my starting-point the 'punitive expeditions' of the Fascist action squads in Italy, then look back to the representations of violence in revolutionary syndicalism, reactionary nationalism and Futurism, which were among their precursors, and finally consider the *Freikorps* in Germany and Nazi genocide.

In working towards such an end-point I do not intend to suggest an inevitable teleology of escalating violence. Nor do I wish to imply, in focusing on Fascism, that an imaginary of sanitary violence belongs exclusively to the political right. What I want to demonstrate is, first, that all manifestations of this imaginary have a displacement in common, through a sort of inversion or negation of the violent act from a hurting to a healing one, and, second, that this displacement, whether in aesthetics, social theory or political discourse, has real effect and therefore needs to be identified and challenged.

Fascist action squads were formed in Italy after the First World War. Just as the *Freikorps*, which were active in Germany during the same period (1918–23), the Fascist squads were constituted around a group of men in their twenties and thirties who had fought in the war as reserve officers and who, after demobilisation, were unable to return to peacetime occupations. They found an outlet for their ideological radicalism and aggression in attacks on domestic targets – socialists, communists, Catholics, trade unionists. In Italy the actions of the *squadristi* characteristically took the form of 'punitive expeditions' against those held responsible for strikes and occupations of the land: a group of *squadristi* would arrive in a town or village by

truck, set fire to buildings of the Socialist Party or the Catholic Popular Party
and assault leaders of these parties or the agricultural workers' movements.
Sometimes stabbings or shootings ensued; more often the assaults were
confined to beatings with a club or cudgel (*manganello*) and the forced
drinking of castor oil.

The acts of the *squadristi* were frequently and grotesquely described by
them and their sympathisers in comic or carnival terms, as sporting
encounters or practical jokes. On occasion the victims died, yet the Fascists
repeatedly claimed that their aim was not to kill but to 'teach a lesson'.

The ritual aggression at once humiliated the victims and subjected them to
a symbolic purgation: the drinking of castor oil was associated both with the
cleansing of the body by the administering of a purgative and with the
administration of corrective punishment to naughty children by parental
authority. The wearing of black shirts and leather boots contributed a
fetishistic aspect to the ritual. In one of the squads' songs the actions are
represented as curative blood-lettings:

> Cudgel, cudgel,
> bludgeon the socialist brain.
> If you don't know us don't swagger
> because we fascists like blood-letting.[3]

All these aspects of squad violence are to be found in a statement by
Mussolini reported in Margherita Sarfatti's early biography, *Dux*:

However much one might deplore violence, it is clear that, in order to impose our ideas
on people's brains we had to use the cudgel to touch refractory skulls. The expeditions
must always have the character of a just retaliation and a legitimate reprisal. We do
not make violence into a school, a system or, worse still, an aesthetic. Violence must be
generous, chivalric and surgical.[4]

Let us consider this statement. It legitimates Fascist violence by representing it as reactive. The squads do not initiate, they retaliate against the
violation of property rights. It portrays violence as imparting a lesson: the
beatings are inflicted upon 'refractory skulls', they are a gesture of corrective
authority which brings the transgressor to heel. This is why the violence is
'generous': it helps the victims, puts them on the straight road. Violence is
'chivalric': it is an adventurous deed which rights a wrong. Finally, violence is
'surgical': it cuts something out in order to make better.

The metaphor of surgery is to be found again and again in later Fascist
discourse. Francesca Rigotti has investigated the use of it in Mussolini's
speeches and writings. In 1922, referring to the need to reform the state
administration, he says: 'it is necessary . . . to use the scalpel inexorably to
take away everything parasitic, harmful and suffocating that has latched on
to the various offices'. In 1935, in an article in *Il Popolo d'Italia* opposing the
League of Nations's economic sanctions against Italy because of its military

aggression against Ethiopia, he attacks 'Genevaism' as 'that horrendous medicine of senility and false youth which may be apt to preserve mummies but which kills the strong or weakens them to an invalid state'. Against 'Genevaism' he sets Fascism, which works by 'the irruption of Fascist blood into the tainted organism of international politics begins to yield its fruits. . . . Will we need to use surgery? . . . In any case one can rest assured: it will be straightforward, radical surgery.' In 1942 Mussolini promises that the Fascist Party 'will take responsibility for defending law and order and cauterising any boils that may break out'.[5]

The use of metaphors of the body in political discourse is an old one, and at one level these and other instances of Fascist rhetoric can be seen as continuations of the discourse of the state as body, the body politic, the corporation, the commonweal. Such political ideas became central to the self-presentation of the Fascist regime in Italy after 1925 and their appropriation belongs, with other aspects of 'traditional legitimation', to mature Fascism: the use of the myth and symbols of ancient Rome, the proclaimed rejection of political modernity in the form of democracy and the parliamentary system, the return to the organic ideal of the 'corporate state' above class interest, the co-optation of the traditional ruling classes and the conservative élites of the Catholic Church.

Yet such discourse is also aimed at distinctively modern ills, for which they claim to offer efficient cures. The body of the state administration is bloated with bureaucracy, infested with parasites which must be cut out. The body of international politics is weakened by bad medicine and requires a blood transfusion. The boils that erupt on the body of modern society can be cauterised by the Fascist Party. In all these variations on the metaphor, it is assumed that modern society is sick and that appropriate forms of political intervention – by the state, the party, the movement – can make it well. Such forms will be made clean, in operations carried out with sterile instruments: the scalpel, the drip and needle, the cauterising iron. These are the commonplaces of a medicalising rhetoric of violence which will be found also in Nazism.

The other characterisations of violence in Mussolini's statement – as retaliatory, as teaching a lesson and as chivalric – are also, at one level, traditional. The shift of blame to the victims as initiators of violence, deserving what they get, is a common way of justifying acts of aggression, as can be seen from research on rape.[6] Many of the men who rape, and many male judges, continue to excuse and justify rape by claiming that it was the result of deliberate provocation, that the victims had 'asked for it'.

The depiction of squad violence as 'chivalric' was also a way in which those with a literary memory could insert Fascist *squadrismo* into literary tradition – that of the *gesta*, in which retribution is carried out by a knight on the body of the transgressor. One of the texts which both pro- and anti-Fascist intellectuals saw as a precursor of *squadrismo* was Ardengo Soffici's *Lemmonio*

Boreo (1911), a novel in which the eponymous hero, disgusted with the petty injustices he finds as he wanders the Tuscan countryside, pairs up with a muscular sidekick and, like a latter-day knight errant or Robin Hood, metes out *ad hoc* punishments. 'Not a day went by but the two comrades did not teach some little lesson, did not defend some poor weak person. . . . They washed a few heads, as they passed, with energetic rinsing.'[7]

Sarfatti likewise depicts early Fascism as 'the militia of a new order of chivalry'. She slots the punitive expedition into the tradition of the *beffa*, a sometimes vicious practical joke, and puts the cudgel in a line of descent from Punch's stick:

With the historical rebirth of sects and factions, the avenging, imaginative, joyful and slightly cruel Italian *beffa* was also reborn; sometimes subtle, more often hearty and clownish, almost always part of the spirit of personal vendetta, outside and against the law. . . . The cudgel itself had associations of the *beffa*, as a concrete entity and a symbolic fetish, in line with the tradition of the *commedia dell'arte*, which was continued in the puppet play all over the world – from Guignol to Punch – and especially in Italy. . . . the rhythm of the stick delights young and old, when it carries out swift justice against delays and sophistries, and the injustices of legal quibbles.[8]

Fascist squad violence was also linked to comic traditions of corrective ritual by admirers outside Italy. An interesting example is a story in the *Boys' Own Paper* in 1924, where the public-school hero proposes to set up 'a company of Fascisti – like that Italian bloke who got fed up with excessive rags and organized a counter-party of orderly creatures'.[9] Here too the retaliatory actions and the chivalric deeds are imagined as targeted against specifically modern enemies: the malfunctioning parliamentary system, the corruption of the law and the administration, the socialists and 'Bolsheviks' who have committed an outrage by opposing the war, preaching an ethic of levelling, asserting the rights of the dispossessed producers. All these agencies are a sore or a wound in the social body. They must be corrected or destroyed to make the body whole again.

In an article published in Mussolini's newspaper *Il Popolo d'Italia* in May 1921, Ardengo Soffici represents Fascism as killing off the already putrid body of the Socialist Party, referred to by the punning acronym 'Pus', or 'Partito ufficiale socialista' – a label given it by former Socialists who, like Mussolini himself, had left the party because of opposition to its neutralist stance on the issue of war.

So the Pus is dead. Some say of cholera, through having spent too long regurgitating and gorging itself on its own excrement and anti-war vomit; some say of indigestion, through having for too long stuffed its 'evolved and socially aware' belly with brains and leathery sweetbreads; some say of Asian plague; there are even some who claim it died of simple diarrhoea [i.e. fear], after the first punches and clubbing dealt it by the Fascists.[10]

Fascism thus presents itself as a modern form of heroism, a righting of a new kind of social and political wrong. Ultimately, all these components of this rhetoric of 'just' violence can be seen as converging on the notion of Fascist violence as therapy, as designed to heal and make whole the imagined body of society and the state.

Among commonly cited precursors of the Fascist cult of violence are revolutionary syndicalism, reactionary nationalism and Futurism. For the first of these, the link is customarily made with Georges Sorel's *Réflexions sur la violence*, the draft version of which appeared first in Italian in 1906.[11] This had a deep impact in Italy even outside syndicalist circles. Benedetto Croce wrote the introduction to the Italian edition and Antonio Gramsci was later to appropriate a number of Sorel's key concepts – revolution as a 'scission' or clean break from the dominant social order, the 'morality of the producers' – and to attribute his own concept of 'historical bloc' to Sorel.[12]

The Italian edition of Sorel's book was also reviewed by Mussolini, who was to remain an admirer. And yet, despite the affinities which undoubtedly existed between revolutionary syndicalism in Italy and the so-called left wing of early Fascism, the latter's relationship with Sorel's ideas is complex.

Central to Sorel's conception of violence is not the violent act itself but the myth of violence, seen as having an organising effect on the subject of the violence, the proletariat, by constituting it as a self-conscious class. Myths in Sorel are conceived as collective 'idea-forces', representations which enable a social group to strive towards a particular goal: he cites the myth of martyrdom for the early Christians and the myth of the nation for the nineteenth century. His key idea is that parliamentary socialism will never be able to overthrow the bourgeois social order because it negotiates with the bourgeoisie, and this attenuates the class struggle as well as the character of the bourgeoisie and the proletariat as a class.

By threatening the bourgeoisie with proletarian violence while at the same time promising to contain it through their own responsible leadership, the parliamentary socialists, like the reformist trade unionists, mediate between classes, put off revolution, perpetuate capitalism. By contrast, revolutionary syndicalism, by means of the myth of proletarian violence and the general strike, will reconstitute both proletariat and bourgeoisie as class-conscious entities. The two classes will then confront each other in struggle. 'Acts of proletarian violence . . . are, purely and simply, acts of war; they have the value of military demonstrations and serve to mark the separation between classes.'[13]

To this end, real acts of violence are less important than the imaginary violence which serves to create cohesion and collective identity in the minds of the workers.

What we find useful in violence is the influence it exerts on the spirit of the workers, enabling them to view all incidents of everyday life as so many images of a great battle to the finish between two rival classes who contend the destiny of the future. This result can be obtained without great acts of violence, as occurs in those countries where the capitalist class is energetic and asserts its will to defend itself: it in a sense collaborates, through its openly and consistently reactionary stance, with the deepening of the scission, the idea of which the revolutionaries seek for their part to develop.[14]

James Joll has remarked of passages such as these that 'Sorel sometimes writes as if, for all the purifying effect of violence, physical violence might not actually be needed and the proletariat's faith in its own power might be sufficient to cause the revolution.'[15]

Against the view that violence is always immoral and a form of barbarism, Sorel argues that proletarian violence is both moral and civilised because it makes possible the transition to a higher, socialist, form of civilisation.

Proletarian violence, exercised as a pure and simple manifestation of the feelings of class struggle, thus appears as something very beautiful and grandly heroic; it is at the service of the primordial interests of civilisation; it may not be, perhaps, the best way of obtaining immediate material advantages, but it is a way of escaping from the world of barbarity.[16]

Sorel takes pains to distinguish his conception of proletarian violence from the episodes of Jacobin violence during the French Revolution, episodes which he describes as 'abuses of strength by the bourgeoisie'. Like Tocqueville he sees the revolutionary tribunals of the Jacobins as continuing the tribunals of the *ancien régime*. In Sorel's view the Jacobin conception of justice did not serve the interests of the people, but those of the state, since 'its principal aim was not the law but the state'.[17] By contrast, Sorel believes that in revolutionary syndicalism justice meant the free development of the social ownership of production.

It is legitimate to conclude therefore that the syndicalist violence of the proletariat on strike, intent upon overthrowing the state, cannot be confused with the acts of barbarism which superstition of the state suggested to the revolutionaries of 1793, when the latter came to power and could hold sway, according to the principles they received from the Church and the Monarchy, against the vanquished. It is legitimate for us to hope that the socialist revolution to which the pure syndicalists aspire will not be stained by the abominations that sullied the bourgeois revolution.[18]

Sorelian violence would seem to be, then, more spiritual than material, more image than reality; with a minimum of bloodshed it crystallises the class-consciousness of the proletariat, allows it to break away from the domination of the bourgeoisie and effect the passage to a higher level of civilisation. In all these respects it seems, and is, a long way away from the punitive violence of Fascist squads acting as strike-breaking thugs on behalf of the propertied classes.

But there are other respects in which, I would suggest, there are affinities between these two imaginaries of violence. In both, violence is seen as making society whole again, as healing and restoring order where there has been division. In both, the imagining of violence involves a series of displacements of its effects. In Sorel it acts more on the subject of violence, the proletariat, than on the object, the victims of violence, who remain more or less invisible. In Sorel's conception there need be few real heads broken because violence will have done the major part of its work in creating proletarian class-consciousness.

For the Fascist squads both aggressor and victim are visible and real acts of violence happen, yet at the same time they are not really visible to them as real acts of violence, since in their imaginary the relation between aggressor and victim is inverted or otherwise displaced. The victim becomes the initiator of aggression and the aggressor acts in defensive retaliation. In addition, the violent act is imaginarily displaced from an infliction of pain into a comic ritual, an act of chivalry, a generous healing. The victim becomes the patient, the aggressor the dispenser of the cure.

The connection between Sorelian violence and Fascist violence is therefore indirect. Sorel minimises violence, Fascism exalts it. The connection is present at the level of the imaginary, where it consists in the common displacement of violence into something other: a social medicine, a creation of order, a revolution-recomposition.

In the case of nationalism and Futurism the links with the Fascist imaginary of violence are more direct. Not only did many right-wing nationalists and some Futurists, officially launched as a group in 1909, join the ranks of the Fascist movement when the latter was constituted in 1919; they, together with syndicalists, provided Fascism with aspects of its early ideology.

One key component of this ideology was militarism. Marinetti's first *Manifesto of Futurism* (February 1909) declared: 'We will glorify war – the world's only hygiene.' In an article of 1910 called 'What is Futurism?' he elaborated the idea:

We thus exalt patriotism and militarism. We love and hasten war, only hygiene of the world, proud flame-burst of enthusiasm and generosity, noble bath of heroism, without which races lie dormant in slothful egoism, economic *arrivisme*, miserliness of the mind and the will. . . . It has been observed that there is a flagrant contradiction between our Futurist ideal and our praise of war, which allegedly constitutes a regression to barbarous epochs. We reply that great problems of moral health and hygiene must necessarily be resolved before any others. Is not the life of the nation similar to that of the individual, which fights infections and plethora with douches and blood-letting? We assert that peoples too must follow a constant hygiene of heroism and allow themselves, every ten years, a glorious shower of blood.[19]

Here again violence is seen as a cure upon an imagined body: in this case it is war which works on the body of the nation. As in Sorel, though in politically different terms, violence is seen as on the side of civilisation against barbarism, as enabling society to be made whole. For the therapy of warfare, in Futurist and nationalist discourse, acts primarily not on the body of the enemy nation but on that of the nation at home. 'Infected' nations, those affected with internal disorders, must go to war, let blood, in order that those disorders may be cured and their health be restored.

The term 'hygiene', from the Greek word for health, originally designated a branch of medicine concerned with the maintenance and regulation of health; by extension it came to mean the maintenance of a sanitary environment, as in the term 'public hygiene', and the day-to-day care of the body. These meanings are condensed in Marinetti's slogan 'guerra sola igiene del mondo'. War is imagined as regulating the health of the national and global body by cleansing and purifying.

One of the most disturbing elaborations of such a militarist imaginary is 'Let Us Love the War', an article written by the nationalist Giovanni Papini in 1914 shortly after the outbreak of the First World War and well before Italy's own intervention in it (May 1915). In it, he states: 'Let us love the war and savour it as gourmets while it lasts. The war is frightening, and precisely because it is frightening and awful and terrible and destructive we must love it with all our manly heart'.

Italy needs 'a hot bath of black blood' because it has been made soft by 'the siesta of cowardice, diplomacy, hypocrisy and pacifism'. To Papini the war is a Malthusian inevitability, needed to get rid of 'a surplus of us over here and over there', and that few who would be lost to war would be worth more as living men than as dead soldiers.

Papini argues, only half tongue-in-cheek, that the war is good for agriculture: 'What fine cabbages the French will eat where the German infantry are piled up and what fat potatoes they will guzzle in Galicia next year!' It is also good for 'modernity' because 'those filthy villages which the soldiers burned will be rebuilt better and more hygienic. And there will still be too many Gothic cathedrals, churches, libraries and castles.' A new art will be created by those who are 'refreshed by destruction'.[20]

Papini's rhetoric at first sight seems markedly different from the standard pro-war rhetoric of 1914 which worked by effacing or masking the violence of war, representing destructive aggression, mutilation and death by euphemisms such as 'glory', 'deeds of valour', 'sacrifice', 'giving one's life'.[21]

The conscription propaganda issued by the belligerent governments deployed this rhetoric, as did the popular press, political and church meetings, even the variety theatre, the school and the workplace. It is chillingly portrayed in Remarque's *All Quiet on the Western Front* (1929) where the schoolmaster Kantorek exhorts the 'iron youth' in his classroom to do their duty to the fatherland, and the boys go off to die.

Papini, by contrast, does not try to cover up the fact that wars consist of people bleeding and dying, instead he says that it is needed as 'a good watering of blood for the searing heat of August, a red racking for the September wine harvests'. But Papini is no more talking here about the reality of war than were its official propagandists. He is not describing the First World War as we know it turned out to be, a war of attrition in which eight million soldiers died and which developed the new military technologies of poison gas and tanks.

Papini, writing in the autumn of 1914, still conceived the future war as one which could be fought mainly with nineteenth-century tactics and weapons and which was likely to be over by the end of the year. Papini was imagining war. With his celebratory fantasies of mass destruction he wanted to shock and provoke his domestic enemies, the socialists, pacifists and humanitarians who deplored the outbreak of war.

It is important to grasp this distinction between a war that is primarily imagined and a war described, and to understand that Papini's text is a case of the former, not the latter. Descriptions involve imaginings too: we can only describe something by inscribing it in a set of imagined categories which enable us to represent that thing in a particular way and not in others. The difference in this case is that Papini's imagined war is a projection of a mass destruction that has not yet taken place rather than a set of imagined categories interacting with an empirical war of mass destruction already under way. Moreover, his text – like the pro-war discourse of glory, valour and sacrifice, albeit in a different way – is made up of a series of rhetorical displacements of violence and death which are also euphemistic, also a 'good-speak' of violence. Papini talks about blood, but the blood is, like Marinetti's sanitising 'shower', a 'bath', a 'watering' of the earth, a cleansing, a fertilising, a regeneration. In other words it is symbolic blood, endowed with magical, thaumaturgical functions. He talks about slitting throats, slashing bellies, ripping out guts, tearing and crunching, but in a way that dematerialises the acts by foregrounding the sound of the words (reinforced in the Italian by alliteration: 'si sgozza e si sbuzza, si sbudella e si sbrana; si spezza e si sfracassa').

Texts like this, and Marinetti's various writings on war, raise the question of the relationship between violence as fantasy, as aesthetic violence, and real acts of violence. Marinetti (unlike Papini, who in the course of the war was to suffer a crisis of guilt over his own fanatical militarism and to convert to Catholicism) enlisted in the Italian army and fought both in the war between Italy and Turkey for control of Libya in 1911–12 and in the First World War. He also took part in street fights against leftist demonstrators in 1919 which he described in his notebooks. Yet all of his writings on war and on violence continue to represent them – despite certain inputs of 'realism' such as descriptions of soldiers scratching themselves in lice-infested uniforms – in a fantastic, aestheticising way. In 'Bataille, Poids + Odeur ' ('Battle, Weight + Smell'), a prose-poem of 1912, a battle is depicted in a stylised piece of 'mots en liberté', with a series of what Marinetti elsewhere theorised as 'increasingly wide analogies' (analogie sempre più vaste[22]), yoking together terms belonging to distant semantic sets: for example the sight—sound analogy 'mitrailleuses = galets + ressac + grenouilles' ('machine guns = pebbles + ebb tide + frogs').[23] This is a poetry of cool detachment, a reworking of the battle into a series of technical innovations. In *La Bataille de Tripoli*, a prose text originally serialised in the Paris magazine *L'Intransigeant* in December

1911, the narrator represents himself flying in an aeroplane above the fighting: 'I fly riding bareback on the battle, which gallops as if crazed. . . . And I clutch its mane of furious sounds.'[24] In 'La guerra elettrica (visione-ipotesi futurista)' of 1915 there is a fantasy both of aeroplanes without pilots (i.e. missiles) remote-controlled at a sanitary distance from the enemy and of ascent into the air as a liberation from the gross body, a release of the intellect made possible by modern technology:

Now that the necessity of doing tiring and degrading tasks is over, intelligence finally reigns everywhere. Muscular work finally ceases to be servile, and has only three goals: hygiene, pleasure and fighting. Now that man no longer has to struggle to win his food, he conceives at last the pure idea of the altitude record. His will and ambition become immense.[25]

Marinetti's writing displaces the violence of war by various techniques of removal into symbol, analogy, fantasies of detachment. These then become the real subjects of his writing. The same applies to violence on the streets. His notebook entry for 15 April 1919, a day in which a general strike had been declared in Milan, describes part of a clash between war veterans (*arditi* or shock-troopers) and Socialists in such a way that the metaphors occupy the foreground, they become the reality of the event:

An *ardito* sets off like a bullet at full speed down the deserted road and hurls himself onto the monument to Garibaldi which bristles with a black crowd.

He climbs up and stabs a speaker who is shouting Long live Lenin.

In a flash the monument turns white. The black crowd which had clad it slips down and flees left and right. Down away there in front of the Castello Sforzesco to left and right down 200 metres in Foro Bonaparte.

Flight of sparrows. Speed of dead leaves which the wind tears from the trees.[26]

When a militaristic writer like Marinetti aestheticises violence, it is not because he is a naive intellectual or an artist who has no experience of actual violence, does not know what it is and does not really know what he is saying. He knows exactly what it is and what he is saying. He has fought in two wars and in the same notebook entry on the street-fight he can also write: 'I see blood on the ground and I feel a deep anxiety at seeing these impetuous young mercenary kids [hired by the 'Bolsheviks'] beaten up with clubs.'[27]

Marinetti aestheticises violence because doing so provides him with a way of imagining it, representing it, and probably experiencing it, as something other than itself: as glorious, joyous, modern, heroic, life-affirming. I would suggest that these representations became real for Marinetti in that they constituted the imaginary categories in which he framed and made sense of reality. This does not mean that his readers are obliged to share his representations and his reality. They are free to object that real violence is never like this for those who have it inflicted upon them: it hurts, it wounds or it kills. They can also say that to represent it as heroic, as life-affirming, indeed as anything other than itself is to play a dangerous game in which sympathy with other human beings becomes suspended and different sentiments get in the way. The myth of war as hygiene, Papini's imagining of war as a 'Malthusian operation' which gets rid of 'surplus', 'useless' people, are deeply dangerous, inhumane and anti-human, and it is not surprising that various forms of Fascism developed their own versions of the same divisive, 'eugenic' rhetoric. For Marinetti meant just what he said when he wrote in 1919:

Futurism has been and will always be a school of spiritual and physical courage. A formula of hygiene for the spirit.
Spiritually and physically courageous and fast.
The lame and the slow will be punished along with the able cretin who lets himself be taken in by the familiar American-style swindle *much more than the thief.*
The idiot of the library and the *village idiot* must disappear. Equally dangerous encumbering retarding for the rapidly turning gears of civilisation.[28]

There was nothing inevitable, in this period, about an equation of this kind between violence, modernisation and civilisation. It was a position like any other and an opposite view was possible. Karl Liebknecht wrote in 1907 that 'the proletariat knows that . . . in every war a volcano of Hun-like brutality and baseness erupts among the peoples involved, and that for years civilization is set back and barbarism reigns'.[29] According to Rosa Luxemburg, writing in 1915, 'War is methodical, organised, gigantic murder. . . . Bestiality of action must find a commensurate bestiality of thought and senses. . . .'[30]

Klaus Theweleit's study of the ideology of the *Freikorps* deals with it as a specifically masculine imaginary of violence. He interprets this imaginary as centring upon men's terror in relation to women and their desire to re-establish control over them when they perceive that control – that is to say, patriarchy – to be momentarily threatened or upturned. He finds in their representations of real or imagined acts of violence against women many variations on the same imaginary: women are a threat to the male subject; an 'unnatural', devouring sexuality is ascribed to them; they are dirty, unruly, enraged, 'sluts' or 'whores', sources of defilement, flowing and flooding which must be stopped up and laid to rest; men must bond together in camaraderie to maintain their integrity, to police the boundaries of their own erect, column-like bodies against the threat constituted by the female body and its disorderliness, its uncontainable, engulfing flows.
One of the many examples in his book of vindictive acts against women comes from an account written by Manfred von Killinger, a storm-troop leader in the Ehrhardt brigade:

I am presented with a slut. The typical bad girl from Schwabing. Short, stringy hair; seedy clothes; a brazen, sensuous face; awful circles under her eyes.
    'What's her story?'
She slobbers out, 'I'm a Bolshevik, you bunch of cowards! Lackeys of princes! Spit lickers! We should spit on you! Long live Moscow!' Whereupon, she spits into the face of a corporal.

'The riding crop, then let her go,' was all I said.
Two men grab hold of her. She tries to bite them. A slap brings her back to her senses. In the courtyard she is bent over the wagon shaft and worked over with riding crops until there isn't a white spot left on her back.
'She won't be spitting at any more brigade men. Now she'll have to lie on her stomach for three weeks,' said Sergeant Hermann.[31]

This, and many of the other passages cited by Theweleit from the diaries, memoirs and novels of the *Freikorps* men, is consistent with what I have been analysing so far. Proto-fascist violence is imagined as a restoration of order after a moment of disorder and provocation. The communist woman is imagined at the end like a convalescing patient, lying. In other examples, the women are shot, but here too the narrative dwells on the restoration of order, on the unruly woman 'put to rest', 'put in her place' by her male attackers.

What Theweleit's analysis distinctively adds is the emphasis on the sexual nature of these violent fantasies and specifically their links with masculine anxieties (fear of engulfment, of castration) and hence with patriarchal power. Much of the same sort of sexually-grounded fears and desires can also be identified in the Italian examples I have discussed: in Soffici's description of the Socialists as a foul, diseased body; in Papini's imagining of war as a cleansing, a washing-out followed by a rebuilding of more hygienic houses; in Marinetti's fantasies of flying as separation and detachment. These too can be seen as sexual anxieties about regulating bodily boundaries and controlling or eliminating dirt.

At the same time, given that not all proto-Fascist and Fascist violence was directed against women, Theweleit's work also poses a problem: how far can it help us make sense of Fascist violence and Fascism in general? One of the ways in which he deals with this is to suggest that many other apparently unrelated aspects of Fascism in fact belong to the same core imaginary. For instance he suggests that the ritual of upright ('erect') male bodies marching on mass rallies, and the material trappings of those rallies (columns, etc.), provided a reassuring sense of maintaining the boundaries of the male body against disorder, against the 'flow' that was always imagined as feminine, replacing it with the 'tamed flood'.[32]

This kind of speculation is seductive, but there is a problem with it which is raised by Barbara Ehrenreich in her foreword to the American edition, namely that if Fascism was deeply male and misogynistic, it does not follow that Fascism and misogyny 'are somehow "the same thing" ':

the Jewish (and Communist) men who fell victim to it were not substitute women, symbolic whores, or anything of the kind, but real men whose crime was their Jewishness, or their politics. Neither feminism nor antifascism will be well served by confounding Fascist genocide with the daily injuries inflicted by men on women.[33]

Theweleit, as Ehrenreich acknowledges, avoids such a confusion; nevertheless, it is not clear where he stands on the relation between Fascism and patriarchy, since in some places he recognizes the internal heterogeneity and complexity of Fascism, disclaims a totalising interpretation of it and stresses the exploratory character of his research, while in others he represents Fascism as a historical subset of patriarchy and insists that male–female relations are central to its imaginary.

The problem with adopting a strong version of this position is that, while it may work straightforwardly enough to explain Fascism's oppression of women and homosexual men, it is harder to make it account in a non-reductive way for Fascist oppression of other groups: Jews, Communists, the working class, Poles, Slavs, gypsies and others who were marginalised, such as the mentally ill. What can, I think, be taken productively from Theweleit's work is the idea that the oppression of these various groups had in common an anxiety over the health of the imagined body (implicitly a male body) and over the maintenance of bodily boundaries and that this anxiety was an important element in Fascism. One can acknowledge this without needing to make a case for this anxiety being the 'true' cause or source of all Fascist oppression.

Anxiety over bodily contact was, however, central to the discourse of Nazi anti-Semitism. The links between hatred of Jews, the obsession with 'blood purity' and sexual repression were first pointed out by Wilhelm Reich in 1933, commenting on Hitler's *Mein Kampf* and Rosenberg's *Mythus des 20. Jahrhunderts*:

The creed of the 'soul' and its 'purity' is the creed of asexuality, of 'sexual purity'. Basically, it is a symptom of the sexual repression and sexual shyness brought about by a patriarchal authoritarian society. . . . the core of the fascist race theory is a mortal fear of natural sexuality and of its organism function.[34]

Nazi racial discourse had its theoretical precursors in the nineteenth- and early twentieth-century 'scientific' racialists (Houston Stewart Chamberlain, Arthur Gobineau and others) who represented the modern world as divided between superior and inferior races, with the blood of the former threatened with contamination and dilution by the latter through 'miscegenation' or mixed-race procreation. *Mein Kampf*, dictated by Hitler in prison in 1925–26, combines a rehashing of these ideas with a personal account of his encounters with Jews in pre-First World War Vienna which is characterised by an obsessive aversion to bodily contact and a constant metaphorical spillage from the physical to the 'moral'.

The smell of Jews, he claims, made him sick. They became 'positively repulsive when, in addition to their physical uncleanliness, you discovered the moral stains on this "chosen people". . . . Was there any form of filth or profligacy, particularly in cultural life, without at least one Jew involved in it?'

The metaphor of infestation of the body, of disease, is pivotal to this imaginary. 'If you cut even cautiously into such an abscess, you found, like a

maggot in a rotting body, often dazzled by the sudden light – a kike!'[35] The
Jews, with no nation of their own, were depicted by Hitler as greedy parasites
in the bodies of other nations.[36]

On 22 February 1942, as the policy of the 'Final Solution' began to be put
into practice, the same metaphorical language was brought into play. Hitler
spoke of Nazi Germany as fighting, like Pasteur and Hoch, a 'bacillus'. He
spoke of the Jew as being 'the cause of innumerable diseases which . . . would
also have ravaged Japan if it had continued to be open to him.' On 15 March
he claimed the Jews had masterminded the defeat of Germany in the First
World War and the revolution that followed and he accused them of
becoming the 'principal carriers of the Bolshevik infection'. He called the
Jews a 'world pest'.[37]

In 1943, attempting to put pressure on Horthy to assist with the
deportation and murder of Hungarian Jews, he stated: 'the Jews should be
treated as tubercle bacilli, contagious for healthy organisms'; to exterminate
them, he argued, was not cruel, since 'even innocent creatures like rabbits and
deer have to be decimated to prevent spoliation'.[38] Nor was this language
limited to Hitler. In March 1943 Goebbels wrote in his diary that Hitler's
prophecy was 'beginning to be fulfilled in the most horrible ways' but that not
to kill the Jews would mean waiting to be destroyed by them in 'a struggle of
life and death between the Aryan race and the Jewish bacillus'.[39] And Hans
Frank, head of the General Government of Nazi-occupied Poland, wrote in
his diary that 'the Jews were a lower species of life, a kind of vermin, which
upon contact infected the German people with deadly diseases'. When the
Jews were killed in the area of Poland under his rule he said 'now a sick
Europe would become healthy again'.[40]

These medical metaphors had real effect because they helped the Nazi
leadership legitimate genocide to itself and its followers and to carry it out. In
a sense they 'derived' from the metaphors of nineteenth-century racialism,
particularly that of 'blood purity'. But they also involved something new,
namely the idea of a therapeutic intervention, the translation of racial 'theory'
into policy in order to restore the imagined Aryan body to health. The 'Final
Solution', in this bodily imaginary, was of a piece with the territorial struggles
of the Second World War: to gain *Lebensraum* for the German people, to
defeat Bolshevism in the East and 'plutocratic capitalism' in the West, both of
which were associated with the alleged conspiracy of international Jewry for
world domination. In this way the racialist imaginary of a hierarchical
separation of bodies and the preservation of the purity of the 'superior race'
were placed in the service of violence of an historically unprecedented type
and magnitude. Once again, however, as in the earlier examples I have given,
the imaginary of this violence worked by displacement and non-recognition,
by turning violence into something other than itself. Mass murder became
'healing'. It was carried out not in the heat of passion but according to a cool,
systematic 'medical' rationale.

In research based on interviews with twenty-eight former Nazi doctors, Robert Jay Lifton found that the method of killing large numbers of people by gas in sealed vans or chambers functioned as 'a way of protecting the killers from the psychological consequences of face-to-face killing'. According to one doctor's testimony, 20 per cent of those who did the actual killing often had 'significant psychological difficulties'. Lifton concluded that 'surgical killing provided a means to overcome those impediments by minimising the psychological difficulties of the killers'.[41] The method of killing by gas was first tried out in the Nazi 'euthanasia programme' of 1939–41 in which an estimated 100,000 German adults and children with incurable disabilities or disorders, patients in mental institutions and the mentally handicapped, were killed on Hitler's orders. The motivation was 'race hygiene', the elimination of so-called 'Ballastexistenzen' ('human ballast') and the consequent freeing of hospital beds, doctors and nurses needed for the war.[42]

Lifton sees a continuity of 'medicalised killing' between the sterilisation programme of 1933, the euthanasia programme and the killings in the concentration and extermination camps. In the latter, the medicalisation of killing involved, as well as the use of gas chambers itself, killing by lethal injection and the deployment of SS doctors for initial 'selections' (the separation of relatively fit young adults from the old people, children and women with children who were immediately sent to die), for the supervision of gassing, the pronouncement of death and the consignment of bodies to crematoria. The presiding doctors' vehicles were usually marked with a red cross.[43]

What can these displacements of violence and murder into acts of healing tell us about the relationship between Fascism and modernity? The view taken by some of the early works on totalitarianism that Fascist violence, like Fascism itself, was a reversion to barbarism on a massive scale, in other words a form of anti-modernity, a regression in relation to the progress of enlightenment and civilisation, seems inadequate as a historical explanation.[44]

It has a rhetorical value, even a necessity, in the sense that we need to be able to say that it is barbaric to kill and to carry out mass murder. This is why statements such as those I quoted earlier by Liebknecht and Luxemburg against war can be politically so effective. But such rhetorical expedients are of little help if we are trying to understand the mentality of people who represented violence and killing, to themselves and to others, in civilising, modernising terms as a way forward, a way of getting society into a healthier, purer state. Nor can they account adequately for the historical existence of those representations themselves. It is not convincing to treat the medical metaphors and rituals which legitimated violence and killing simply as a piece of conscious and cynical deception by barbarians, sheep's clothing worn by Fascist wolves. These people did not think of themselves as neo-barbarians but as the new civilisers of the Thousand Year Reich. At worst, despite intentions to the contrary, the anti-modernity or barbarism thesis can provide

Fascism with an ideological justification by portraying it as a sort of atavistic relapse, an aberration from the normal state of things, a coming to the surface of innate aggressive drives or instincts, and therefore as something that 'could not be helped', rather than as the product of historically particular ways of organising society and sexual difference.[45]

It is also mistaken, in my view, to go too far in the other direction and see Fascism simply as a logical consequence of modernisation. Adorno and Horkheimer's *Dialectic of Enlightenment*, first published in 1947, is the most celebrated example of this position, with its argument that Fascism, and its controlled violence, is a culmination of enlightenment rationality developing along its 'dark side': control of nature and society by science and technology, bureaucratisation, mass culture. This thesis can certainly help us make sense of the medicalisation of violence in Fascist discourse as a technique of distancing it and regulating it with scientific protocols, but it goes too far because it makes it impossible to disentangle modernity from Fascism: all of modernity becomes, for Adorno and Horkheimer, like Fascism. Civilisation as a whole, far from 'lapsing' into barbarism, progresses towards it. The negativity of this vision of modernity is overwhelming.

If a modernising imaginary of violence is closely bound up with Fascism and belongs to its self-representation as a modern civilising movement, it does not follow that all of modernity is implicated with violence in exactly the same way as Fascism. Let us compare the Fascist state with the parliament-ary–democratic state. We may concede that the latter, like the former, rests upon violence and coercion and not just upon consent or voluntary accept-ance: it too exercises its authority, particularly at moments of crisis and in places where that authority is openly challenged, through a police force and an army.

This is no more than to say, as Weber did in 1918, that all states possess a monopoly of the legitimate use of physical force or violence.[46] We might also say that it is characteristic of the democratic state, perhaps even more than of other states, to deny or mask its own use of violence by calling it something else: law and order, defence of the realm, anti-terrorism, protection of the public interest, maintenance of sovereign authority, a just war in defence of democracy. It may even use medical metaphors: the sanitary cordon, the mopping-up operation, the surgical strike. And we may also agree that, with legitimation, the democratic state can carry out sustained and systematic violence against whole populations or whole sections of populations sub-jected to it through various forms of political, economic or military control.

Yet despite all these areas of overlap what remains distinctive about Fascism is crucially the way it enlarges the area of legitimate violence, justifies wholesale violence systematically as therapy and at the same time closes up the spaces from which legal opposition to it could be mounted. Fascist violence, as we have seen, begins outside the state as illegal violence repre-senting itself as cure. It then moves to conquer the state and when it does so its violence becomes, by definition, legitimate; it also becomes more controlled, less visible and less accountable to any regulation since, as a state, Fascism quells all legal opposition.

Finally, it is not, I think, facile or naively optimistic to suggest that modernity offers other positions, such as the various discourses of individual and collective rights and freedoms, from which to criticise both political ideologies which harass and coerce subordinate groups and the modernist art movements which supported these ideologies. The Fascist imaginary is para-noically obsessed with the body (whether of the individual, the state, the nation or the race) and with the regulation of the boundaries between it and other bodies: there is an effortless sliding from literal to metaphorical bodies and back again. It is an imaginary obsessed with control, cleansing, healing. It applies a 'medical' or 'surgical' rationale. But what it, and the artistic ideologies like Futurism which converged with it, mask or displace with these slidings and metaphors, are actual or possible violent acts on real human bodies. If we want to make a political critique of these ideologies from within modernity there is no better place to start than with its imaginary of the body and with those real bodies which it coerces, humiliates, injures or murders.

Elizabeth Wright

Dismembering the body politic:
Brecht's early plays

Brecht's early plays differ from his later work and the *Lehrstücke* as examples of Jean-François Lyotard's notion of 'experimentation' aimed at eliciting new criteria for rules in each pragmatic situation,[47] rather than as examples of the author's own view of an experimental 'theatre of the scientific age' in which he and his co-workers self-consciously probe history for its repression of the political facts of life.

The early Brecht is different from the later Brecht who produced the split subjects of the 'great' plays and who attributed this split to the divisive nature of bourgeois capitalism. In the Brecht of the early plays ideas are enacted rather than defined, with the result that accidental meaning subverts any didactic intention. In Walter Benjamin's terminology, it is a case of 'Erlebnis' (experiencing the random shocks of life) replacing 'Erfahrung' (experiencing life as a continuity).

Where in the 'great' plays the didactic story-line provides sense and meaning despite the disruptions of the epic mode, in the early plays theatricalisation of experience undermines reference, so that anything can happen in the communication process, between characters, and between stage and audience. To theatricalise is to engage in a fictive experiment with the interaction of language and experience, to explore the very ground of representation. According to Lyotard the language games one is nevertheless forced to play expose the players to dire risks as they pursue the satisfaction their subjectivities demand:

The social bond, understood as a multiplicity of language games, very different among themselves, each with its own pragmatic efficacy and its capability of positioning people in precise places in order to have them play their parts, is traversed by terror, that is, by the fear of death.[48]

In Brecht's early plays there is no appeal to the audience to solve the contradictions outside the deliberately unfinished work. The work of the plays is on language, with the effect that the characters are not self-present but continually constitute themselves via some other. This other may include the individual subject, but the audience as such is not inscribed in the text. On the contrary, there is rather a move away from soliciting any kind of collective perception.

The plays have certain elements of negation in common. That is why they cannot be reduced to a *fabula*, although both Marxists and humanists have tried to appropriate them. Marxist critics see them as subjective, impressionistic, and self-indulgently aesthetic. Humanist critics fall back on biography and talk about the anarchistic tendencies of the young Brecht, citing the author's much later comment on *Baal*: 'I admit (and warn you) the play is lacking in wisdom.'[49] Meanwhile Marxist critics cite another part of the same comment: 'The play *Baal* could present difficulties for those who have not learned to think dialectically. They are not likely to find anything in it apart from the glorification of a blatant egotism.'[50] But as Brecht himself was never satisfied with the results of his work,[51] it is not hard to make out a case for either position.

The present discussion will concentrate on *Baal* and *In the Jungle of the Cities*, written by Brecht at the age of twenty and twenty-three respectively. It will be seen that the power of the two plays resides not in their documentary effectiveness, but in their formal characteristics. Their content can be appropriated one way or another, but if they have any political use-value it is more likely to be found in their formal properties than in any uniform conceptual view, such as vitalism, nihilism, anarchism, or even Marxism. Their politico-aesthetic function resides in the way Brecht manages to make the spasmodic, discontinuous perceptions of a reality-in-process into a theatrical object. They challenge our interpretations of the concrete and our assumptions that words are able to define that which we perceive with the senses. Most of all, the plays are an attack on assumptions of stable identity, our own and that of others.

Baal and *In the Jungle of the Cities* offer a challenge to representation in a different mode from that of the later plays of Brecht, which tend to be purges of the shocks to our mimetic understanding. They do not yield a relatively ordered collage of happenings, conveniently subtitled in a way which foregrounds the *fabula*, being anti-narrative in form. Impossible to package for consumption, they disrupt normal modes of perception and merely point to happenings, postures, and processes. They cannot be reduced to any particular ideology, because this would amount to an attempt to join up a deliberately de-centred view of reality. Instead they expose the spectator to an onslaught on representation from within.

Brecht is out to redefine our understandings of concrete limit-experiences; he restages the dramas of birth, love, sickness and death in the attempt to articulate alternative meanings. The plays provide a knowledge of the condition of representation for a subject (character and spectator): she/he can only have access to such knowledge via a theatricalisation of experience. That is to say, Brecht makes limit-experience into a theatrical object.

Baal

The form of the play is that of a series of fragmentary scenes centred around a poet (seen by some critics as a Verlaine/Rimbaud figure)[52] who lives out his life by eating, drinking, reciting, singing in grog houses and cafés, procuring sexual encounters which are enacted in attic rooms, streets, fields and forests. Women (and a male lover) only too readily make themselves available to him as sexual objects, and he moves from one to the other, leaving a trail of corpses in his wake. He dies unrepentant and abandoned by all. 'He plunges grinning into every extreme of moral and physical squalor; and emerges – this animal tormented by possession of a soul – gasping: "It was all beautiful!" '

Baal, Brecht argues, is 'asocial, but in an asocial society', for here an 'I' confronts a world only able to recognise a productivity which can be exploited rather than one that can be utilised, which has given grounds for some critics to argue that Baal is an active anti-bourgeois, an anarchist in a society which pays lip-service to bourgeois individualism but then cannot accept it when it appears in its extreme form.[53] The asocial Baal thus exploits the exploited, putting the basic drives on show for all to see. In 1918 Brecht wrote to Caspar Neher, his old schoolfriend and life-long collaborator: 'I am writing a comedy: Baal guzzles, Baal dances, Baal is transfigured! A hamster, a great sensualist, a clod who leaves grease spots in the sky, a crazy fellow with immortal intestines.'[54]

The general argument is that the early Brecht wanted to affirm the subversive energy of the basic drives in the context of a bourgeois society which insisted on putting the reality principle before the pleasure principle. An undialectical interpretation would be that this drive-bound creature acts as a provocation to a society which demands that the drives be repressed and as a shock reminder of what this entails. This might be turned into a dialectical interpretation if one points out that Baal does not withdraw from society, but on the contrary, uses others, particularly women, in order to gratify his needs; his being 'asocial in an asocial society' is thus not wholly to be laid at society's door. Yet on the other hand perverse sexuality can become a positive act against bourgeois morality, a more revolutionary move than cravenly surrendering in the style of *The House Tutor* and *Man is Man* by committing acts of self-castration in order to stay in the system. Brecht himself, however, expressed misgivings about the political effectiveness and documentary use-value of his new model, though he held to the radical effects of the asocial: 'How can the conceptual world of *Baal* possibly be made effectual in a world which nowhere conceptualizes the individual as a phenomenon, but as something to be taken for granted?'[55]

The scandal of *Baal* is the ubiquitous nature of the central figure's desire. The whole world is libidinised for Baal; he appears to have no sense of any boundaries, living in a flux of perceptual experience and continually seeking out situations of extreme limits which might bring new forms of subjective experience. This mode of being involves using others as objects for a catalyst, a trigger for desire, rather than as ends in themselves: the libidinal aim is the desire of another, not the person as such, who becomes expendable once the circuit of desire is completed: 'When a woman, says Baal, gives you her all / Let her go, for she has nothing more.'[56] This libidinised world of pleasure and pain is seen retrospectively in the 'Chorale of the Great Baal', which precedes the play as a hymn to nature, to the real in which Baal lives and dies. Beauty and ugliness are indiscriminately experienced, and vice is as productive as virtue: 'All vices are good for something/And so is the man who practises them', says Baal.[57] In the real world everything is productive, nothing is wasted, and dirt – which, as Freud observed, is only matter in the wrong place – can become an object serving a non-squalid function. One of the lumber men in the forest who observed the onset of Baal's death comments: 'He had a way of laying himself down in the dirt; but then he never got up again and he knew it. He lay down as if in a bed already made.'[58]

For Baal there is nothing that is not there to be absorbed by his voracious senses. Indeed, the world is waiting for him before he arrives, mediated in the process of his growth in his mother's womb and retained by him as his body rots away in the womb of the earth. This cyclical process is theatricalised in Baal's 'chorale' which addresses itself to the audience. The dominant image is the sky which is also the word for 'heaven' in German: metaphorically 'Himmel' stands for material nature, and it becomes a near-blasphemous paradox in its presence as mere cyclorama to desire. For Baal is inserted into a material process, where the presence of an indifferent nature is inescapable and indeed celebrated: he capitalises on the indifference of nature by allowing himself total licence. The bare sky and the wide world form a steady back-drop, there before him and after him, giving the same cover in pleasure or pain. When Baal dies 'he has so much sky under his eyelids / That even in death he still has sky enough.'[59] Baal will have absorbed so much life that the difference between life and death becomes eroded.

Throughout the text, fragmentary scenes, clusters of images and snatches of songs act as metaphors for a theatrical reality, access to which can only be had subjectively. The function of the subjective, however, is not that it acts as a precondition for a new reality, as the Expressionist project conceived it, but that it marks an attempt to get back to the concrete. By the same token, a Marxist reading which argues that all this is symptomatic of the fragmentariness of bourgeois life[60] presupposes a unity which could be obtained if only things were otherwise. This is precisely what the material production of this text does not allow, for it shows a natural process where creatures prey on each other: the vultures wait for Baal and Baal knows it and preys on them in turn. As the corpse of the woman who drowns herself because of him glides Ophelia-like downstream, far from leaving a gap in nature, her death facilitates other life:

Wrack and seaweed cling to her as she swims
Slowly their burden adds to her weight.
Coolly fishes play about her limbs
Creatures and growths encumber her in her final state.

. . .

As her pale body decayed in the water there
It happened (very slowly) that God gradually
    forgot it
First her face, then her hands, and right at
    the last her hair
Then she rotted in rivers where much else
    rotted.[61]

Snatches of elegies, celebrating the materiality of life and death, recur in the text, prominently as a contrast between the whiteness of bodies and fresh linen and the blackness of mud, earth and filth, the delicacy of the women and the grossness of Baal, all indiscriminately libidinised. The process of life is represented as an anti-narrative, a circulation of matter, where identities are always precarious and, if anything, shunned, because they interfere with participation in the process. Baal and his companions consciously seek to dissolve all boundaries, all naming: 'Yours is a face, in which the winds have room to blow . . . you haven't a face at all';[62] 'Once she has been laid, she may become a heap of flesh, which no longer has a face'; 'D'you know what I'm called, then? My name's Sophie Barger.' 'You've got to forget it.' Baal celebrates the circulation of desire irrespective of identities and personal destinies: 'As the juniper tree has many roots, all twisted, so you have many limbs in one bed, and in them the heart beats faster and the blood flows.'[63]

This imagery comes uncannily close to such postmodern conceptualisations as 'a body without organs', or 'rhizome'[64] – anti-categories which have been coined in order to open on to a project that seems very similar to that pursued by the young Brecht, namely 'to overturn the theatre of representation into the order of desiring production'.[65] To do this they reject psychoanalysis for what they call 'schizoanalysis', whose task it is to discover the nature of the libidinal investments in the social field. The 'rhizome' combats Aristotelian logic-trees that divide genera, species and differentiae on a binary basis. Rhizomatic categories produce the heterogeneous, enabling the conception of asignificant particles, not defined by a master signifier, but by the interaction of flows and currents of desire. Schizoanalysis, as much the author's as the reader's project, then serves as a new model for artistic production, tracing 'lines of flight' which facilitate escape out of the hierarchical system. The revolutionary reader/writer (author and spectator each taking up this dual role) conducts experiments, trying to find a way out of representation, providing what Deleuze and Guattari call 'deterritorialised' images, unformed material offering itself to temporary investments, demolishing totalising structures and revealing heterogeneous elements. Desire flows and is constantly on the move, mapping new territories, fluid boundaries that are constantly shifting.

Instead of a 'politics of interpretation' going over the past in the realm of unconscious fantasy, they call for a 'politics of experimentation', taking hold of existing intensities of desire to get the desiring mechanism in touch with historical reality. Under historical reality Deleuze and Guattari do not want to recover Oedipal experience; on the contrary, what they are after is memory functioning as a 'childhood block: it is the only real life of the child; it deterritorialises; it displaces itself in time, with time, in order to reactivate desire and to multiply its connections'.[66]

Evidence in Baal points towards an attempt to recover such experience, manifesting itself in the energy with which Baal sets about investing the world with new 'intensities', 'enjoyment, by God, is no easy thing'[67] and in the few utopian elements which involve the kind of past illuminations Deleuze and Guattari have in mind. As Baal begins to feel the onset of his decline at the age of twenty-five, he reminisces, declaring himself full of champagne and happy in the dark, feeling 'nostalgia without memories':

> Sick from the sun, and eaten raw by the weather
> A looted wreath crowning his tangled head
> He called back the dreams of a childhood he had lost altogether
> Forgot the roof, but never the sky overhead

. . .

> Loafing through hells and flogged through paradises
> Calm and grinning, with expressionless stare
> Sometimes he dreams of a small field he
>   recognizes
> With blue sky overhead and nothing more.

There is much that speaks thematically in the text against a simple appropriation of this as evidence of the utopian: not only Baal's exploitation of and brutality towards women and their readiness to lend themselves as victims, but also the collapse of his bravado and deliberate staging of his ignominious death. Yet formally, in the theatricalisation of nature as the material rather than the ideal, the ambiguity of the social bond is exposed, a bond feared in life and desired in death, a reversal that subjects are exposed to in confronting concrete reality. Baal himself is quite unfitted as a character to give shape to the revolutionary impulse of this exposure even though he has access to the unrepresentable ground from which it springs. In his undirected savagery he is the evidence of that ground and there is a pathos in his failure to make use of it on behalf of the oppressed around him. Baal is unable to 'reactivate desire' and 'multiply connections'. His defeat is a cautionary tale for revolutionaries.

It is not surprising that Brecht had misgivings about his play 'lacking wisdom' and about its being useful as a blueprint.

In the Jungle of the Cities

This play, first performed in 1923, shares certain thematic features with Baal: a sordid setting, a character or characters whose behaviour seems totally arbitrary, a sadistic attitude to female figures who are represented as wallowing in such treatment, a homosexual relation which culminates in death. It too is in the form of fragmented scenes, originally set in Chicago's Chinatown but extended to Chicago as a whole in the 1927 version. The action revolves around an apparently motiveless fight between an older and a younger man. The older man, the active agent in this play, is a Malay timber merchant by the name of Shlink, who provokes a young American, George Garga, to enter into conflict with him, as a result of which Garga gets sacked from his job as a library assistant. In the course of their power-struggle the economic fortunes of the contestants go back and forth, while Garga's family- and love-relations become pawns in the odd couple's all-absorbing master/slave game. Just as in *Baal*, the female figures readily offer themselves as victims to the power of the male. Shlink is eventually defeated in the struggle and dies by his own hand in the surrounding thickets and swamps. The conflict is played out against a sordid background, the scenes being set mainly in the workplaces and sleeping quarters of Shlink and Garga: a lending-library, a timber merchant's office, a Chinese hotel, Garga's home, a bar, and the wilderness surrounding Lake Michigan.

Brecht was as ambivalent in his utterances about this play as he was in the case of *Baal*. The only thing that is clear from the fragmentary notes he made over a period of time is that he was working towards an understanding of what he was trying to do. What troubled him earlier and later is the nature of the fight that he is attempting to stage. He prefaced the play with an injunction to the audience not to worry about the motives for the fight, but to keep in mind what is at stake for the contestants, to make an impartial judgement on the technique of the fighters and to concentrate on the finish.[69] But both at the time of the first performance and in his later retrospective notes on the early plays he feels he has to defend the lack of motive. He does not seem to be able to make up his mind whether it is a fight over material things, such as family and business, or whether it is a fight conducted for the sheer joy of fighting, but he does seem to be aware that the conflict is somehow over-determined, that its source is not exhausted by a single factor:

What was new was a type of man who conducted a fight without enmity but with hitherto unheard of, undepicted, methods, together with his attitude to the family, to marriage, to his fellow-humans in general, and much else – probably too much.[70]

Yet Brecht could not leave this 'too much' alone. In another set of notes to this play he wavers between maintaining that there is such a thing as fighting for pure enjoyment (something he calls an 'idealised fight', in contrast to the fight over women or property so common in the bourgeois theatre), and wondering whether the 'idealised fight' with which he was so fascinated might not be an allegory of the class struggle, which would make it into a revolutionary fight instead of a competition for what ever was going in capitalism.[71]

What Brecht returns to again and again in his comments is the idea of a furious fight engaged in for no other reason than the pure pleasure of fighting, a kind of 'mythic fight' conducted only for the sake of determining who was the 'best man'.[72] Yet there is no indication that the contestants experience their fight as an enjoyable sport; on the contrary, they show every sign of being caught up in a paranoiac structure. If this is a sport it is only so to the extent that it is a struggle about who can torment the other most. It is not so much about the pleasure of winning as about the seemingly perverse pleasure of destroying or being destroyed. It ends with Shlink dying as ignominiously as Baal, with Garga proclaiming that the most important thing is not to win, but to stay alive.

So what gives this fight its energy, if it is not, as Brecht would like it to have been, the sheer love of fighting? Someone (Garga) is unreasonably provoked and yet quick to take up the challenge, taking up the fight 'unconditionally'. This includes his acceptance of Shlink's terms, that he is to play the evil master in a master/slave relationship, which Shlink defines:

From now on, Mr Garga, my fate's in your hands. I don't know you! From now on I'm going to be your slave. Every look that comes into your eyes will trouble me. Every one of your wishes, known or unknown, will find me willing. Your cares will be my cares, my strength will be yours. My feelings will be dedicated to you alone, and you will be an evil master.[73]

The staging of conflicts and quarrels works as part of a theatrical moment in the constitution and reconstitution of subjectivity and bears out Lacan's theory of the formation of the subject. That which gives rise to that particular form of aggression he terms 'aggressivity' is the fear of dismemberment, the threat to the body image posed by the supposed unity and wholeness of another: 'Subjective experience must be fully enabled to recognize the central nucleus of ambivalent aggressivity, which in the present stage of our culture is given to us under the dominant species of resentment.'[74]

In Brecht's text it is possible to discern certain paranoiac structures and images of disintegration which might make an otherwise motiveless fight between 'comrades of a metaphysical action'[75] more readable in terms of the text's own figurations.

In *In the Jungle of the Cities* the dominant images are clustered around the fear of losing face, and these images are shared out among the characters and are not confined to the main protagonists. Unlike in *Baal* dissolution is feared rather than desired, but as in *Baal* the male figures constitute themselves at the expense of the female ones, who again masochistically turn themselves into sex objects. The obsessive dwelling on the face as a likely index to identity is present throughout and provides one of the few conceptual links in the otherwise non-narrative stance of the play. It is partly by this means that the fear of disintegration is made representable.

Dramatically the text is made up of a series of face-losing encounters within a paranoiac structure of pursuers and victims. The opening scene immediately strikes this double note in that the challenger, Shlink, seems to have a sufficient knowledge of Garga's life to mock, harass and hustle him. Shlink is well informed as regards the whereabouts and abject circumstances of Garga's father John, his mother Mae, his sister Marie and girlfriend Jane, and even about Garga's private dream, his longing to go to Tahiti, factors which empower his persecution:

GARGA   Are you running a detective agency? Your interest in us is flattering, I hope.
SHLINK   You're just shutting your eyes. Your family is headed for disaster. You're the only one who makes any money, and you can indulge in opinions! When you could be on your way to Tahiti.
Shows him a sea chart that he has with him.[78]

Shlink taunts Garga with ever increasing sums of money in a deliberate move to provoke and humiliate him:

GARGA   What do you want of me? I don't know you. I've never seen you before.
SHLINK   I never heard of this book and it doesn't mean a thing to me. I'm offering you forty dollars for your opinion of it.
GARGA   I'll sell you the opinions of Mr J.V. Jensen and Mr Arthur Rimbaud, but I won't sell you my opinion.
SHLINK   Your opinion is as worthless as theirs, but right now I want to buy it.
GARGA   I indulge in opinions.[77]

As a result of Shlink's manoeuvres Garga is dismissed. In order to save his face and his family he now has no option but to take over the timber business which Shlink forces on him. The persecution and its effects on the driven set of characters manifests itself not merely on a thematic and fragmentary narrative level, but via a persistent set of configurations which orchestrate the sufferings undergone by all as they literally face humiliation, rejection, hunger, sickness and death. The metaphor of losing face recurs in a variety of sensuous images whose meaning and connections are withheld: 'May I see your face?' 'It's no longer a face. It isn't me'; 'People stay what they are even when their faces disintegrate'; 'My mother, Mae Garga . . . went missing three years ago in October and has even vanished from memory, she no longer has a face. It fell off like a yellow leaf.'

Causing another to lose face seems to act as some guarantee of identity. A Salvation Army officer who stands to make a gain for his cause maintains 'I have always kept my face clean', only to have Garga incite Shlink to 'spit in his face . . . if it so pleases you', as the price for receiving the gift. Shlink relates how he was maltreated working in the junks on the Yangtze, 'a man trod on our faces every time he came on board. We were too lazy to move our faces out of the way. Somehow or other the man was never too lazy.' One of the women's faces is described as looking like 'a lemon ice that's starting to thaw', another woman asks 'does my face seem bloated to you?' Shlink describes Garga's face as 'hard as amber, transparent, here and there one can find dead flies in it'. Shlink begs Marie, 'throw a cloth over my face, have pity', just before he dies.

When Shlink and Garga finally confront each other in the undergrowth and gravel pits of the lakeside, it is only Shlink who is still committed to the metaphysics of the conflict, and who mourns the impossibility of a bodily relationship, whether it is grounded in love or hate. Garga divests himself of all responsibilities and sets off alone to begin again in a new city. Like Baal he affirms the past, regretting nothing: 'It's a good thing to be alone. The chaos is spent. That was the best time.'[78]

Chaos is good, because it leads back to the concrete, out of the repressive representation, but only for the male protagonist, to which the text testifies: 'You have opened her eyes to the fact that she will always be an object for men.' Women are no more than props in the maintenance of men's solipsistic fight; they have to submit to the constant masculine desire for representation together with the fear of feminine excess. But whereas in *Baal* the themes and figures of the text incline towards a celebration of dissolution and a defiance in the face of decay, in *Jungle* dissolution, decay and death are feared and fought by all. Both plays, however, are preoccupied with the concrete, figured as uncontrollable bodily fluids – spittle, tears – or bodily grossness and sickness in the ravages of time: what is shown is the uncanniness of dismemberment rather than the comforts of metamorphosis. Being is in the body; the subject is preoccupied with evolving a bodily image of itself. The body therefore becomes highly eroticised: the effect of this is aggressivity as a reaction to the threat of bodily disintegration, loss of continuity, or loss of self-esteem. The characters under subjection to this threat are put to the utmost test in their attempts to form a libidinal relationship to the world (Baal) or test out its constancy (Shlink). Narcissism and identification emerge as part of the conflict with an other, as each tries to verify itself by trying to take the other's place (Shlink and Garga). Narcissism – fear of losing face – is not pathology but part of self-formation. The source of energy, the 'meta-physical' element in both plays, is narcissistic passion, the goal of energy being the interaction with the other – a mirror image rather than with the Other – the power structure. Yet the Other is clearly present in the theatricalisation of the general oppressiveness of the living and working conditions of the characters and in the language which cannot articulate their concrete experience.

These plays pose a challenge to the spectator, and even more to the reader who misses out on the stage production on which these texts depend perhaps more than any other of Brecht's plays. The spectator needs to be drawn into the production process in order to experience the shifting and contradictory choices of stage subjects/objects. The work of engaging the audience is not done on the stage via specific V-effects, but pressure is put on the audience to co-produce in order to avoid the unpalatable alternative of placing her- or himself in a psychotic position and abandoning meaning, and thus becoming dismembered subjects themselves.

Rod Mengham

From Georges Sorel to *Blast*

Wyndham Lewis composed his works as the enemy outsider of English culture; he relished the position of permanent adversary expressed through a rhetoric of violent aggression and frequently acted out in a series of conflicts with other artists and artistic groups. His sustained effort of going against the grain of British cultural politics was most conspicuous during the 1930s, when a fascination with the Hitler phenomenon was initially ambivalent enough to call his judgement into question and attract charges that he was a Nazi proselyte. Such reactions were only confirmation for Lewis that his goads were having effect; but his continued waywardness and deliberate provocations should not be seen principally as the means by which an aberrant psychology achieved satisfaction. The viperish subversions for which he has become notorious should rather be understood as part of a political method that had clear determinants in the French cultural milieu with which Lewis enjoyed immediate contact during his lengthy stays in Paris between 1903 and 1908. There was a body of social and political thought developing during these years, both on the syndicalist left, and among those on the extreme right who would form the Action Française, by whose lights a chronic antinomianism could represent a principled stand with both moral and intellectual legitimacy. In particular, Lewis's attitude towards the avant-garde art group as a kind of terrorist cell, engaged in guerrilla warfare against bourgeois philistinism, while it could be translated into the series of rhetorical moves that he employed with increasing facility, should also be seen as having emerged naturally from French thinking about the uses of violence in political life. And in this connection the key figure, both in the original French context and in the mind of Lewis himself (as frequent references in a number of his texts convey) was Georges Sorel. This essay confines itself to exploring the possibility that Sorel's emphatic recommendations of violence resonate in the various aspects of Lewis's career as editor, entrepreneur and writer.

Sorel's most celebrated publication was *Réflexions sur la violence*, first published in 1908. The first English edition in the translation by T. E. Hulme (with whom Lewis had personal and professional relations) was published in 1916. In Lewis's study of 1926, *The Art of Being Ruled*, both *Réflexions* and Sorel's other major text *Les illusions du progrés* (also first published in 1908) are repeatedly quoted from and analysed, Lewis's estimate of their significance being encapsulated in the ultimatum that 'George [*sic*] Sorel is the key to all contemporary political thought.'[79] Sorel's central tenet in *Réflexions* is that the ethical life is inseparable from violence. A distinction is made between violence proper, since its agents are the 'producers', and force, which is the means employed by the state to impose a false consciousness of social unity. Since the reality is disunity and a conflict of interests, violence is not only the recourse of the proletariat, but also the guarantee of its integrity. A successful act of violence represents a defeat of hypocrisy, but according to Sorel the revolutionary disturbances of the nineteenth century had all, without exception, waylaid violence into force by complying with the interests of the state, 'reinforcing the power of the state'.[80] The ethical life is only preserved in small groups whose violence detaches them from the state; the model for this activity is syndicalism, but Sorel traces a similar dynamic operating in different periods of history. In Chapter VI, 'The Ethics of Violence', he argues that the persistence and success of Christian ideas throughout the first millennium depended on the early Christians' engagement in situations of violent conflict. In his view, the availability of the Gospels was not enough to ensure the survival of Christianity, which is why the apocalyptic books were added to the existing corpus of texts; the Acts of the Martyrs should be regarded as a further stage in the attempt to supplement a code of meekness with the advertised strength of ideas proven in combat: 'the Acts of the Martyrs were drawn up in such a way that they might excite the same feelings that the Apocalypses excited; it may be said that they replaced these'. [81]The potent mixture of apocalypse, violent separation and autonomy is one that Sorel himself is prepared to transplant from one sphere of operation to another, from politics to religion and vice versa, in respect of societies historically very different from one another, and in Lewis's case, this transfer can be effected just as easily in respect of avant-garde artistic practice in England.

What makes Sorel's ideas particularly amenable to the practice of an avant-garde is their insistence on the need for splinter groups, social fractions, cadres, cells, small nuclei of enemies of the state. Just as Sorel refused to lament the marginalising and atomising of proletarian organisation, because he recognised separatism not only as a tactical expedient but also as a form of moral insurance, so the avant-gardes of pre-war London tried to preserve the separate identity of artistic values that a mass culture would only ever endure in adulterated form. Both the Rebel Art Centre and the Vorticist project *Blast* conducted their business in a dissident and apocalyptic register that is wholly compatible with Sorel's articulation of the General Strike as the enabling myth of syndicalist activity. The Strike is needed as a replacement for political debate, which would only draw the proletariat into a movement of 'social capillarity',[82] a process that other commentators have described as 'embourgeoisement': ' the assimilation by the working classes of bourgeois norms, ideas and modes of behaviour'.[83] The exclusion orders that result from this resemble the avant-garde's embargo on vulgarisation of its practices, which it prefers to introduce into the context of everyday life by means of violent irruption, imposing its own terms of reference on kinds of experience that conventionally do not exchange views with art. At the same time, the Strike does not figure in syndicalist discourse with reference to considered analyses or detailed plans, but in the form of a myth, or occasionally a drama, intended to evoke 'as an undivided whole the mass of sentiments which corresponds to the different manifestations of the war undertaken by socialism against modern society'.[84] According to Sorel, 'the whole of socialism' is concentrated by this means into the myth, which cannot therefore be subjected to analysis, but must be grasped 'by intuition alone'; this gives it a function rather like that of artistic symbol. Moreover, the tension between analysis and intuition is reproduced in the differentiation of kinds of language employed by reform socialism and syndicalism respectively, the one concerned to define the mode of its progress, the other marking its progress by a gesture to infinity, 'because it puts on one side all discussions of definite reforms and confronts men with a catastrophe'.[85] The sabotaging of definition and, more generally, the destruction of instrumental language, provides the basis for a broad comparison with avant-garde practice that will be given a little later on. The social organisation of syndicates and artistic groups alike reflects the paradox of a minority attacking consensus on behalf of the majority. As J.C. Talmon argues, in what is a largely mistrustful examination of Sorel's teachings: 'what they are in fact is a Nietzschean repudiation of bourgeois mediocrity and deceit and a Nietzschean philosophy of élitism applied to the proletariat'.[86]

   It is Sorel's enthusiasm for the intactness of the small group and the inviolability of its separate identity that makes his project especially compatible with avant-gardism. But at the same time, fear of contamination by extraneous forces (a motive that is heavily stressed by Edward Shils)[87] could also serve as a link between syndicalism and other very different kinds of fervid interest in belligerence and purity. From one point of view, a rather technical one, it is only a contraction of scale that removes the separatism of small groups from the same field of operations as an aggressive right-wing nationalism. Historically speaking, the link was actually made effective for a short period of time during the experimental collaboration of syndicalists with members of the Action Français.[88] Aggressive nationalism was equally popular in England at the time; Lawrence caught the mood in 1916 in *Women in Love* where he makes Gerald Crich give a representative little speech on national 'emulation'. Lewis's own writings are copiously supplied with illustrations of the eagerness for national rivalry, though it is revealing that all his most pungent examples are French. In *Rude Assignment*, his intellectual autobiography, he refers to the claim of Edouard Berth that the 'true nature' of a state is to be 'war incarnate'; 'a State is, in other words, a society organized for war. What is natural for all states is to be bracing themselves to spring upon another state.'[89]

Mutual aggression in the national and international spheres, group solidarity and the demand for programmes of total change are vital components of the background to Lewis's involvement in cultural politics in the period, just before the First World War, up to and including the publication of his most notorious editorial venture, *Blast*.[90] His conduct during this time was marked by a series of disaffiliations from one-time colleagues and friends. In fact, his rate of turnover in respect of both artistic allies and personal friends was quite phenomenal; he seems to have alienated virtually everybody.[91]

Once again, the recurrent need for expulsion and outsiderdom, which could be regarded merely as an individual character trait, is strictly in line with Sorelian principles, in that it allowed Lewis to occupy a position from which to unlock 'the mystery of historical development', a mystery which, Sorel argues, 'is only intelligible to men who are far removed from superficial disturbances; the chroniclers and the actors of the drama do not see at all, what, later on, will be regarded as fundamental; so that one might formulate this apparently paradoxical rule, "it is necessary to be outside in order to see the inside" '.[92] In other words, the Bohemian squabbles and betrayals that provide copy for a melodramatic psycho-biography are indistinguishable from the series of moves that Lewis the strategist would have to make in order for his work to avail itself of the scope guaranteed by critical distance.

Lewis distanced himself from Impressionism, Cubism, Futurism (Marinetti in particular), the Omega workshop (Roger Fry in particular), his associates at the Rebel Art Centre and finally certain of his fellow Vorticists, even though he owed allegiance to each and every one of them in turn. In the epigraph to his journal *The Enemy*, which first appeared in 1927, he was to advocate hostility to the very idea of friendship, and carried out his threat by attacking an old ally and patron, Ezra Pound. As Sue Ellen Campbell points out, 'his attack on Pound advertised the seriousness of his new role as a critic; an Enemy who will publicly criticize even an old and valued friend will not easily be daunted by lesser social pressures'.[93] Pound's own estimate in 1914 was that 'in Mr Lewis's work one finds not a commentator but a protagonist. He is a man at war.'[94]

Lewis deplored Impressionism for its obsession with biological nature and ridiculed the subject matter of Braque and Picasso canvases of the Cubist period which he felt were more likely to depict the objects on a bourgeois table-top than anything else, and which would therefore reproduce without critical distance the preferences of a standard bourgeois sensibility. Despite his own preference for unfamiliar and dynamic subjects in painting, he soon became sceptical of the Futurists, whose flirtation with machinery he regarded as an evasion because its replacement of carafes and mandolins with trains and planes did nothing finally to free painting from its enslavement to the mimetic. Pound referred to Futurism as 'accelerated Impressionism' and this matched Lewis's observation that while the Futurists set themselves up in competition with their French precursors, there was an important sense in which both could be cast in opposition to his own preferred practice. In the final analysis, what Impressionism and Futurism shared was a supine attitude towards the given forms of the visible social world, whereas the Lewisian project involved the formation of a style that would not be based on the representation of given forms.

Nevertheless, he was attracted by the Futurists' massive investment in the principle of dynamism and had to exercise ingenuity in finding ways of distinguishing his own practice from theirs. Richard Cork, who has written most fully and astutely on Lewis's activities as a visual artist, draws the distinction in the following terms:

Lewis and his colleagues always preferred staccato, angular forms and sharp diagonals which broke masses up into fragments rather than rendering them in a rounded, flowing sequence. Curvilinear multiplication characterized the Futurist style, after all, and the Vorticists would have nothing to do with the Italians' obsessive interest in speed.[95]

What the interest in speed produced, amongst other things, was the exaggerated mimeticism of blurred contours, while the Vorticists retained 'an insistence on precise contours and a solidity of construction often', says Cork, 'almost sculptural in its weight'.[96] Perhaps the most successful Vorticist artist was the sculptor Henri Gaudier-Brzeska. A majority of both Vorticist painters and Vorticist sculptors pursued their interest in form to a point of abstraction far beyond anything achieved by most Futurists.

It is worth recalling what exactly the term 'vortex' might signify in this context. According to Pound, the vortex was 'a radiant node or cluster . . . a VORTEX, from which, and through which, and into which, ideas are constantly rushing'.[97] A focus, then, for dynamic energies, and a focus of intellectual dynamism. According to Lewis, however, the artist who is at the centre of this vortex, the Vorticist artist, is 'at his maximum point of energy when stillest'.[98] The vortex is simultaneously, then, the locus of great rushing energies and the locus of a great stillness. The paradox is not as problematical as might at first appear. The integrity of the individual artist is to be maintained precisely in the face of conflicting energies; the individuality of the artist defines itself against the claims of extraneous energies rushing through it and round it, just as for Sorel, the highest endeavour that humanity is capable of must stand the test of opposition and conflict. There is a formal parallel between the structural perfection that Lewis imagines at the heart of motion and the moral perfection that Sorel believes can only be generated from within a context of prolonged antagonism.

But the parallel that can be drawn between the ethics of Sorel and the principles or programme of Vorticism is less striking than the way in which the history of Lewis's actual involvements in a whole succession of separatist movements reflects a Sorelian insistence on the necessity for a permanent adversarial stance; it is revealing to go into a certain amount of detail concerning those episodes which prepared the way for *Blast*.

Lewis's employment at the Omega Workshop was crucial. The influence of Bloomsbury taste over the style of decoration promoted by the Omega could not have been ideal for Lewis, and the presence of two dominant personalities – his and Roger Fry's – at the workshop was a recipe for dissatisfaction. The differences between the two men emerged in their violent altercation over a commission for the Ideal Home Exhibition, which Fry may have rather clumsily steered away from his difficult colleague. Or Lewis may have turned what was only a misunderstanding over the negotiations into a full-scale dramatic confrontation, which led to his storming out of the Omega and taking four other artists with him. The situation was further exacerbated by Lewis's publication of a 'round robin' letter denouncing Fry. The trenchant satirical abuse of this document was effectively a rehearsal for the vituperative manifestos of *Blast*.

After breaking away from the Omega, Lewis founded, in March 1914, the Rebel Art Centre, at 38 Great Ormond Street. It did not take him long to estrange his fellow Rebels by putting their canvases on display while he locked away his own, on the suspicion that his colleagues would want to steal all his own ideas. Rebel activities reached a climax in a combination of intellectual rivalry and sexual jealousy involving Lewis and T. E. Hulme. The personal quarrel between the two men ended with Lewis being suspended, upside-down, by his trouser-cuffs from the railings of 38 Great Ormond Street. It was perhaps the most straightforwardly, if reductively, Sorelian episode of his entire career. Soon after this pantomime the momentum that had gone into the creation of the Rebel Art Centre petered out.

Lewis also set himself up as a sparring partner with Marinetti, who completed several reading tours of London venues during these years. Lewis was in the habit of taking gangs of hecklers along to the readings to barrack the proceedings from start to finish. Even so, he admired Marinetti's resourcefulness and facility with shock tactics and borrowed from him what became some of his own most effective and characteristic manoeuvres. Marinetti's 'Vital English Art' manifesto, published in the *Observer* on 7 June 1914, could almost have been a preliminary sketch for *Blast* in that much of its material is divided up into two columns headed 'WE WANT' and 'AGAINST', just as the *Blast* manifesto divides its targets up into those who are cursed and denounced and those who are blessed and encouraged. The Vorticist movement as such evolved as a fragile project; it had very little coherence except in so far as Lewis managed to make both issues of *Blast* almost single-handed ventures – he supplied the bulk of the writing himself.

Even before publication of the first issue, the editor's habitual bullying meant that several of the most important and interesting potential signatories to the manifesto, David Bomberg in particular, had already dropped out.

Lewis's psychological, and sometimes actual physical, pugilism, and the habits of execration and cat-calling that determined his public relations are permanently enshrined in the style and content of Blast. 'It is no accident', suggests Richard Cork, 'that as many as eleven professional fighters and music hall entertainers were blessed in Blast No. 1: the manifestos combine the aggression of the boxing-ring with the raucous aplomb of a music-hall song.'[99] Although he had parted company with Hulme by this time, Lewis would almost certainly have found common cause with the point of view put forward in Hulme's 1914 essay 'Modern Art and Its Philosophy'. This referred to the art of those who have since become associated with Vorticism as a 'new modern geometrical art' that was quite distinct from the productions of either Futurism or Cubism. Hulme predicted that 'the new "tendency towards abstraction" will culminate, not so much in the simple geometrical forms found in archaic art, but in the more complicated ones associated in our minds with the idea of machinery'.[100] Most important of all, he noted the significance of an amalgam of mechanistic energy with savage primitivism, and he associated the idea of machinery not so much with the Futurist emphasis upon speed and automation as with the desire to create 'an artificial world of order'. As H. Stuart Hughes expresses it, Sorel himself 'disliked what he called "natural nature", as contrasted with the "artificial nature" that scientists and technicians imposed on the chaos of reality';[101] and in Réflexions, Sorel argues that the need to control a refractory nature is what links art and mechanisation and allows one to be seen as the forerunner of the other: 'whenever we consider questions relative to industrial progress, we are led to consider art as an anticipation of the highest and technically most perfect forms of production'.[102]

A direct influence on Sorel's thinking on this topic was the German philosopher and Professor of Engineering Franz Reuleaux, whose major work, *The Kinematics of Machinery*, was published in English in 1876. Kinematics dealt with the science of movement and the changes wrought by movement: Reuleaux had a quasi-Marxist awareness of the social changes wrought by mechanisation and of the threat of alienation it posed to the labour force, but he also stressed the creative possibilities of technological invention. His terminology is extremely suggestive in the context of the present discussion, particularly in its concentration on the 'restriction' of motion, and the 'constrainment' of force:

The whole inner nature of the machine is, as our investigations have gradually made clear, the result of a systematic restriction, its completeness indicates the increasingly skilful constrainment of motion until all indefiniteness is entirely removed. Mankind has worked for ages in developing this limitation. If we look for a parallel to it elsewhere we may find it in the great problem of human civilization. In this the development of machinery forms indeed but one factor, but its outline is sufficiently distinct to stand out separately before us. Just as the poet contrasts the gentle and lovable Odyssean wanderers with the untamable Cyclops, the 'lawless-thoughted monsters', so appears to us the unrestrained power of natural forces, acting and reacting in limitless freedom, bringing forth from the struggle of all against all their inevitable but unknown results, compared with the action of forces in the machine, carefully constrained and guided so as to produce the single result aimed at. Wise restriction creates the state, by it alone can its capacities receive their full development; by restriction in the machine we have gradually become masters of the most tremendous forces, and brought them completely under our control.[103]

Reuleaux himself employs the vocabulary of 'restriction', 'constrainment', 'limitation', to compare the guiding of force in the machine with that which determines political structures. Sorel might almost have derived his insistence on separatism from this, as also his distinction between hypocritical force and ethical violence from Reuleaux's distinction between 'latent' and 'apparent' force. The description of the machine also resembles the characterisation of the vortex, at the centre of great rushing energies 'acting and reacting in limitless freedom', which it organises and from which it separates. Reuleaux, Sorel, Hulme and Lewis all stress the role of the intellect in the invention of artificial order, as opposed to the serendipitous discovery of natural motions by means of what Hulme, following Worringer, terms 'empathy'.[104] This is Reuleaux's version:

This constrainment is obtained only as the result of thought, man has had to create it through an intellectual act, in other words to invent it. Discovery on the one side, invention on the other; in this antithesis we have the difference between the dynamic and the kinematic development of the machine.

It is also an antithesis that might help to differentiate between two very different artistic enthusiasms for the machine, the one accompanied by a zest for adrenalin, the other by a respect for order; between the Futurist embrace of sheer dynamism and what we might now think of as the kinematic priorities of Vorticism. Curiously, Reuleaux's point-path diagrams, revealing the order behind mechanical motions, bear a family resemblance to the designs of Vorticist paintings and drawings.

Of course, the creation of an artificial order involves making its outline 'sufficiently distinct to stand out separately', by means of the removal or destruction of all 'indefiniteness', and it is the tone and vocabulary of destruction and eviction that has the most immediate impact in the Vorticist idiom. Even now, it is difficult not to be impressed by the strident vulgarity and the ferocity of the language used in *Blast*, as well as by the hammered-out boldness of its visual style. The initial statement of its lurid pink cover branded with the heavy black lettering of the title could not be more unabashed and swaggering. In *Vorticism and the English Avant-Garde* William C. Wees observes:

The mood created by that cluster of words [employed in the opening pages] – 'violent', 'exploded', 'bursting', 'burst up', 'volcanic', 'bomb' – reinforced *Blast*'s aggressive vision of artists as fighters, mercenaries, savages, barbarians, and revolutionaries, whose violent energies suited the dynamic, potentially violent modern world. 'The Art-instinct is permanently primitive', said the manifesto, 'the artist of the modern movement is a savage'.[106]

The title of Lewis's subsequently written memoir covering this period suggests the degree to which he identified his activities with the occupations of fighters, mercenaries, revolutionaries. That title, *Blasting and Bombardiering*, marks no difference between the business of propagating experimental art and the kind of work one is called upon to carry out as a soldier in the First World War trenches. 'Killing somebody', Lewis says in 'Futurism, Magic and Life', 'must be the greatest pleasure in existence; either like killing yourself without being interfered with by the instinct of self-preservation – or exterminating the instinct of self-preservation itself!'[107] 'The gladiatorial instincts', the manifesto defiantly pronounces, 'are the springs of Creation.'[108]

The first issue of *Blast* includes the manifestos, a string of reviews and notes by Lewis, two independent statements on 'the Vortex' by Pound and Gaudier-Brzeska, a review by Edward Wadsworth of a book by Kandinsky, a few of Pound's most feeble poems, a couple of barely appropriate pieces of fiction by Ford Madox Hueffer and Rebecca West, and finally the only piece of writing that has any real claim to revolutionise its medium, Lewis's peculiar and elusive text *Enemy of the Stars*. The title – which is archaic and futuristic at one and the same time - announces yet another scenario of conflict. The text proper is composed in a conflictual language held in a tension between the conventions of several different genres: drama, fiction, essay, poetry. The action is given a stage-setting that it would be impossible to stage. One cannot conceive of realising in theatrical terms the following directions: 'HE LIES LIKE HUMAN STRATA OF INFERNAL BIOLOGIES. WALKS LIKE WARY SHIFTING OF BODIES IN DISTANT EQUIPOISE. SITS LIKE A GOD BUILT BY AN ARCHITECTURAL STREAM, FECUNDED BY MAD BLASTS OF SUNLIGHT.[109]

The characters, Arghol and Hanp, are introduced as 'protagonist' and 'second actor', recalling the conventions of the Greek tragic theatre with its agonistic confrontations. Perhaps also one is supposed to think of the tragic conflict as it has been described by writers such as Hegel and Nietzsche, the two actors representing values that have become divorced from each other as much as they should be united. The sequence of events, culminating in a fight in which one actor murders the other, followed by the suicide of the survivor, illustrates the thesis that the two halves of the self can neither be successfully separated nor live together in peace. The element of confrontation is compounded by the instruction to the reader that the drama is to be 'VERY WELL ACTED BY YOU AND ME',[110] raising the possibility of an agonistic confrontation, actually a fight to the finish, between the writer and the reader. At the centre of *Blast*, then, the reader is issued with a challenge to a duel, shaken out of his or her habitual passivity, forced to act (in imagination at least), forced to collaborate in a Sorelian type of contest: the reader as co-conspirator, revolutionary, gladiator.

In an essay entitled 'The Physics of the Not-Self', appended to a revised version of *Enemy of the Stars* published in 1932, Lewis distinguishes between the 'self' and the 'not-self'. What he means by the self is not the individual ego but just the opposite. The accumulated effects of the environment on the individual – everything that attaches to the individual from her or his involvement in the socio-cultural continuum – comprises the self and has a deleterious effect on the achievement of true individualism in the not-self. At some level, this is what the struggle between Hanp and Arghol is supposed to signify.

What this position resembles is the platform for a radical individualism occupied most spectacularly at the time of early Modernism by the theories of Max Stirner. Stirner's book *Der Einzige und sein Eigentum* (translated as *The Ego and His Own*) had first been published in 1844 but had then gone into nearly total eclipse for more than fifty years before being revived for the English-speaking world in 1907 in the translation by the American anarchist Benjamin Tucker. After revival, the translation went into no less than forty-nine editions over the following twenty-two years. It became an immensely influential book.

Michael Levenson, in his study *The Genealogy of Modernism*, outlines the Stirnerian position and offers an account of its role in the formation of early Modernism.[111] For Stirner, the wilful individual was the sole source of truth. The ego was the centre of the world and its circumference, while religion, morality, democracy, simply dropped from consideration. Concepts such as 'equality', 'unity', 'humanity' and 'law' were regarded as futile and irrelevant. Only properties such as 'will', 'life' and 'self' were celebrated as healthy, because egoistic. All political programmes were ridiculed, especially those depending on 'humanitarian' or 'progressive' opinions.

Clearly, the attempt to separate out the ego from other constituents of subjectivity, to cut away everything that does not pertain to a central core of pure self-interest is to conceive of the subject in terms of an internal division – an internal conflict – that answers to the terms of Lewis's schedule for the divergence of the self from the not-self (the 'not-self' standing, for the sake of argument, for Stirner's ego). It also involves a degree of violence between the constituents of the subject (the Cain and Abel scenario of *Enemy of the Stars* makes this glaringly evident) which is a kind of internalisation of the violence among social groups that Sorel conceives of as the condition of moral and political integrity. Stirnerian egoism is a form of internal separatism, corresponding to the political separatism of warring factions that Sorel would argue allows for the possibility of self-determination in the social order. Both require a form of violence. *Enemy of the Stars* displays the projection of conflict into the elaboration of subject matter, but for Lewis himself the same principles came to govern his method of composition; in *Time and Western Man*, he refers to the movement of his thought as the outcome of a violent competition between possible lines of pursuit: 'I have allowed these contradictory things to struggle together, and the group that has proved the most powerful I have fixed upon as my most essential ME.'[112]

Fredric Jameson has explored how in another text of this period, Lewis's novel *Tarr*, written just before, during and after the First Word War, the business of detaching the self from the not-self is overtaken by the processes of history.[113] The novel is set in Paris, a city invaded by an astonishing range of foreign nationals, cultural refugees from a Europe whose old power-structure, determined by the relations of nation–states, is crumbling away and being replaced by the emergence of new forces that provide a different context for socialisation. Jameson proposes that the new model for the formation of social identity consists of political forces in the form of international movements: specifically, Fascism and Communism. But if in the general historical process, the gradual corrosion of national identities is seen as the result of damage inflicted by emerging transnational patterns of organisation, that is not exactly what is going on in *Tarr* at the level of narrative dispositions.

At the level of the narrative process, the subtraction of national identity is just part of a more general dislocation of stereotypes, and for each of the main characters the sense of self is most acutely realised in moments of syncopation between the different constituents of the self. For a character like Kreisler, in whom the conflict of self-images is most intense and most violent, his sense of how he relates to the most important organising categories of his imagination (stereotypes of Germanness, for example or stereotypes of what it means to be an artist) is a sense of distance and disconnection. He becomes disconnected from various accretions to the self or, perhaps one should say, not-self, but does not become connected instead to any substitute for them. He experiences the disjunction between 'self' and 'not-self' not as a great opportunity but as a painfully yawning gap.

As in *Enemy of the Stars*, the rivalry of constituents in *Tarr* culminates in a duel. But this particular competition of national identities (German and Polish) is not, *pace* Fredric Jameson, overtaken and overshadowed by the much greater violence of the impending First World War which would, of course, inevitably hasten the dispersal of patriotic realities. Reed Way Dasenbrook argues in his edition of *The Art of Being Ruled* for the view that Lewis's writing embodies a perception of the 'nation-war' of 1914–18 as no more than a background for three other wars: the 'class-war', dominated by the fortunes of socialism; the 'sex-war', a conflict deepened by the rise of feminism; and the 'age-war', illustrated by the 'cults' of childhood and homosexuality. *The Art of Being Ruled* itself shows how individuality, imprisoned in an oppressive social structure, becomes little more than the 'net effect' of these simultaneously waged wars: people are defined less and less in terms of who they are in themselves and more and more in terms of their membership in a warring party or parties.[114]

To conclude: what is particularly unusual about the texts and avant-garde activities of Wyndham Lewis during this period centres on their recognition of the social and political role of violence, and it is in their relationship to a variety of kinds and conceptions of violence, I think, that one can measure the aptness and adequacy of their response to the conditions of knowledge obtaining in European culture at the start of the First World War. For Lewis, the seminal figure in all this was Georges Sorel, and his view is best expressed in a characterisation of Sorel's work that could serve equally well as an accurate self-portrait:

George[*sic*] Sorel is the key to all contemporary political thought. Sorel is, or was, a highly unstable and equivocal figure. He seems composed of a crowd of warring personalities, sometimes one being in the ascendant, sometimes another, and which in any case he has not been able, or has not cared to control. He is the arch exponent of extreme action and revolutionary violence *à outrance*; but he expounds this sanguinary doctrine in manuals that often, by the changing of a few words, would equally serve the forces of traditional authority, and provide them with a twin evangel of demented and intolerant class-war . . .

He is, in brief, a symptomatic figure that it would be difficult to match. As to his standing in the world of letters and politics (and in that as in everything else he is a fabulous hybrid, attacking himself, biting his own tail, kicking his own heroical chest, his own unsynthetic flesh, and showing his wounds with pride – self-inflicted, self in everything) he has an enviable position.[115]

Michael Minden

Expressionism and the First World War

Expressionism and the First World War relate to each other like a form and a content which do not quite match. They exceed, miss, engulf each other. To paraphrase the words of one critic: 'The Expressionists at first prophesied and then opposed the War, and were finally rendered superfluous by it.'[116]

In this chapter I want to give an idea of the effect the war had on the Expressionists, then I want to look at the representation of and response to the war in various Expressionist texts, and finally I want to refer briefly to the Bloch–Lukács debate about Expressionism in the 1930s, which gives a model for thinking about the true relation between the phenomenon of artistic Expressionism, the first German Modernism, and historical reality.

Expressionism was a generational ferment, inspired with Nietzschean vitalism, starting in about 1910, and the war both interrupted and confirmed it. The apocalyptic tendencies of pre-war Expressionism sometimes produced a yearning for war, or visions of it, as a relief from a hostile and spiritually unsatisfactory reality. The first Expressionist to die in the war was Alfred Lichtenstein, who was killed on 25 September 1914. Before the war he had written: 'We have enjoyed peace for too long . . . if only a wind would blow . . . tear the gentle world with its talons of iron. That would be a real distraction.'[117] The profoundly felt dissatisfaction, indeed agony, of the early Expressionists not infrequently found definition in visions of war. Perhaps the best known such intimation of war comes in the famous poem of 1911 by Georg Heym, 'War'. It finds its voice, draws its power, from the rhetorical business of evoking the advent of the god of war, and from the contrast to the minor key reality which will be swept away:

> It falls far into the noise of the evening,
> Frost and shadow of an alien darkness.

The vision of war provides the other, against which reality is alienated, caught by the poem as it vanishes into worldwide conflagration and oceans of blood. The emphasis is upon mass movement: not revolutionary, but mythical or cosmic:

> He who has long slumbered has arisen,
> Arisen from deep vaults below.
> In the halflight he stands huge, unrecognised,
> and crushes the moon in his black hand.

The conventional reference of the lyric, the moon, is crushed within the chillingly regular lyric metre. Heym's poem is as complex and ambivalent and the celebration of war is mixed with terror. But in famous diary entries, Heym was less ambiguous: 'If only we would start a war, it doesn't matter whether the cause was just. This peace is so unwholesome, oily and sticky, like the gluey polish on old furniture.[118]

Heym himself did not live to see his dreams come true (he drowned while skating in 1912), so there is no way of knowing how he would have reacted in 1914, but according to John Willett the actual arrival of the war came as 'a bolt from the blue' to the generation of intellectuals and artists who had been responsible for the German avant-garde before August 1914.[119] This is the mismatch, the shock, I referred to above. Reality exceeds the dreams. Very soon, not only are the brilliant young men scattered, but many of them are dead. But not before the general predisposition to great change and apocalyptic renewal of their vigorous artistic oppositional attitude had merged for a moment with the almost universal 'Hurra-Patriotismus' of the outbreak of war. Apart from the apocalyptic fever provided by the outbreak of war, certain other deep-felt needs of that generation of artists were apparently met: notably the prospect of a sense of community to overcome the artist's isolation, and the sense also of political identity within the surpassing cause of war.

Franz Marc wrote, for instance, from the front in autumn 1914: 'The German nation sensed that it had to go through the Great War before it could form for itself a new life and new ideals.' For Marc a moral universe was still in place, but only just:

Only the good things remain, the genuine, substantial, true ones; they come through the purgatory of the war purified and strengthened. . . . If the war is to give us what we ardently desire and what is commensurate with our sacrifices – this gigantic equation takes your breath away – then we Germans must avoid nothing more passionately than narrowness in our hearts and our national aspirations.[120]

To make sense of the war is almost impossible. The objective failure to make sense of the war is held in the fact that this essay of Marc's was published in *Der Sturm* in 1916, after his death at Verdun, a circumstance which profoundly modifies his expressed meaning, and catches the strange refraction of the generations' aspirations in the reality of the First World War.

The fact is that after the initial enthusiasm of some Expressionists (apart from Marc; Toller, Kokoschka, Lichtenstein, Sorge, Döblin) the opposition of that intellectual–artistic generation to the war was implacable. The Expressionist milieu became the source of the most powerful pacifist voices. Its journals, both within Germany and more explicitly (because of censorship) outside Germany in Switzerland, were the principle organs of opposition to the war. Indeed, Pfemfert's journal *Die Aktion* had never supported the war and was uniform in its opposition, in the face of all the constraints placed by censorship, throughout the period of the war. (Incidentally, a considerable number of prominent young artists, among them Werfel, Hasenclever, Becher, had also conspicuously failed to join in with the general war fever.) By a curious reversal, it was now the anti-war cause, the passionate appeal to end the war, which lent substance and focus to the Expressionist project, so much so that Willett feels able to write: 'It was the war which turned the young poetic movement of 1910–14 into what became known as the Expressionist school.'[121]

The real experience of war certainly provided one of the key motifs of later Expressionism, the motif of transformation. To this we shall return in the context of the most famous literary representation of such a conversion, Toller's *Die Wandlung* (*The Transformation*). On the strength of experiences at the front, artists, intellectuals and writers were put in touch with a new spiritual immediacy and urgency which they strove to translate into effectiveness through their artistic, literary and political practice. It is interesting that the 'transformation' of Piscator, whose book *Das politische Theater* (*The Political Theatre*) opens with the words 'My chronology begins on the fourth of August 1914', was not to a more intense artistic commitment, an ever more concentrated appeal on behalf of humanity, but to a wholesale rejection of the whole edifice of art in favour of an unambiguous commitment to political praxis. Here too we see how the war both focused and outflanked the Expressionist movement.

For it is clear that opposition to the war no more supplied a smooth content for the angular forms of the Expressionists, no more delivered them the alternative reality they so sincerely craved, than had the war itself in the first place. It is the unreal reality of the First World War without precedent which gave rise to the hopes it also inevitably failed to fulfil.

In the revolutionary situation after the war the political aspirations of the Expressionists which it had brought to definition proved incapable of fulfilment. Nevertheless, this definition was sharp and real, and genuinely committed to entry into the political arena. Some Expressionist factions, such as those around Pfemfert and Rubiner, looked to the Soviet Union, others distilled a political programme out of artistic–intellectual pathos, as was the case with Kurt Hiller and those like him. In the Bavarian Republic of Councils Toller became first vice-chairman of the Central Council of Workers', Peasants' and Soldiers' Councils, then chairman of the Independent Socialist Party in Munich and finally commander of the corps defending the northern suburbs of Munich against the right-wing private army of General von Epp.

He thus commanded real political power for a brief period, yet none of the attempts by the Expressionists to permanently influence political reality came to anything.[122] They never connected with genuine popular support. This is because they could not come to terms with the contradiction inherent in the apotheosis of individualism which they proposed and a historical situation in which the foundations and assumptions of individualism as an ideology lay in ruins.

This is, of course, the difference between Piscator's, and Brecht's wartime conversions, and that of Toller and others who remained within the Expressionist horizon. It is also, some might argue, the contradiction with which they began, simply twisted a couple more turns.

But in order to explore the relationship between Expressionism and the war it is necessary to turn to specific texts, and especially the lyric. Expressionism was oriented towards the lyric even before the war, and in some ways, as a literary mode, lyric poetry suits the visionary and subjective tendency of the movement as well as its desire for brief and penetrating utterances, of an experimental and innovatory nature, calculated to shock or provoke a reader from his or her normal habits of response. At the same time the lyric is a mode in which immediacy can best be represented, since it is a reduced, truncated form, not bound in to the logic of drama or narrative, which tend to impose meanings by their very extension.

The First World War also produced a sort of immediacy. Immediacy in the sense of a sustained confrontation with death and suffering which resisted assimilation into any official discourse, be it the propagandistic labels of government and military leadership, or the heroic mode which literature had in store to deal with the subject. It is said that over a million poems were written in Germany on the occasion of the outbreak of the First World War.[123]

One of the most famous statements on the effect of the Great War upon poetry comes from Owen:

> Above all I am not concerned with Poetry
> My subject is War and the pity of War
> The poetry is in the pity
> all a poet can do today is warn.

Poetry retains a role in human affairs as response to a moral scandal which beggars coherent discourse. Poetry has a role because it can get the closest to speaking without lying. It is not an institution, although it has a strong tendency to be, but a certain quality of experience and language. That is why Owen spells Poetry with a capital P when he rejects it but with a small p when he says where it really lies, within the pity.

The Expressionists did generally care about Poetry with a capital P and about the Poet. In contrast to many English poets of the period they lacked what a German critic calls 'Gegenständlichkeit', and an English one 'particularity'.[124]

Nevertheless, some poets combined a strong enough poetic integrity with aspects of Expressionism which (as we saw) is equipped to the representation of apocalypse, catastrophe and mental limits, to produce front poems of great power. First among these is Georg Trakl. He produced only two genuine front-line poems, 'Lament' and 'Grodek'. Trakl was a volunteer, like Toller and several other contemporaries. He went in 1914 to Galicia as a lieutenant–pharmacist. During the battle of Grodek he was responsible for some ninety severely wounded men lying in a barn with no doctor available for two days and with insufficient drugs to alleviate their suffering. One of the men shot himself in Trakl's presence. Unable to bear the sight, Trakl walked outside only to see a row of bodies hanging from trees. This experience is the background to the composition of the two poems. Soon afterwards Trakl committed suicide. Thus real experiences coalesced with Trakl's already dark and disturbed vision.

Lament

Sleep and death, the dark eagles
Sweep round this head all night:
As if the golden image of Man
Were consumed by the icy wave
Of eternity. Upon grisly reefs
The purple body breaks
And the dark voice laments
Across the sea.
Sister of stormy sadness
Look, a frightened boat sinks
Beneath stars,
The silent face of the night.

The poem does not once refer to war directly. Although 'The purple body' breaking 'upon grisly reefs' might be an image of real mutilation, such verbal configurations had occurred previously in Trakl's poetry. Actually it is the non-visual quality of the poem that is most compelling. The language is opaque, not transparent upon a natural description or indeed upon a mental or emotional experience. The experiencing subject is decentred: sleep is a personal experience, death terminates personality, yet these two qualities surround the 'head' which is curiously objectified, the poet's or another's. There are fragments of poetic discourse (of which the 'head' is an example, since it is a piece of poetic diction), with all the spiritual warmth that attaches to poetry, juxtaposed with the coldness of otherness. Most clearly in the content of the head's dream held half in sleep half in death: 'the golden image of man' and 'the icy wave of eternity' for either could be subject or object. A battle between a whole image and construction of mankind and another vision which petrifies the visionary into death.

If this poem is self-referential – 'And the dark voice laments' – it refers to itself as poetry with a small p, as the spiritual nakedness at the edge of language (note the brute repetition, the signal of violent unreconciled adversity in the sounds of the phrase about eternity). Not as the institution of poetry, the glories of which are nevertheless still reflected in fragments. It is the smashing of the human body that is the pity of this poem, and the power of its idiom is that it fuses the real and the symbolic without false pathos. The World War manifest as the end of humanism.

Humanism (to say nothing of the First World War for civilisation) was a masculine affair, and the turn of the poem is towards the asocial sweetness of incest. Words melt alliteratively into one another, the subject constitutes itself in speech, in appeal ('look'), humanity at a more immediate level than the official construction of it that lies in crimson shreds around him. The incest motif is, of course, notoriously peculiar to Trakl, yet not uncommon in Expressionism in general (it figures prominently, for instance in *Ein Geschlecht*), as part of the radical search for the alternative to the patriarchal order, the taboos of the father. Here there is no connection between the appeal, and the sight it is called upon to witness. The diction of poetry ('Antlitz' or 'countenance') faces the silence, the end of language, the point beyond which poetry cannot reach.

GRODEK

In the evening the autumn woods resound
With deadly weapons, the golden plains
And blue lakes, above them the sun
Rolls by darker; the night embraces
Dying warrior, the wild lament
Of their broken mouths.
Yet quietly in the willow hollows red clouds
Gather, in which an angry god resides
And spilled blood, lunar coolness;
All roads end in black decay.
Beneath the golden twigs of the night and the stars
The sister's shadow sways through the silent grove,
To greet the spirit of the heroes, the bleeding heads;
And softly the dark flutes of autumn sound in the reeds.
Oh, prouder mourning! You brazen altars
The hot flame of the spirit is fanned by a mighty pain,
The unborn grandchildren.

'Grodek' is more directly connected with the frontline experience of which I spoke. Its title identifies it, as does the mention of 'dying warriors'. Otherwise its context is indeterminate. The word 'warrior' is heroic, poetic. Again the 'gold' of a poetic, heroic culture breaks on the reefs of the war. The poem is impaled upon the line 'all roads end in black decay'. This line is both descriptive and apocalyptic. On either side of this perfect expression of an experience of finality the balance between the human spirit and its antithesis in the war is poised. The first part begins with the war dominant. In the original German the sound of 'tödlich' (deadly) echoes 'tönen' (plains), but it is the dominant image; the sun sets darkly upon the once familiar and benign landscape, poetry is only a breath away from unanimated noise: 'the wild lament of mouths'. With the line beginning 'Yet' there is a move toward myth, a god of war not a little like Heym's now animates the landscape. But the key line insists that the landscape has been emptied of every trace of familiar humanity. On the other side of this divide, the human spirit regains dominance. The night is inhabited by spiritual visions replacing physical sight. Again the alliterative ghost of the sister furnishes a spiritual reference point, by reference to which the heroic implication of 'Warrior', seems confirmed, as the war dead are transfigured into heroes received in heaven. Yet, just as the war vision was indelibly touched with the spirit, so the spiritual vision, the light of 'the hot flame of the spirit', is touched by a sense of the Fall, of the death of the spirit as well as of the soldiers, in the final phrase, the greater mourning, not for the presently dead, but the unborn children, the discontinuity wrought by the war which finishes an entire culture.

A personal vision and experience of the war fuse here in Trakl's poetry with remarkable results. August Stramm too found the content for his style in the experience of the war which claimed his life (he was killed on 1 September 1915). I reproduce two of his poems here.

Storm Attack

From all corners shriek fears willing
Screech
Whips
Life
Before
It
Gasp death
The skies tatter.
Blind slaughters wildabout with terror.

Fear Storm

Shudder
I and I and I and I
Shudder Roar Rush Shudder
Dream Split Burn Blind
Starblind Roar Shudder
Rush
Shudder
I

The mixture achieved by Stramm's strange idiom, as difficult in the original as it is in translation, is peculiarly suited to what must have been the psychological disassociation of the war, where habits of thought evolved in normal circumstances adapt, bend and break in the context of the front, as indeed do grammatical categories. The word 'blind' is, for instance, syntactically indeterminate, as is the phrase 'skies tatter', which is Stramm's version of the apocalyptic overtone buried in particularity: a sense of doom before it finds words with which to console itself. 'Willing' connotes the psychological category of discipline, self-control, applied in a situation which in its universal meaning questions the ground of discipline, leaves the sure structure which discipline emplaces hanging in space. Stramm's poetry usually deals with disembodied experience, it does not identify and distribute experience by a conventional use of personal pronouns. The impersonality is perhaps like Trakl's. When the first-person pronoun does occur, it is in trauma, as we see in the second poem, no longer a smooth and familiar token for negotiating relations between self and world, but a syllable that has become opaque, material, resistant.

To turn now to the drama. Here the deficiencies of Expressionism, that mismatch with which we started, are harder to avoid. The dramatic requires a higher degree of systematic articulation than the lyric. Pre-war Expressionist drama tended to derive its conflict from a father–son antagonism.

The War was not amenable to the sort of assimilation that entails. The pathos and intensity of the Expressionist idiom and the topic of the war, its historical and social implications, gave rise to thematically and stylistically extreme pieces like Unruh's *Ein Geschlecht* or Kaiser's *Gas* plays. Unruh's play, written at the front in 1917, pushes the unleashing of violence of the war to its extreme in the case of one individual, the eldest son, who self-destructs. Hence individual self-assertion, and the turn to barbarism of the state are dimly related to each other as moments of the same patriarchy, the answer to which is to be found in the attitude of the mother, from whom, so the play suggests, the real anti-war revolution will come. The attempt to develop the sort of connections evoked in Trakl's references to the sister, by founding hope for revolution in the figure of the mother, reveals the gap between the spiritual predicament of the Expressionists and the objective situation in which they found themselves.

The *Gas* plays, composed in 1918 and 1920, ultimately dispense with the matriarchal pathos and present instead the auto-destruction of the Expressionist movement itself. This is represented, first, by a son who cannot manage the inheritance of his father, against the hostile, anti-idealistic logic of technology and economics, and then by a son's son, who cannot manage the inheritance from his mother, namely the prophecy from her mouth, at the end of the first play, that she will give birth to the New Man. The First World War made manifest the contradiction of European patriarchy so drastically, that the Expressionists felt themselves no longer secure in the role of sons turning against their fathers. The self-destruction of the father is dimly echoed in that of the son. The Expressionist turns upon the father in himself.

Goering's *Seeschlacht*, written in a sanatorium in Davos and dedicated to 'the Mother', is an interesting variation on this grim confusion. It finds a way of achieving Expressionist concentration, but relating it to the sort of particularity and immediacy which saves the best lyric poetry aesthetically, and anticipates *Neue Sachlichkeit*, the post-war style which seeks to reflect the post-war sensibility to which Expressionism seemed overblown. The concentration is achieved by representing the war through the motif of the approaching battle of Jutland, for which the characters in the play, nameless but numbered sailors confined within the same gun turret, attempt to prepare themselves psychologically and spiritually. We have the same sort of effect Stramm achieves in his extreme concentration, namely that of the testing, and resultant scattering of ordinary human psychological sets in the face of institutionally sanctioned technological barbarity. One of these characters is an enthusiast for human spiritual values. Before the battle breaks, he is a loner, an outsider, one who distinguishes himself from the automatic discourse of the ordinary sailors, and of the Christian sailor. He alone considers mutiny, refusal to acquiesce in the fight. But when the battle does break, his spiritual enthusiasm transfers effortlessly to the euphoria of the fray, since this provides him as well as his earlier aspirations, with a way out of ordinary experience, and into a new sense of collective purpose. 'I shot well, didn't I? I'd have mutinied well too!'[125] The other sailors are better placed to register the unspeakable collapse of humanity with which the reality of war, that is to say the smoke, shells and death, which implode into the stage space, confronts them. In this way the play criticises the problem the Expressionists had with relating their extreme individualism to any sort of collective, and highlighting the danger inherent in the Expressionists' excessive idealism, which in some cases led it to Fascism.

Toller's *Die Wendung* is perhaps the play which most clearly demonstrates the mismatch between the war and the response it called forth from Expressionism, the gap between intense and utterly sincere spiritual anguish and aspirations and reality. It is perhaps also the most central Expressionist war play, and draws on considerable stylistic originality to seek to bend idea and suffering upon each other and link them to a political position. Toller's hero is also an enthusiast whose enthusiasm first goes with war, then turns against it. He takes Goering's argument a step further (which is not to say that he necessarily improves upon it!), such that Friedrich sets off saying 'The struggle will unite us all. . . . The great time will make us all great',[126] only to perceive the contradiction in such destructive idealism. The stylistic achievement of the play is to operate a dialectic between naturalist and visionary scenes, thereby giving force to the interpenetration of reality and idea. The 'transformation' itself, and the place where reality turns to symbol, is marked by the presence of the sister, who, characteristically, as I have been arguing, provides guidance in the spiritual impasse:

FRIEDRICH   My path is buried beneath rubble and impassable
SISTER   Your path leads you upwards
FRIEDRICH   Back to our mother?
SISTER   Higher, but also to our mother
             Your path leads you to God
             Your path leads you to Man.[127]

The extreme experience of the war (the front-line experience), here feeds the passion of the political commitment to humane uprising. The play ends in a direct plea to revolution, as though the 'limit situation' of the war could sanction that 'limit situation' in which an appeal to common humanity might have a galvanising effect, in disregard of class and national rivalry, of self-interest and industrial–military interests.

But these two things do not match up together in that way. Social–cultural apocalypse is not spiritual apocalypse (not immediately, anyway). Toller's play exhibits the contradiction of Expressionism in a particularly glaring light. It is an attempt to imbue classical bourgeois values ('the Eternal Feminine' among others) with revolutionary force in the service of the overthrow of the modern state. It lacks a language for its passion and agony (which does not make them less real), and remains ensnared in the old languages. As Brecht said in an early review of Toller: 'There was the pleasure derived from ideas, but no ideas',[128] or in Sokel's words,

there is an element of eighteenth-century rationalism and eudaemonism hidden under the Dionysiac surface of much of Expressionism. The Expressionist activist intensifies the Socratic faith in persuasion and reasoning until it attains a white-hot lustre of ecstasy; but this ecstasy is based on reason, this flame is the white light of reason.[129]

It is noteworthy that Toller's play, intended as a call to outstretched arms, became instead a triumph of style. In the successful 1919 production by Karl-Heinz Martin (a leading Expressionist), the differences between the symbolic/visionary passages and the naturalistic one were apparently suppressed, thus depriving the play of its main aesthetic–political thrust. After the war Expressionism had lost its edge as avant-garde, becoming an important commodity in all areas of the culture industry from cinema to soft furnishings.

But the domestication of Expressionism is too negative a note on which to conclude. Expressionism is, in any case, a label used to denote a vast and diffuse phenomenon, which is only partially understood beyond certain recycled generalisations. It is too simple to dismiss it as a late bourgeois aberration, transfixed upon the contradictions of the culture it sought to oppose. The terms of the Bloch–Lukács debate in the 1930s revolve around the question of the objective status of Expressionism, and can supply a model in terms of which to begin to think about the real relations between modernism and history.[130]

Lukács denies Expressionism the status of progressive literature, because its subjectivity is not artistically related to the objective determinants of the world, and thus reflects only the partial and distorted vision of a class whose historical moment has passed. Bloch argues that the contradictions displayed in Expressionist art are historically authentic ones.

Are confusion, immaturity and incomprehensibility always and in every case to be categorized as bourgeois decadence? Might they not equally ... be part of the transition from the old world to the new? Or at least be part of the struggle leading to that transition?[131]

Given that its transition to politics failed, as art Expressionism 'undermined the schematic routines and academicism to which "the values of art" had been reduced, and directed attention to human beings and their substance, in their quest for the most authentic expression possible'.[132] This reading seems more sensitive to the complex construction of subjectivity, and the vital if enigmatic role played within it by creativity. This respect for the refraction of the objective in the subject, this acknowledgement of their complex and continuous mingling, seems appropriate at a time when it seems unclear whether that transition from the old world to the new, mentioned by Bloch, and in which Expressionism and the Great War for civilisation were most certainly both implicated, has actually been effected.

Richard Cork

Images of extinction: Paul Nash at the Western Front

Now that the extent of Paul Nash's achievement in the First World War is fully appreciated, his paintings and graphic works of 1918 can be seen as the most impressive images produced by any British artist during the conflict. Before the hostilities commenced, however, Nash would have seemed ill-equipped to place this lacerating tragedy at the centre of his work. Confining himself to modest watercolours and drawings, he had gained a precocious reputation as a gentle landscapist with pronounced leanings towards the visionary. More indebted to the previous century than his own time, Nash was obsessed by Blake, Palmer and above all Rossetti. While many painters of his Slade-educated generation grappled with machine-age modernity, he hid himself away in sequestered corners of the English countryside to pursue his quest for the elusive 'spirit of a place'.

Having joined the Artists' Rifles as a home defence private in September 1914, this nervous and highly imaginative young man was selected for officer training two years later and sent to the Western Front early in February 1917. Serving as a second lieutenant in the Hampshire Regiment, Nash could scarcely be expected to respond to a terrain so removed from anything he had cherished at home. But life in a front-line trench at St Eloi sharpened his senses with phenomenal swiftness. 'This has been the most interesting week of my life', he wrote to his wife, explaining that 'my inner excitement and exultation was so great that I have lived in a cloud of thought these last days'.[133] Although the Ypres Salient was relentlessly shelled, Nash did not witness a major engagement or, probably, encounter a single corpse.[134] His awareness of destruction was at this stage countered by the joyful and consoling realisation that nature still reasserted itself throughout the blasted landscape – just as Otto Dix had noticed in his charcoal drawings of the same period. Nash delighted in the sight of dandelions 'bright gold over the parapet',[135] and was even able to refer to 'those wonderful trenches at night, at dawn, at sundown'.[136] Filled with a spirit of zest and renewal, he found the time to make drawings of this enthralling new world and send them home.

They would, no doubt, have been very different if Nash's stay at the Front had lasted longer. But in May 1917 a broken rib caused by a fall at night sent him back to London for hospital treatment. It was a fortuitous release: the Hampshires attacked Hill 60 only three days later, and many of his fellow-officers were slaughtered. Although the news of their deaths must have affected Nash, the drawings completed during his recuperation concentrate on the land rather than the soldiers who fought there. It was a wise decision. Human figures would always be the weakest element in his work, which now gained enormously from their virtual exclusion. His style also changed, in order to encompass the vision he had confronted at the Ypres Salient. The lines defining attenuated trees and gouged mud took on a more jagged, Vorticist-like harshness, proving that Nash was finally prepared to learn from the austere language of his most innovative British contemporaries. Nevinson's earlier war pictures were a particular source of stimulus. In March 1917, around the time when he drew the spiky, almost surgical *Wytschaete Woods*, he asked his wife: 'Do you remember Nevinson's small etching of the 2nd bombardment (or was it the first) of Ypres? I should like to have it if possible. . . . It is part of the world I'm interested in.'[137] Nash probably recalled this stark image of gutted, scorched houses from Nevinson's one-man show at the Leicester Galleries. The two men met in July 1917, perhaps for the first time since they were students together at the Slade,[138] and Nevinson's ability to define the Western Front in all its staccato grimness elicited Nash's admiration at this crucial stage in his development.

Even so, most of the work he displayed in a June one-man show at the Goupil Gallery stopped a long way short of tragedy. One exhibit bore the disconcertingly playful title *Chaos Décoratif*, and resembled at first a woodland scene where a ladder, duckboard and shattered tree hardly disrupt the prevailing mood of pastoral calm. None of these early war pictures is informed by the profound sense of moral outrage which fuelled his sub-sequent front-line work. Nash's experience of the battlefield was at this stage too limited, unmarked by the horror which could only be felt when hostilities were at their fiercest. But the success of the exhibition prompted him to seek out a commission as an official war artist. His request encountered consider-able opposition from some of the government's advisers. Campbell Dodgson complained that 'Nash is decidedly post-impressionist, not cubist, but "decorative", and his art is certainly not what the British public will generally like.'[139] Buchan agreed, and yet he bowed with reluctance to the enthusiasm of others. In November 1917 Nash returned to the Salient with a plentiful supply of paper, crayons and chalks.

Some artists deteriorated once they gained this official status: Nevinson changed, in the main, from harsh denunciation of front-line conditions to heroic celebration of air combat. But despite the comforts of a life removed from active service further cushioned by a manservant and chauffeur-driven car, Nash did not lapse into complacency. On the contrary: his expeditions to the battlefields transformed him into an angry, wholly engaged opponent of the war's destructive futility. His long-held belief in the sanctity of landscape hastened this inner metamorphosis. Nash's love of nature was outraged when he discovered the shocking change in the Salient. The terrain which had previously been replenished by signs of spring was now entering winter. Rain had been more or less incessant since August, and it gathered in muddy shell-holes rather than sinking beneath the clay. Nature, no longer capable of alleviating the damage wrought by incessant gunfire, appeared everywhere to have suffered irrevocable extinction. Passchendaele had been fought for three harrowing months while Nash was in London, and nothing could conceal the grievous wounds it inflicted on the countryside. The battle of the mud, as Lloyd George so aptly dubbed it, claimed over 300,000 British casualties. Even the most hardened soldiers were demoralised by the inhuman conditions in which this purposeless struggle was enacted. When Haig's Chief-of-Staff visited the Passchendaele Front for the first time in November, and found his car shuddering with the effort of moving through the churned and waterlogged ground, he began to cry and said: 'Good God, did we really send men to fight in that?'[140]

No wonder Nash was so shaken by his investigations of this benighted region. The shelling nearly killed him at times, for the privileges available to war artists offered no guarantee of protection of a man bent on 'getting as near to the real places of action as it was possible to go'.[141] But he survived to set down his anguished reactions in image after image, using 'nothing but brown paper and chalks'[142] as he rapidly defined the hideous reality of the killing fields. At the same time Nash attempted to write about the horror he had experienced, in the privacy of an eloquent letter to his wife. 'I have just returned, last night, from a visit to Brigade Headquarters up the line', he reported,

and I shall not forget it as long as I live. I have seen the most frightful nightmare of a country more conceived by Dante or Poe than by nature, unspeakable, utterly indescribable. In the fifteen drawings I have made I may give you some idea of its horror, but only being in it and of it can ever make you sensible of its dreadful nature and of what our men in France have to face. We all have a vague notion of the terrors of a battle, and can conjure up with the aid of some of the more inspired war correspondents and the pictures in the Daily Mirror some vision of the battlefield; but no pen or drawing can convey this country – the normal setting of the battles taking place day and night, month after month. Evil and the incarnate fiend alone can be master of this war, and no glimmer of God's hand is seen anywhere. Sunset and sunrise are blasphemous, they are mockeries to man, only the black rain out of the bruised and swollen clouds all through the bitter black of night is fit atmosphere in such a land. The rain drives on, the stinking mud becomes more evilly yellow, the shell holes fill up with green-white water, the roads and tracks are covered in inches of slime, the black dying trees ooze and sweat and the shells never cease. They alone plunge overhead, tearing away the rotting tree stumps, breaking the plank roads, striking down horses and mules, annihilating, maiming, maddening, they plunge into the grave which is this land; one huge grave, and cast up on it the poor dead. It is unspeakable, godless, hopeless. I am no longer an artist interested and curious, I am a messenger who will bring back word from the men who are fighting to those who want the war to go on for ever. Feeble, inarticulate, will be my message, but it will have a bitter truth, and may it burn their lousy souls.[143]

It was not an attitude which Buchan, the effective paymaster of Nash's activities, would have been eager to promote. The aim of the war artists's scheme centred, after all, on propaganda for the British cause, and Nash's despair was hardly likely to boost the war effort. To its credit, though, the Department of Information provided firm support after his final return to England in December. Armed with more than '50 drawings of muddy places'[144] produced at the Front, he worked in a frenzy to complete enough pictures for another one-man show in May 1918. Nash's fears that his work would be 'feeble, inarticulate' proved groundless. An impressive number of the images he produced during that period, when the memory of his visit was still at its most intense, did indeed turn out to possess 'a bitter truth'. Without degenerating into crude polemics, he defined the utter negation of a locale brutally shorn of either sustenance or hope.

Figures appear in some of the pictures, and they are handled with unusual conviction. *Nightfall. Zillebeke District* includes a number of soldiers walking in both directions along a narrow, zig-zagging duckboard. They are diminutive enough to ensure that Nash could draw them without any apparent difficulty, and their modest proportions also serve to emphasise man's helplessness in the face of overwhelmingly hostile surroundings. They look just as broken and vulnerable as the stripped trees projecting so nakedly from the land beyond. No shelter can be found against the rain as it lances down, piercing both troops and ground with the same needle-thin sharpness which Nevinson had earlier conveyed in his painting of a *Flooded Trench on the Yser*. When Nash carried out a lithographic version of the Zillebeke scene, he changed the name from *Nightfall* to *Rain* and reinforced the assault of each stroke. Instead of simply falling in one direction, they now form a criss-cross structure of cruel lines. A few more figures can be discerned, too, but they do not appear any more capable of withstanding the storm on their exposed and unstable pathway.

Perhaps emboldened by the expressive power of these beleaguered silhouettes, Nash also produced a lithograph where marching men play a more prominent role in the composition. Nevinson's precedents are again evoked, most notably his early war painting *Column on the March* which likewise makes use of a dramatic perspective.[145] The differences between the two images are, however, far more significant than their similarities. Nevinson's troops proceed in daylight under an open sky, and a considerable amount of vigour still animates their limbs. Nash's nocturnal travellers are huddled and forlorn. The legs of the men at the front are bent in a strangely uncertain way, as if physical collapse were imminent. Their bodies move along diffidently like a column in retreat, and the trees flanking them on either side accentuate the sense of oppression. Rather than offering protection, these tall columnar forms signify confinement. They almost seem to imprison the figures, condemning them to trudge in an apparently unending procession on a road as monotonous and inflexible as the war itself.

In the main, though, Nash's use of figures was more sparing. He became preoccupied by the belief that the wasteland of Passchendaele was inimical to human life, and in *After the Battle* a few corpses are the only soldiers visible in an otherwise deserted setting. The foreground body is already sinking into the mud. In order to stress the anonymity of dissolution, Nash leaves the face without any distinguishing features. The figure near the centre, subsiding into the broken slats behind him, has already taken on a skeletal appearance. He looks as forsaken as the landscape around him, where everything is derelict. The duckboard at his feet has been severed; the trench is eroded by shell-holes and land slippage; and the barbed-wire fencing has been broken up into a mêlée of tilting stakes. They are almost as sharp as the thin spears of rain falling from the sky. The dense ink-hatching scored into the paper by Nash's surgical nib does not prevent him from summarising the terrain in a sequence of bare structures, all redolent of desolation and despair.

But most of these elegiac drawings dispense with figures altogether, confronting us directly with the emptiness of a region which seems to have devoured everyone who previously inhabited it. Nobody could survive for long in *The Landscape – Hill 60*, where explosions tear through the sky above a pummelled mass of mud and wire. Even the water in the shell-crater is peppered with tracer-bullets, determined to ensure that any soldiers who might be still lurking there will never emerge. The intricate system of dykes and ditches which had drained this Flanders country for many centuries was obliterated by the bombardment of Passchendaele, giving way to the subdued, featureless morass defined so uncompromisingly in this image. If God had indeed abandoned the battlefield Nash scrutinised, he saw no reason to minimise the ensuing nullity.

Precisely because Nash had cherished nature with such visionary fervour in his pre-war work, his outrage over her subsequent desecration knew no bounds. In *Wire*, one of the largest and most powerful of all the 1918 drawings, he unleashes the full force of his indignation by emphasising the shattered foreground tree. Figures are no longer needed here, for the remains of this grievously abused trunk are as pitiful as any human martyr. Enmeshed in barbed spirals, which circle around the tree like the thorns crowning Christ's head, the tree symbolises the degradation and extinction of all living things. If there are echoes of the cross on Calvary, Nash nevertheless makes sure that no hint of a future resurrection is allowed to counter the prevailing emphasis on death. The coiled wire holds both the tree and the surrounding landscape in its possessive grip. Defilement could hardly be more thoroughgoing, and apart from the pale pink flaring in the sky he restricts the composition to the unrelieved chill and dampness of dull green, umber and grey.

Nash did not deal exclusively with the aftermath of battle. When he turned to oil painting early in 1918, for the very first time in his career, he was soon able to produce an arresting image of bombardment in progress. Nash realised that the transition from drawing and watercolour to oil paint might prove difficult, and confessed that he felt guilty of 'a piece of towering audacity'[146] when faced with a canvas. But the outcome was surprisingly assured. *The Mule Track* is an impressive achievement, carrying over the intensity of his graphic work to the new medium without any loss of conviction. Indeed, a new emotional vehemence enters Nash's art with the advent of oil painting. Some tiny silhouetted soldiers can be detected at the heart of *The Mule Track*, struggling to prevent their pack animals from panicking and falling off the crazily zig-zagging duckboard. But the shelling around them is an absolute inferno, and they could easily be overwhelmed by its savagery. One figure is already plummeting into the water, while further up the duckboard an animal has broken free and bolts through the glaringly lit mayhem like a demented refugee.

The expressive resources of paint prompted Nash to be more ambitious with colour than he had been hitherto. The trees which were so sombre in his works on paper are irradiated, all over *The Mule Track*, by ferocious yellows, oranges and mustards in the explosions. Colour used to frighten Nash, but he now deploys it to arouse the sensation of terror in his viewers. Nor did he rely solely on his imagination to give this image of bombardment its authenticity. As an official war artist, he had consistently flouted the attempts by General Headquarters at the Front to keep him safely away from the conflict. Nash later remembered how he managed to 'evolve a technique' which eventually enabled him to 'get where I want to be'.[147] His desire to approach the battle area, and witness far more of the action of war than he had experienced as a second lieutenant the year before, was facilitated by his 'mad Irish chauffeur'. Once, while travelling along the Menin Road, the driver 'piloted the car so skilfully, that he timed the constant shell bursts on the road, any one of which might immediately have killed' them both.[148] Confrontation with danger no doubt acted on Nash as an energising force, stimulating him into an enlarged awareness of what warfare really entailed.

All the same, the most profound and despairing of his 1918 paintings draw back from the thick of the fighting to meditate, once again, on the waste of battle. One of these canvases, *Void*, still shows the conflict proceeding in the distance. A strafed aeroplane appears to be falling towards the ground, and shells explode near a duckboard where men carry out a slow, funereal retreat from the maelstrom. The rest of the picture, however, is devoted to the terrible stillness of a landscape already shattered and deserted by the opposing armies. Nash concentrates on the violation of nature with even more perturbation than before. The entire composition is sliced up into a network of angry, disruptive diagonals. A damaged lorry has slewed off the road, spilling its cargo of ammunition and rifles across the foreground. There they lie, along with the body of a soldier who appears to have been driven into the earth by a vehicle heedless of its callous progress. He has become one more piece of detritus, a discarded remnant like the helmet floating in water nearby. The guns are equally useless, their heavy wheels bogged down in the mud which grows ever more treacherous as the rain continues its interminable assault. *Void* justifies Nash's terse title by stressing the nullity of a land where everything has been abused, stricken and robbed of its former identity. This pitiless emptying-out, summed up by the abject corpse whose very substance is brutally flattened out on the furrowed ground, haunted Nash's imagination. He called his May 1918 one-man show at the Leicester Galleries *Void of War*, and accompanied it with a stark monochrome poster design which reduced his memories of the killing fields to a stark combination of trees, rain and dank, stagnant craters.

Nash may well have owed the notion of a void to William Blake, whose work he had venerated for many years. In September 1917 he produced three illustrations for 'Tiriel', a gruelling poem about a 'blind & aged' man whose Timon-like curses summon up a vision of destruction as catastrophic as the scenes Nash was about to witness at Passchendaele:

> Earth, thus I stamp thy bosom!
> rouse the earthquake from his den,
> To raise his dark & burning visage
> thro' the cleaving ground,
> To thrust these towers with his shoulders!
> Let his fiery dogs
> Rise from the center,
> belching flames & roarings, dark smoke!
> Where art thou, Pestilence,
> that bathest in fogs & standing lakes?
> Rise up thy sluggish limbs
> & let the loathsomest of poisons
> Drop from thy garments as thou walkest,
> wrapt in yellow clouds![149]

The apocalyptic virulence of this damnation may have returned to Nash's mind as he surveyed the Front only a month after completing his 'Tiriel' designs. But Blake deals with the void itself in his Second Book of 'Milton', where the trembling Virgin Ololon responds 'in clouds of despair' to Milton's insistence that:

> All that can be annihilated must be annihilated
> That the Children of Jerusalem may be saved from slavery.

In Ololon's reply, which Nash could well have read while executing the 'Tiriel' pictures, she poses the kind of anguished question he must have asked himself when surveying the wasteland of Flanders:

> O Immortal, how were we led to War the Wars of Death?
> Is this the Void Outside of Existence, which if enter'd into
> Becomes a Womb? & is this the Death Couch of Albion?
> Thou goest to Eternal Death & all must go with thee.[150]

A similarly tragic mood informs the masterpiece of Nash's war paintings, where he wonders whether regeneration can ever occur after such wholesale destruction has prevailed. The image grew out of a drawing called *Sunrise: Inverness Copse*, where a pale yellow sun begins to illuminate a scene stripped of everything except trees and mud. There is still a hope, in this otherwise dejected study, that light and heat will one day nurture the graveyard of nature's forms. But by the time Nash executed a painting of the same subject, he decided to dispense with the reference to a particular locality and make the prospect of a rebirth far more doubtful. *We Are Making a New World* is the bitterly ironic title he bestowed on his definitive, universalised image of front-line devastation. All the incidental detail found in *Void* and *The Mule Track* has here been dispensed with, so that we are forced to confront the issue of extinction alone.

No corpses, animals and abandoned equipment prevent the eye from moving over the mounds of pummelled earth towards the blackened, severed trunks punctuating the land beyond. They have the pathos of amputated limbs, for Nash regarded these trees almost as an extension of his own body. In his pre-war work they had often played the role of people, and long before hostilities commenced he took time off from depicting the elms in his family garden to tell Gordon Bottomley that 'I have tried to paint trees as tho they were human beings . . . because I sincerely love & worship trees & know that they are people & wonderfully beautifuly [*sic*] people'.[151] Now, aghast at the wanton dismemberment of these cherished growths, he was able to convey the horror of human carnage by focusing on the withered stumps rising so mournfully from ground no longer capable of nourishing their roots. One tree has fallen over already, its topmost branches submerged in the water. The rest could easily follow, and the emergent sun no longer seems capable of preventing their demise. Unlike the disc in the Inverness Copse study, this new orb is restricted to a cold whiteness. Moreover, the dull brown clouds in the drawing have been transformed here into the colour of dried blood. The sun's rays lighten the clouds a little, but cannot disperse them. They clog much of the sky with their oppressive weight, as if all the blood spilled on the Western Front had coagulated on the horizon and threatened to choke nature altogether. Instead of responding to the shafts of light, the trees remain despondent and inert. Their branches dangle from the trunks like melancholy tresses of hair, implying that the entire group of trees could be seen as chorus-like presences mourning the death of the world Nash so ardently held dear.

Looking at this profoundly moving canvas today, we are confronted not only with an image of Nash's belief that 'sunset and sunrise are blasphemies, they are mockeries to man', but also with a reflection of our own contemporary nightmare. For the parallels between the extinction of Passchendaele, and the nuclear winter threatening the planet now, are inescapable. They help to explain why *We are Making a New World* continues to exert a special hold over our imaginations, giving pictorial coherence to a prospect of total annihilation. The warning which Nash sounded in 1918 has, if anything, grown in pertinence, now that we contemplate the possibility of a global disaster far more calamitous than the devastation he forced himself to survey. When photographs of his war work were sent to Colonel Lee for censorship, however, they elicited a very different response. After dismissing the idea that 'Nash's funny pictures' could 'possibly give the enemy any information', the bewildered officer complained: 'I cannot help thinking that Nash is having a huge joke with the British public, and lovers of "art" in particular. Is he?'[152]

The answer, so far as most visitors to his *Void of War* exhibition were concerned, favoured Nash rather than the disgruntled colonel. Moreover, the Department of Information supported his work by reproducing fifteen of the war pictures in Volume III of *British Artists at the Front*. Timed to coincide with the opening of his one-man show, it helped Nash's uncompromising vision gain a wide and receptive audience at home. His desire to be 'a messenger who will bring back word from the men who are fighting' was thereby fulfilled, and in the book of reproductions Jan Gordon, writing under the pseudonym 'John Salis', acknowledged Nash's ability to comprehend how the immensity of the tragedy could best be conveyed. 'It is not possible to paint truly how this war has swept man', conceded Gordon, 'because horror will not permit this truth to be said. It is possible to depict the devastation of Nature, partly because we cannot understand the full horror, and partly because through it we may come to a deeper realisation of what the catastrophe may mean to man.'[153] This meaning had nothing to do with crude polemics. In August 1917, before Nash had produced any of his finest war images, Francis Stopford told John Buchan that Nash's pictures of the Ypres Salient provided 'a much better understanding of German brutality and of the needless havoc and destruction which German armies are committing under orders in occupied territories'.[154] But the truth is that Nash's work of 1917–18 transcends propaganda entirely. Man's inhumanity in general is arraigned in these poignant pictures, which convey an artist's deep-seated revulsion at the barbarism inflicted by both sides on each other and, by extension, the whole of the natural world.

Katharine Hodgson

Myth-making in Russian war poetry

Russian Futurism had the stated aim of re-creating and renewing literature and art by the rejection and destruction of all former culture. The movement projected a rebellious and confrontational image, an image which mirrored the increasing levels of political violence in early twentieth-century Russia. The Futurists, however, drew their battle-lines in the field of literature and art. Their activities were intended to shock the public by transgressing established rules, whether in art, dress or behaviour. Violence, in an abstract form, was an essential ingredient of the movement. Implicit in the title of an early manifesto 'A Slap in the Face of Public Taste', violence informed much of the imagery used by Futurist writers. Their approach to language and artistic form was characterised by a fierce rejection of convention, as word and meaning were set adrift, syntax disordered and rhyme made an area for bold experimentation. Preconceived notions about art, all established writers, and the expectations of polite society were targets for an often vituperative attack.

This chapter will examine the wartime poetry of two prominent Futurists, Vladimir Maiakovskii[155] and Velimir Khlebnikov,[156] tracing the evolution not only of the use of abstract violence in their work, but also of their ideas about war in general, as well as of the effect that *the* war had on their work.

The outbreak of war in August 1914 provided the Futurists with a theme which seemed ideally suited to their enthusiasm for conflict. The Futurists initially welcomed the war for two distinct reasons. The chaotic violence of war was felt to be a vindication of their artistic methods, as they claimed that only Futurism had the means to represent the speed and intensity of war effectively. Secondly, Maiakovskii and Khlebnikov shared a romantic view of war in general, which they associated primarily with glory and heroism, rather than with death. As the war continued, their response became increasingly qualified. War in the abstract was seen as a positive, dynamic experience; *the* war involved senseless suffering and destruction which seemed to have little in common with the creative violence of Futurism. By

1915 they had begun to replace their patriotic and artistic belligerence with pacifist longings for a world without war.

The Russian Futurists, unlike their Italian counterparts, had no fixed ideological stance on the subject of war, being in any case a movement which was fragmented into various, often hostile, factions. Some of the Russians' theoretical pronouncements on war were close in spirit to the position put forward by Marinetti in his 1909 manifesto.[157]

In folklore Khlebnikov and Maiakovskii found an example of what they considered the proper depiction of war in art. They contrasted modern writers' association of war with suffering and death with folk-song celebrations of heroism and presentation of battle as the fulfilment of noble ideals. For Khlebnikov in particular war was associated with figures from legend and history, ancient Slav warriors who fought for their people's freedom; in his early poetry Khlebnikov strongly identified with these heroes.

The First World War failed to live up to the archaic and glorious image of warfare presented in folk-song. Maiakovskii's reactions to the war were ambivalent from the start: 'As a Russian', he wrote, 'every effort by a soldier to wrest land away from the enemy is sacred to me, but as an artist I am forced to think that this whole war has been thought up simply as an excuse for someone to write a really good poem.'[158] Maiakovskii found the war an occasion more appropriate for declaring that Futurism had come into its own than for indulging in patriotic sentiment. In a series of newspaper articles on literature and art published towards the end of 1914 he wrote that Futurism was flourishing as the only artistic means capable of giving an effective portrayal of war's high-velocity violence: 'Isn't this simply an embodiment of our ideas? It's called "war": people writhe in nightmares, arrive home without arms or legs, and in reality there's nothing apart from some kind of sky from Tokyo to London, criss-crossed every day by a new pounding geometry of shell-fire.'[159]

Those who had subjected the movement to ridicule now found their own work disparaged. Painters of the realist school who objected to Futurist art on the grounds that the colours and forms used were 'unnatural' were told by Maiakovskii that their palettes were suited only to painting snails and the like, but could not depict 'the ruddy-cheeked beauty War, in a dress as blood-bright as the desire to beat the Germans, with the suns of her searchlight eyes'. He challenged them, if they wished to copy nature, to count how many legs there were in a cavalry attack and depict accurately a train hit by a shell.[160]

Maiakovskii accused other writers of failing to depict the war effectively. To prove his point about the monotony and uniformity of contemporary war poetry, Maiakovskii combined three stanzas by three different authors to produce a poem which showed no signs of its disparate origins. The root cause of such blandness, Maiakovskii wrote, lay in seeing poetry not as an end in itself, but as 'a draught animal whose purpose is to convey knowledge', that is, to see the information contained in a work of art as its primary purpose.[161] One of Futurism's basic premises contained in the 1912 manifesto *A Slap in the Face of Public Taste* and expanded in the following year's *A Trap for Judges 2* was that the meaning of a word should not be seen as the predominant criterion for its selection and positioning in a work of literature; its phonic and graphic qualities were equally important. Language had to be shaken loose from its traditional restraints. Declaring a hatred of previously existing language, the pioneer Futurists set themselves the task of creating new words, both arbitrarily and by derivation. Their verbal experimentation was carried out under the banner of slogans such as 'the liberation of the word', 'the word as such'. Language was finally to be freed from 'the tyranny of meaning'.

Maiakovskii's 1914 articles repeated the Futurist principle that each new phase of ideas demanded its own unique form of expression, and that only the Futurists were able to encapsulate the new age in their art. He cited the Russian capital's change of name as proof that a new Futurist age had dawned: 'On yesterday's pages there stood the name "Petersburg". With the word "Petrograd" a new page of Russian poetry and literature has been turned.'[162]

The war, as a new phase, required that all words be tested to see whether their sound related convincingly to their meaning; if not, they must be discarded and new words invented to replace them. In 'War and Language' Maiakovskii wrote: 'We must demand language which gives a concise and accurate representation of every movement. We want words to explode like shells, or ache like wounds, or thunder joyfully like cheers of victory.'[163] The 'gunshot-word' was, he wrote, a fitting expression of war. Attempts by poets to bring their work up to date by inserting words like 'machine gun' amidst otherwise archaic diction were derided.

Maiakovskii made a strong case for Futurist methods as an effective means of evoking the violence of war. The Futurists were, after all, well versed in the portrayal of all things shocking. But since real life had begun to imitate the violent actions which the Futurists had presented as abstract gestures of rebellion, the tension between their theoretical view of war as glorious and the artistic principle of revelling in the gruesomely distasteful was unavoidable. If the war was not believed to be a heroic enterprise, then all that remained was violent and pointless slaughter; elation was replaced by despair. Theoretically, both Maiakovskii and Khlebnikov welcomed, or at least accepted the war – Maiakovskii on artistic grounds, Khlebnikov on the basis of his theories about fate.

The massive loss of life in the Russo-Japanese War of 1904–05 had provoked Khlebnikov to embark on extensive numerological studies founded on the dates of significant battles, with the aim of discovering the laws of fate which determined events and finding the reasons behind the deaths. In late 1914 he published a treatise called *Battles 1915 to 1917: A New Teaching*

About War, which claimed that the number 317 was important in determining the amount of time which elapsed between significant battles, and that reversals of fortune were linked with the conquest of rivers and the sea.[164]

Neither Maiakovskii nor Khlebnikov could maintain for long the detached stance of the theoretician. Their theories, rooted in an abstract view of war, were called into question by *the* war. Maiakovskii's poetry demonstrates considerable ambivalence towards the war, which seemed to both fascinate and repel him. His portrayals of war as a dynamic experience are tempered by a distancing awareness of suffering and tragedy. In 'Wonderful Nonsense', written in 1915, this distancing is achieved by the narrator's inability, or unwillingness, to believe that the dreadful sights he is witnessing are really happening and are not just an amusing party trick:

> The host's bass voice is gentle,
> it only seems similar to a cannon's.
> And the mask isn't there to protect from gas,
> it's simply a playful joke.[165]

In this poem Maiakovskii creates an ironically aestheticised picture of war made harmless. Blood is transformed into red carnation stains and gangrene is described as yellow-leaved flowers on corpses who are only playing dead. A similar kind of alienation appears in an early wartime poem, 'War is Declared', which combines contrasting images of aggressive excitement and innocent suffering in a world where the boundaries between animate and inanimate are highly fluid. War intrudes into the city in the form of rivers of blood and a red snow of human flesh; blind to this horror, people, even bronze statues of generals, are seized with the urge to join battle. The suffering of war is revealed, however, on a cosmic scale. While human beings are shown as unfeeling automata, nature is animated: the sky is torn by bayonets and the stars weep. Pity personified is trampled underfoot and squeals for mercy.[166]

The apparent detachment shown by Maiakovskii in his critical articles is set aside in his poetry. During the early stages of the war Khlebnikov's poetry was, by contrast, in complete accordance with his theories on fate. Believing that events were determined by fate, Khlebnikov could not sustain his belligerent nationalism. In his poetry of 1915 he shows a fatalistic acceptance of a war in which enemy action appears to play no part in the deaths of Russian soldiers. But passive acceptance of fate was, for Khlebnikov, only a temporary solution. He was unable to reconcile acceptance of the inevitable with a growing sense of revulsion against the war. In 'Funeral' he asks 'Are we men or spears of fate?'.[167]

His answer is given in the cycle of poems 'War in a Mousetrap', written between 1915 and 1922. Here, Khlebnikov rejects passivity in favour of militant action against war, death and the older generation, in whose interests the war is being fought. Fate becomes a force which must be tamed and controlled rather than accepted.

The disenchantment with the war which appeared in the poetry of Khlebnikov and Maiakovskii was not the result of a direct encounter with the horrors of battle. It is, however, questionable to what extent this encounter might have influenced them, as other Futurists who saw active service at the front, such as the poet Nikolai Aseev, wrote in terms which were not significantly different from those used by non-combatant colleagues.

Maiakovskii was called up in October 1915 and Khlebnikov in April the following year, but neither reached the front line. Maiakovskii was considered too politically unreliable to fight, having once been briefly imprisoned for revolutionary activities, and so spent the war safely in Petrograd as an army draughtsman. Khlebnikov was sent to Tsaritsyn for military training, where the strain of drill and confinement to barracks caused him to fear the loss of his inspiration and his sanity. In a short lament he wrote: 'In the 93rd infantry regiment, I died as children die.'[168] He was eventually released shortly before the February revolution of 1917. Army life had no romantic or heroic appeal for him. In 'War in a Mousetrap' Khlebnikov describes himself as the 'captive of wicked elders' for whom life offers only destructive monotony:

> I too shall take up a rifle (it is large and silly,
> Heavier than a manuscript),
> And I shall march along the road,
> Measuring out 365.317 steps a day precisely,
> And I shall forget the dear kingdom of twenty-two year olds,
> Free from their elders' stupidity.[169]

Immediate experience of battle played little part in the two poets' rejection of the war. Another possible source of opposition, political ideas, particularly those based in Marxist thought, were almost absent from their anti-war poetry until 1917. Maiakovskii and Khlebnikov both refer in passing to the Marxist interpretation of the war as a struggle between imperialist powers, fought by workers in the interests of capital and not for their own benefit, but this strain plays only a small part in their views of the war, which were highly personal. While progressive thinkers in Russia were united in the belief that revolution and social change would be an inevitable result of historical progress, Khlebnikov and Maiakovskii found their solutions to the evils of war in an escape from historical time.

Khlebnikov's 'War in a Mousetrap' proposes to nullify time by the poet's prophetic ability to understand and control fate. In 'War and the Universe' by Maiakovskii time is first shattered by the violence of war, then transcended by an act of martyrdom. These are their major works on the war, both using ideas and images drawn from myth and religion, a sphere which, according to Vahan Barooshian, was of central importance to Khlebnikov and

Maiakovskii: 'Both were obsessed with one grandiose mythopoeic vision of universal harmony and solidarity, which assumed the character of a religious hope or belief.'[170]

Their recourse to myth was in tune with the times. After years of civil disorder, strikes, assassinations and the revolution of 1905 there was a general air of optimism, a sense that the war offered Russia a chance to fulfil her destiny, achieve new greatness and wipe out the memory of defeat at the hands of the Japanese in 1905. The war was seen as a potential turning-point in Russia's destiny by Symbolist writer Viacheslav Ivanov, who felt it presaged a renewal of the country's material and physical strength, and a fundamental reappraisal of existing values.[171] The poet Valerii Briusov wrote of it as 'the last war' and prelude to a new age.[172] Some poets, including Anna Akhmatova and Maksimilian Voloshin, wrote of the war as an apocalyptic tragedy; most tended to interpret it as the onset of a messianic age. But whether the war was interpreted as a disaster or a triumph, it appeared in poetry in an abstract, aestheticised form, irrespective of whether the poet was writing from personal experience. The war's significance took precedence over the realities of battle. Censors, anxious to avoid any suggestion of difficulties at the front, removed details which hinted at less than perfect conditions, but for the most part poetry presented them with an inoffensive picture of battlefields peopled with angels and virtuous heroes. The real war was mythologised, conveyed through a selection of religious and legendary images and the use of archaic language. Poetry showed a war in which violence was replaced by heroic acts, the wounded were tended by ethereal, saintly women and the dead were welcomed joyfully into heaven.

It was not the Futurists' concern to explode the mythologised representation of the war by giving a realistic picture of battle. Instead they presented a mythic world in which conventional assumptions were overturned. Their answer to the widespread aestheticised approach was to accentuate, through grotesque hyperbole, the violence and disharmony of war. Maiakovskii's use of religious imagery in 'War and the Universe' is more than tinged with blasphemy. In spite of these inversions, Khlebnikov and Maiakovskii used myth much as conventional writers did. Parallels with myth and legend served to transfer the war into a familiar context which supplied otherwise potentially frightening events with meaning and predictability. By placing their interpretations of the war on a mythic plane, Khlebnikov and Maiakovskii too were able to make sense of a war which challenged some of their theories and ominously fulfilled others. The major difference is that they went further than discerning similarities between myth and reality. Their reality was subsumed in a mythic world, at the centre of which stood the poet, both hero and creator.

In conventional poetry the poetic 'I' often saw the war as a chance to escape the troublesome bounds of private life and seek anonymity in the pursuit of a greater goal. Khlebnikov and Maiakovskii used the war as a vehicle for the exploration and amplification of their personal concerns. Self-effacement was alien to them, as their poetic 'I' represented a hyperbolised self, a sign which encompassed the poet as an individual, a representative for mankind, and as a superhuman figure. Both wrote on a theme fundamental to myth – the act of rebellion, which is associated with the creative violence of Futurism. Their works sought to make harmony and order from the chaos of war, casting themselves as rivals to God by imitating the original act of the creation. To rival the deity is the ultimate form of rebellion, a logical conclusion for the Futurists who rejected all authority and tradition in favour of something new and less flawed. The *personae* they adopted are Promethean figures who perform extraordinary acts with startling results.

In Maiakovskii's 'War and the Universe', after the prologue, in which the poet speaks as a recruit about to set off to war, there follows a lengthy description of the decadent pre-war world, then of furious battles. As the violence reaches its crescendo, Maiakovskii reverts to his initial position at the centre of his work. The apocalyptic visions of a world engulfed in war are countered by Maiakovskii's poetic *persona*, usually larger than life, and here acting as a substitute for Christ as redeemer of the world. Vladimir Markov commented: 'Maiakovskii seems to have found in the war an even better vehicle than the city for his self-hyperbolisation and hysterical emotionality.'[173]

Maiakovskii prefers to see things differently, protesting that his emotions are taken over by the war rather than vice versa. He claims that his poem is no ordinary work of art, squeezed out of paper and ink. It is drawn from his own sympathetic suffering:

> You take the pain,
> let it grow and grow:
> your breast is pierced by every pike,
> your face distorted by every gas,
> the citadel of your head is shattered by every gun
> this is in every stanza of mine.

This insight spurs Maiakovskii into indignant action. He storms the heavens, ready to protest, but finds that the gods have fled in terror. The absence of a god on whom the poet can either vent his anger or from whom he can demand an end to the war forces Maiakovskii to turn his aggression against himself while assuming the role of Christ. Similar motifs of the absent or indifferent god and of the poet as Christ also occur in 'A Cloud in Trousers', written between 1914 and 1915, which centres on the hyperbolised agonies of the poet rejected in love.[175] The absence of love, whether in the poet's private life or in a world engaged in warfare, provokes the same response. Maiakovskii presents himself as a suffering Christ figure with whom he simultaneously identifies and whom he travesties. In both poems the use of religious imagery is heretical and anti-theist, as suggested by the original title of the earlier poem, which was to have been 'The Thirteenth Apostle' until the censor objected.

That both poems inhabit a shared poetic universe, with much imagery in common, suggests that 'War and the Universe' not only shows the poet's response to the outward circumstances of the war, but also uses the war as a hyperbolised dramatisation of the poet's emotional chaos. In 'War and the Universe' Maiakovskii plays a role which is in many ways similar to that of Christ, whose death atones for the sins of the whole world. Christ is associated with unconditional love of humanity, which is the antithesis of war. Maiakovskii, in the poem's prologue, identifies himself with Christ by claiming that he is the sole guardian of 'love for all things alive' and calling himself 'the sole herald of future truths'.[176] But Maiakovskii who saves the world is also the source of all the world's evil, and takes on the role of a scapegoat, tearing out his heart in a frenzy of repentance. Through this act of self-sacrifice the world is miraculously renewed and the poet, resurrected, sees himself as the new world's creator.

Although the *personae* used by Khlebnikov in 'War in a Mousetrap' are not consistent, the most dominant is a hybrid, combining the belligerent qualities of his earlier Slav nationalist self and the detached wisdom of a prophet. This combination of aggression and neutrality reflects his changed attitude towards the problem of fate and determinism. Although his earlier wartime poetry shows a passive acceptance of war and death, Khlebnikov could not countenance the fact that the war demanded the lives of so many young men. As a warrior–prophet, Khlebnikov seeks not only to discern future events, but to control them, rebelling against the laws of fate. In an early poem of the cycle Khlebnikov describes himself as the 'captive of wicked elders' and admits to being a 'timid rabbit' rather than a 'king', the Russian words being, respectively 'krolik' and 'korol' and thus offering scope for word-play.[177] At other times Khlebnikov portrays himself as a figure who is elevated to superhuman status by his prophetic powers. He displays a disturbing tendency to act with arbitrary violence like a delinquent god. The warrior against war speaks of breaking the human race 'like a box of matches' and seizing the globe 'with a madman's paw'.[178] The revelation of the meaning of the mousetrap is brought to Khlebnikov by a devil who appears to be a projection of the poet himself.[179] Khlebnikov conveys a hyperbolised self-image, claiming that wars, like birds, peck grain from his hands, and that he holds the world on one finger, while the 'snail of centuries' crawls along his arm.[180] The poet transcends the ordinary restrictions of time and space, and, finally, death, from which he emerges with renewed warlike vigour:

> I have died, I have died,
> And blood gushed
> In a broad torrent over armour.
> I have awoken, changed, again
> Casting my warrior's gaze over you.[181]

Elsewhere in Khlebnikov's poetry the image of the warrior is closely allied with that of the hunter. 'War in a Mousetrap' combines both images in the figure of the poet leading an attack on war itself:

> Let us go majestically to the giantess War,
> Who combs corpses from her hair,
> Let us shout boldly, boldly as before:
> 'Impudent mammoth, await the spear!
> You're eating Man Stroganoff.'[182]

Although Khlebnikov rejects war, he does not reject violence as such, but presents the reader with the paradoxical *persona* of a militant pacifist. Violence appears in 'War in a Mousetrap' in two guises. The young are portrayed as heroic hunters setting out with their dogs against monsters; they share the nobility of Khlebnikov's Slav warriors. There is no heroism about the actions of the older generation, who ensure that the war continues for their own profit. Their greed degrades the victims of war, the young men killed in battle, to the status of game birds strung up for sale. Human life is cheapened until it is 'cheaper than earth, barrels of water or cartloads of coal'.[183] Khlebnikov's anti-war imagery rests heavily on the taboo subject of cannibalism, the ultimate dismissal of the humanity of others, but, for the poet, it is the logical conclusion to be drawn from the behaviour of those who encourage the war. He describes heaps of human flesh ready for consumption and suggests that people take lessons in cannibalism from the Fijians.[184] The violence Khlebnikov portrays is not the violence of the battlefield. In view of his early poetry on Slav warriors, this would have seemed too heroic a context for the war Khlebnikov rejected so strongly. Instead he shows that this war has debased the heroism of battle into the distasteful operations of a slaughterhouse.

His theoretical writings show that Khlebnikov now refused to see war as an inevitable fact of existence. He devised methods of preventing, or at the very least, controlling war. The creation of an universal language was intended to avoid misunderstandings which might cause conflict; war was to be restricted to a distant island and made harmless by the use of 'sleep bullets' as ammunition. Khlebnikov no longer felt bound by the laws of fate. He assumed the title of the 'King of Time', believing that the most potent weapon against war was the full understanding of these laws, which would allow him to control the destiny of mankind. Fate, its workings entirely revealed, would become as powerless as a mouse in a trap. Notes written with another Futurist for a talk in April 1917 illustrate the idea underlying 'War in a Mousetrap': '1. We are swarthy hunters who have hung on our belt a mousetrap, in which fate fearfully trembles with black eyes. Definition of fate as a mouse. 2. Our answer to wars – the mousetrap.'[185]

Maiakovskii's opposition to the war relies for much of its effect, as does his solution to it, on scriptural references. He depicts war as fratricidal slaughter, associating it with the first murderer Cain. Scriptural references apart, the war is presented through the use of grotesque exaggeration and distortion, and the result is an effective demonstration of Maiakovskii's claim that war and Futurism were symbiotically linked. Maiakovskii comments that even the most monstrous hyperbole is too gentle to depict war; nevertheless he does his utmost to provide a fittingly horrific picture, which he begins in conventionally Futurist terms. Borrowing Marinetti's concept of war as hygiene, Maiakovskii shows the beginning of war in what is literally a 'surgical strike', blood-letting to save the life of a decadent world, a veritable Babylon. But surgery rapidly turns into universal butchery, as battles are described in terms of gladiatorial combat in a world-wide arena, a spectacle never before witnessed, even by the emperor Nero. The magnitude of the slaughter is shown by frequent references to the blood-soaked earth. Blood instead of water runs from a tap, the earth's surface is reduced to a uniform consistency:

> It's all the same – whether
> Stone,
> Bog,
> Or cottage,
> Human gore drenches all.
> Everywhere
> footsteps
> squelch identically,
> wading through the earth's steaming mush.[186]

The poem's final section shows the apotheosis of the world renewed, and acts as a contrasting counterbalance to the grotesque descriptions of war. Using images drawn from the Bible, Maiakovskii describes the resurrection of the dead, the clothing of skeletons in flesh, and, as the ultimate symbol of regeneration, depicts Christ and Cain playing draughts under a tree. Once-warring kings walk arm in arm and cannons graze on green meadows. It is a utopian vision, religious in its essence, but without a god. Maiakovskii himself occupies the position of deity and redeemer in a world purged of violence.

The two revolutions of 1917 were widely perceived in mythic terms as an elemental force for change. The October revolution put an end to Russia's involvement in the World War; it may have appeared to offer the glorious transformation of the world hoped for by the two poets, but it brought civil war and famine instead of redemption. One of the most striking images of the revolution in poetry, in Aleksandr Blok's 'The Twelve', depicts Christ leading a band of revolutionary sailors through the streets of Petrograd. Although religious imagery was out of place in the new atheist state, Blok's paradoxical combination of the anarchic and violent sailors with the peaceful figure of Christ seems to express the sense of the meeting of myth and reality in a new world. Maiakovskii and Khlebnikov both welcomed the revolution by setting aside their pacifist ideas. The violence of the revolution was qualitatively different from the violence of the First World War; it was akin to the violence celebrated by the Futurists, and they portrayed it with excitement rather than horror.

While in some poems Maiakovskii gloried in the violence of revolution, his propaganda verse written during the Civil War shows it in a stylised form. The shocking force of warfare is miniaturised, the graphic naturalism of his First-World-War poetry is replaced by the style of folk-song and fairy tale. General Denikin's White Army is reduced to a horde of insects, easily crushed between the fingernails of a Red Army soldier.[187] Violence becomes symbolic gesture, hyperbole is used to comic effect instead of to shock. The battle against foreign intervention becomes a duel fought between Ivan, a collective Russian hero, and Woodrow Wilson.[188]

Khlebnikov retained his distaste for war to some extent. He objected to Kerenskii's Provisional Government which supported Russia's continued involvement in the World War, and during the Civil War a certain pacifist streak remained in his work. For the most part Khlebnikov evokes the dynamic nature of battle, in which the red wood-sprite shouts her encouragement to the Red Army's soldiers and inanimate objects are endowed with the characteristics of predatory animals.[189] Behind the excitement there remains a yearning for peace. Khlebnikov evokes the coming of spring as a battle fought between flowers with their scents which are 'fragrant bullets', and urges people to imitate their example.[190] There is a deep and fatalistic ambivalence in his depiction of revolutionary violence in the poem 'Night Search', unpublished in the Soviet Union until recently.[191] The rebellious and elemental force which fuels a band of Bolshevik sailors appears to be both misdirected and ultimately provides no protection against the iron laws of fate.

As Soviet literature gradually evolved into the centralised, state-controlled entity which it became by the mid-1930s, there was a distinct change in the representation of violence and war. The rebellious, elemental aspects of violence associated with the Futurists' work could no longer be an acceptable part of state culture. The notion of rebellion against the Establishment had served its purpose; now the new state needed to bolster its authority. The new approach is epitomised in the work of Nikolai Tikhonov, who rose to become a leading official Soviet poet and literary functionary. As a soldier during the First World War, he wrote from personal experience and with increasing disillusion of the loss of life and suffering he witnessed. Subsequently Tikhonov became a soldier in the Red Army, and his poetry was significantly altered. Violence practically vanished from the scene as warfare was purged of all unnecessarily distasteful details. The focus of attention became the loyalty and devotion of the Red Army soldier, obedient to his commander even in death.

While some poets continued to write of the Civil War in elemental imagery, describing the Red Cavalry charging across the steppes like a flood of lava, Tikhonov celebrated not the dynamic force of violence which carried its perpetrators blindly away, but man's ability consciously to channel this force. War, stripped of the dynamic qualities brought to it by the Futurists, was transformed into the stuff of glorious legend, and often appears as such in the poetry he wrote about the Soviet war with Finland during the winter of 1939–40, and during the Second World War. Tikhonov compares soldiers with knights in armour, tanks with their trusty war-horses, and represents battle not as a vast, chaotic panorama, but concentrated into the combat of a few heroes against the enemy.

Soviet society of the 1930s was increasingly based on unprecedented acts of violence against the population, yet in literature, as in other areas of public life, this violence could not be made manifest. A group comparable to the Futurists in their heyday of 1913–14, whose violent gestures reflected social upheavals, would not have been tolerated in the 1930s. As war broke out in June 1941, its events could be shown only through ritualised, controlled actions, presented in legendary terms which, despite the lack of overt religious content, echo the conventions of 1914. Small wonder, then, that Nikolai Aseev, former Futurist and follower of Maiakovskii, complained in 1943 that war poetry had become monotonous and predictable. As Maiakovskii had done in 1914, Aseev put together three stanzas by separate authors in a single poem to demonstrate their stylistic and thematic uniformity.[192]

His gesture was coolly received. Khlebnikov and Maiakovskii had written of war in poetry which was dynamic, intense, rooted in the poet's inner world, but which used myth to expand their personal horizons. Violence, whether it was being celebrated or vehemently rejected, was depicted by them in vivid detail. Their poetry was superseded by poetry which practically denied the existence of violence, replacing its elemental force with the concept of control and restraint rather than creativity. The Soviet poet's individuality, rather than being hyperbolised, was neutralised beneath an official mask of stylistic and ideological conformity.

Alison Sinclair

Disasters of war: image and experience in Spain

Men are executed, women are raped, mutilated corpses are impaled on the branches of trees – the whole set against bleak landscapes devoid of natural life, frequently clouded by billows of gunsmoke. The experience of contemplating *Los desastres de la guerra*, Goya's series of eighty-five etchings stimulated by the war of resistance to the Napoleonic invasion of Spain in 1808 is a harrowing one, the more so when we realise that atrocities of this kind continue to be perpetrated. There is a double layer of violence: the horrors of war are conveyed to the spectator, and there is a second intense violence implicit in the production of a situation by which the spectator is not merely exposed to such horrors but forcefully subjected to them. The possibility of a perverted, masochistic pleasure in the double process cannot be disregarded as the spectator becomes also voyeur of experience that is outside the boundaries of the acceptable.

Though Goya is not part of the European avant-garde of this century, his work, whether in the *Caprichos*,[193] the *Desastres*, or the paintings of the Black Period, contains strong elements of the surreal and the uncanny, and there are, in the spectator's reaction to his work, close connections with the response evoked by avant-garde depictions of violence. When compared with avant-garde visions of violence, the work of Goya is in many respects more effective, more powerful. My aim here is to discuss why this may be so, using Goya as a yardstick for examining the complexities that arise when artists portray or include violence in their work.

The *Desastres* were not an immediate public and political response to the invasion, in that they were not to be published until 1863, long after the violent events which had provoked their creation. The engravings range over a variety of war experiences, with an emphasis on the Spaniards as the victims of the war, and the French soldiers as the antagonists, though Nos 28 and 29, for example, do show the *pueblo* as aggressor. The degree to which Goya was partisan in his selection of victims and perpetrators of violence is a matter of dispute, displaying the desire of critics, perhaps, to annex him for other causes.[194] There is, however, no doubt of Goya's horror at the activity of war itself.

The initial impression of the *Desastres* is of a chilling and sober reportage of subject matter that cannot be viewed coolly. Yet they are not entirely realistic. In the portrayal of the human participants in the war, the engravings present some figures, particularly those of women, with a stylised and Romantic beauty – slender-waisted, hair flowing in the wind like the French Marianne of the Revolution, the folds of their dresses clinging gently to curving forms, as in No. 4 (*Women provide courage*), No. 5 (*And they are fierce creatures*) and No. 7 (*What courage*). The classic form and musculature of some of the men is reminiscent of studies for life-classes, as in No. 16 (*They take advantage*) or No. 33 (*What more can be done?*), but this is at times offset either by heads which suggest the animal rather than the human, or at least the brutal and the ugly rather than the handsome, or by the mutilation of such fine physical forms, as in No. 37 (*This is worse*) and No. 39 (*A fine deed. With dead men*). That is, Goya emphasises for us the violence suffered by an element of idealisation in the portrayal of his human figures, which he then mars wilfully and forcefully.

We can assess just how effective this is by comparing it with the force of certain surrealist paintings in which the disfigurement, distortion or mutilation of human forms is experienced more forcefully by the spectator because the original forms are perceived not only as realistic but of beauty. See for example the chilling effect of distorted muscular beings in paintings by Alberto Savinio, such as *The Return* (1929), *Builders of Paradise* (1929), or *Roger and Angelica* (1931–12) in which a handsome nude male has the head of a cockerel. In the composition of Goya's engravings, we also see the hand of the artist who handles light and shade, rhythm and visual structure, so that the whole is not merely a pre-photographic impression of events witnessed. There is control and selection, shaping and dramatisation.

In tension with this artistic shaping is the impression that the *Desastres* constitute a type of reportage, presenting a series of stills which bear titles that act more as commentaries than labels. Typical titles are *One cannot bear to see this*, *This is worse*, *This I saw*. The individual and the cumulative effect of these titles is that they highlight Goya not just as artist, but as horrified witness: not a witness exulting in the violence, but shocked by it. This is despite the fact that the event in question is, in terms of Spanish history, generally seen as an event to be celebrated, an interpretation that might conveniently pass over the human horror of the event. Goya faces us with the reality of suffering, rather than with a political cause for celebration.

When we turn to the way in which violence appears in the art of the avant-garde, there is a degree to which there is an interference in the inclusion of violence which, I would argue, derives both from levels of overt political commitment and from the theoretical attitudes to its inclusion. That is, instead of a quasi-realist model which seeks to show us the horrors of a certain reality, we find ourselves in an arena where violence is either the stimulus to engage more directly in political propaganda through an artistic channel or the motive through which the artist makes a challenge to propriety – a challenge made by annexing certain types of subject-matter for art, and by simultaneously committing acts of violence or shock upon the consumer of that art. Complications ensue.

Among the avant-garde, violence was promoted as appropriate subject-matter for art in the wave of boundary-breaking of old academy-led attitudes which held that the world of the artistic should be restricted, and be more beautiful, than the world of the real. For the Futurists, and other related movements, the celebration of violence came as a part of the celebration of youth, of (male) sexuality, of the sportsman, the marvels of machinery, the power of the fast car and the aeroplane. This is clear from the manifestos of the first two decades of this century, signal examples being the various Futurist manifestos and the *Manifiesto anti-artístico catalàn* (1928).

The artistic values (and implied social and political values) of such manifestos are aggressively expressed, and determinedly so. And the proclamation that formerly unacceptable subject-matter is acceptable or desirable for the new art of the twentieth century is conveyed in a manner which is itself violent. It is above all anti-bourgeois, and in this sense elitist; it is excluding of its recipients in the way in which it tramples on sensibilities both artistic and non-artistic. By proclaiming that what is proper for art is an area of subject-matter and approach which goes against previously accepted canons of taste, it is revolutionary. The nature of the revolution, however, particularly in the way in which no quarter is to be given in the multi-faceted assault on good (or rather, accepted) taste, is conducted out at the political extremities, and is arguably right-wing, even fascist, as much as it is left-wing.

Violence was appropriated by the avant-garde as proper subject matter for art in company with other unconventional types of experience, such as technology, or even the ordinary. But in the manner of their presentation, these 'new' areas of subject matter for art were thrust before their potential consumers in a manner that virtually defied them to overcome their qualms, their sensibilities, their sense of good taste, in order to accept them either as experience or as artistic experience. Violence, indeed terrorism is contained in the very avant-garde act, in all its elitism, of proclaiming that there should be no allowance made for those who find the new art unacceptable.

A problematic aspect of the attitudes to violence in avant-garde art is the degree to which it is not a question of either/or, that is, either you take a political attitude to violence, and condemn it if others perpetrate it, or glorify if you participate in it out of political commitment, or alternatively you present a challenge to conventional artistic taste in depicting violence within an artistic framework. The more frequent and complicated position is that already exemplified in part by Goya, that is, that political intention and artistic activity are closely entwined. For ease of reference, however, I shall use the term 'communicative' for the first attitude, and 'artistic' for the second. Most frequently the difference of attitude to violence is in fact embedded into the work of art itself, with a variety of results. The evidence of the Hispanic and other texts given here suggests that at the two extremes, one attitude will win out over the other, and that maximum success (in both artistic and communicative terms) is likely to be found at the point of maximum tension between them.

First, an example of the extreme of the spectrum in which the artistic attitude to violence appears to take precedence over the communicative – the slim volume produced in 1917 by Valle-Inclán, *Midnight: Sidereal Vision of a Moment of War*.[195] This volume of supposed reportage from the Front in the First World War is a set of short vignettes of scenes of the war. One might imagine them to be the verbal equivalent of the *Desastres*, and they have elements in common – the human tragedy and the wholesale devastation caused by the war are clearly visible (the trenches, the long lines of refugees, the wasteland caused by the activity of war). Yet the vignettes of the war have a pronounced *modernista* stylishness about them, which protects the reader from their ultimate violent reality. Chapter XII, for example, shows Valle-Inclán perhaps at his most macabre, as he describes the action to send some hundred German corpses floating away from the shore, the horror of which is offset by the vision of the containing frame of those who deal with the dead, and who are 'childlike and credulous souls'.[196] The grim horror is lightened by Valle-Inclán's desire to retain elements worthy of admiration. The distinction between the ideal elements here, and those idealised and beautiful figures who occur in the *Desastres* is that in the latter they are victims, subject to the brutality portrayed, while here they are distanced by their role of spectators curiously untouched by the horror with which they have such close contact. By Chapter XXXIII, Valle-Inclán is engaged in a different mode of portraying violence. He is distant from the emotional impact of Goya and closer in his exultation to the celebration of the violent that we find outlined in the most political of the avant-garde manifestos. He is totally caught up in excitement, in the view of battle perceived from the safe distance of the general's position: 'How the great battle becomes broken and split into separate types of action, marches, flank movements, ambushes, until at length the sidereal vision fades into the tumult of hand to hand fighting, ending in a shout that is like the victorious crowing of the cock!'[197] Here, as in the majority of the sketches, the artist's eye for line combined with a nostalgia for past grandeur converts in an easy movement the communication of the horrors of war into an artistic and aesthetic perception of the war, thus converting it into a vision of the glories of war.

When war is closer to home, the distance of Valle-Inclán becomes less feasible, and political commitment a more likely option. We can see this in the reactions of artists to the Spanish Civil War of 1936–39 whose reaction takes them close to the communicative mode. The situation here is different from the one to which Goya reacted, that of war on home soil. In that situation the aggressors came from outside, and it was possible to lodge responsibility for violence with the invading forces. A civil war changes all this: strife is from within, and the truths about life offered by it are consequently more uncomfortable to deal with. This may account for the degree to which art produced in response to the Spanish Civil War is not noted for its tendency to confront openly the fact that it was a war involving the struggle of Spaniard against Spaniard. It may be significant in this connection that one of the most powerful expressions of reaction against the war was Picasso's *Guernica*, where the violent event was one perpetrated by non-Spanish forces. What is notable, however, is the degree to which responses in poetry and the visual arts are both polemic in intent, and are perceived by others as constituting political action. This status of art as political and immediate action in these cases, makes the art of the Civil War stand in contrast to the 'reporter' stance of Goya (not to mention the private status of the *Desastres* until decades after their time), and with the generalised view of war which is produced by Valle-Inclán. While the level of commitment in Civil War art is evenly present, the level and nature of the communication varies, however, as does the artistic control over the whole.

Located on the communicative side of the balance (as opposed to the artistic) is the response of Pablo Neruda in his collection *Spain in the Heart* (1936–37). Neruda's collection calls on recognition of traditional symbolism. Through the collection, the Republican cause is presented as allied with the natural order, and the potential strength of the natural world. Through images of blood, fertility and the emergence of natural forms, all of which are associated with the resistance of the Republicans to the Nationalist invasion, Neruda evokes a poetic world which despite its grim attachment to the realities of war is none the less also attached to the poetic traditions of rural idyll, and the belief in a natural order which must be restored. The question arises, however, of the extent to which communication of the positive statement of values offsets the communication of the violence of the war itself – a problem bound to arise with all committed accounts of a conflict, whether in the form of media reportage or artistic response.

The poem 'Anti-tank forces' illustrates a number of these points. The title itself refers to avant-garde determination to introduce unaccustomed subject matter and reference into poetry. Those who combat the tanks are presented not just as heroes, but as sons of the earth, linked to the natural world and consequently glorified: 'pure sons of the earth . . . naked sons of the earth and glory . . . sons of victory'. They are 'sown' in the fields as they prepare for action. Their action is perceived not just as coming from gunfire, but deriving from 'your deep smoking heart'. Neruda looks to the fighter's roots (within the well-established Spanish tradition of turning to the *pueblo* to find strength and values). He sees their simplicity, the rightness and honesty of their pursuits. Their past is associated with simple fruitful labours, the olive, the 'nets full of scale and silver'. In their war participation now, he perceives only glory, the terms of reference curiously reminiscent of the Valle-Inclán extracts discussed earlier:

> Here you stand loaded with lightning,
> gripping glory,
> exploding with furious power,
> alone and hard in the face of the shadows.

As the 'anti-tank forces' are made into myth in the course of the poem, so too is the concept of liberty. Thus the final approximation to the physical grim realities of war is first muted by the triumphant lines preceding it, and then defiantly superseded by an affirmation of the lasting meaning of the fallen, 'your burning race of hearts and roots'. And although the end of the poem refers to destruction and death, it is in general terms, and the final note carries the conviction that the men rise again. Individuals die, it is implied, but not the group.[198]

There is a scale in the depiction of violence along which different artists mark different points. Thus at one end there is the glorification of violence, or, as we saw with Valle-Inclán's *Midnight*, the appreciation, revolutionary and shocking, of the aesthetics of violence. Neruda's position marks something different: violence or war can be celebrated provided that the cause is right.

For the Peruvian poet César Vallejo perception of the violence of war could be characterised as deriving from the belief that it is tolerable only because of the writer's conviction of the worth of the cause. Vallejo's writing, in contrast to that of Neruda, expresses a more marked horror on behalf of the victims of violence.

While Neruda's cycle of poems moves around a set of major symbols which anchor and yet elevate the Civil War struggle, so that it becomes grandiose rather than sordid, Vallejo's most impressive poems consist of moments of intimate humanity and human vulnerability. What emerges in the cycle of poems *España aparta de mí este cáliz* (1937) is a sense of the common man who is caught up in this struggle, the common man who suffers and dies for a cause. This is distinct, to some degree, from the links made by Neruda between the soldiers and their *pueblo* roots, and this derives principally from Vallejo's greater degree of individual particularisation. There is no lack of pathos in the miniature scenes of humble men who perish, as with Pedro Rojas in No. III, with his naive spelling the indication of the simplicity of his involvement, but there is still the sense of these men as involved in a struggle that is heroic. Ernesto's broken body and pain dominate No. VI, but the poet invites him to sit on his throne – albeit the incongruous throne of his right shoe, the incongruity puncturing but not destroying the sense that the cause was a worthy one. Dignity and reverence in these poems derive from the sense of dignity of individuals fighting in the cause, so that the poems carry the tone of the sober celebration of sacrifice, in which suffering is acknowledged, but tempered by the communality of suffering and struggle. Thus in IX, in the 'Little Prayer for a Hero of the Republic', there is humble human greatness in the man, and in the way he is treated:

> They bore the hero away,
> and his ill-fated bodily mouth entered our breath; we all sweated, with our
>   burden of man's core; the moons travelled in our wake;
> the dead man also sweated with sadness.[199]

Stylistically Vallejo moves to a level where comprehension–communication on a simple linguistic level becomes impeded, although the communication of sadness speaks through the confused earthiness of the images. Here he stands on an edge of tension comparable with that of Goya, and in the halting, crumbling and surreal images, in which the human suffering rather than the glorious cause is emphasised, he communicates with the greatest power.

Vallejo's poetry derives its strength from its surreal confusion, through images suffused with, but also directly echoing and expressing, human suffering, in which there is no order imposed by conviction about the rightness of the objective. The confusion is itself, however, carefully ordered and balanced. Pain is made the more exquisite, the more delicately it is traced.

Let us now consider how the work of containing emotional impact can enable it to be communicated more forcefully. In my two final examples – 'The Show' by Wilfrid Owen, and Picasso's *Guernica* – there exists not only the general tension between the communicative and the artistic modes, but, more important still, a tension that derives from the flexibility and fluidity of the artistic patterns employed, so that the reader or the spectator has the offer of artistic resolution only to be denied it as a further level of artistic perception comes into view. These works exemplify the success already illustrated in the case of Goya, where the tension is maintained between the artistic and communicative approaches to violence, but take this tension a step further by virtue of the complexity of communication and artistic vision.

Owen communicates a total condemnation of war (as opposed to the bare tolerance of Vallejo), and keeps tight control over the expression of that condemnation, while his artistic image is one of inexorable metamorphosis. In Picasso, the complexity of the various 'readings' of *Guernica* in no way diminishes the sense, conveyed by Owen, of the human suffering that is deplored, but reiterates that sense in a variety of keys.

Owen's power derives partly from his unequivocal attitude to the phenomenon of war, uncomplicated by political commitment to a particular side. 'The Show' illustrates his rejection of those attitudes to war which bypass its real and awful nature. The title itself has all the significant quality of Owen's work: anger, bitterness, controlled but sharp: 'The Show' is the military term for an event, an attack, and the vocabulary indicates that deflection from awful realities that is a necessary part of warfare (as in the modern term of 'taking out').

The poem is based on the development of a complex and unpleasant image, the detail of which is spelled out with awesome meticulousness. The poet looks down on a 'sad land' that is immediately converted into a body ravaged by sickness. We pass with speed through bleak images of realism:

> Gray, cratered like the moon with hollow woe,
> And pitted with great pocks and scabs of plagues

which become subject to a poetic metamorphosis. Land becomes body, it is assigned a beard, and unnatural and horrifying 'thin caterpillars' move over it. While these too are separated from their natural state (they are 'slowly uncoiled', an image stretching back to 'that horror of harsh wire' which is the land's 'beard'), they are also clear and graspable in the repulsive visual image which is suggested.[200]

Owen's relentless pursuit of the minutiae of his image of the caterpillars gives the reader no respite. While superficially one could view him as performing the same type of artistic *tour de force* as was performed by Baudelaire in 'La Charogne' (in *Les Fleurs du mal*), the difference here is the reality, the anger, the commitment. Baudelaire's point we can regard as an artistic one, his poem a feat of daring to test the limits on aesthetic acceptability, to prove that art does not have to restrict itself to the beautiful. Here we have the same poetic power, capacity to maintain artistic tension, yet now with a purpose.

The object under attack is the business of war itself. This is no celebration, but a condemnation of violence. But here it is an attack on war in general, whereas the Spanish examples, while displaying horror and a critique of war, and while concentrating their attention upon the innocent victims of war, none the less have a *parti-pris* at source. The Spanish artists are spurred into (artistic) action by outrage at the horrors committed on specific groups, but this is offset by the belief that one side has justification for its activity. By contrast, one feels that Owen's disgust, like that of many other English war poets, is total, and is no respecter of the political colour or sensibility of either side in the activity of warfare.

Owen's poem shows us how some English war-poetry does not belong to extreme avant-garde writing in form, yet embodies some of the fundamental processes of such writing. By its contained, even conservative, form, it gives greater force to the experience of violence in art.[201] It is not the description of violence, but an act of controlled violence in itself, saved and contained by the artistic form that both subjects us to it and focuses our attention on it.

Picasso's *Guernica* takes us back to the Spanish Civil War. A work often taken to be the emblem of the Spanish artistic response to the Civil War, it is, at first sight, a painting which holds in balance that tension between a work of art, and a work communicating feelings and responses to the horrors of the war that are being portrayed. It is also direct and committed in the sense that it was produced by Picasso as a reaction to a specific violent event in the Civil War – the bombing of Guernica. Yet, like the *Desastres*, it did not come as an immediate response, and had a lengthy and careful gestation. Where Goya's *Desastres* convey the impression of reportage, with the stark commentaries acting as a type of war-correspondent's voice, there is no such mediation in the case of *Guernica*. Nor is there the recognisable realistic human feel of the *Desastres* – since the artistic mode within which it was painted was Cubism. It could be argued that the sense of the non-human that emerges from Cubist dislocations is itself communicative of the alienating experience of war, but there is a distinction to be made between the non-human and the inhuman, in that to communicate the latter adequately a sufficient level of contact with the agonised human experience is necessary.

The German Condor Brigade bombarded the ancient Basque capital of Guernica on a market day in April 1937. The victims were civilians. There was thus political symbolism perceptible in the act, and as an event of war it embodied the suffering of the innocent, devastated by alien and unthinking forces. The fact that havoc was wrought by foreign planes avoided the arguably more uncomfortable truth of the fraternal conflict of civil war. The potential symbolic status of the bombardment was clear from the start, and testimony to this was that its occurrence was significantly both denied and asserted by different sections of the media. Picasso, who was by this stage of the war already involved as an artist (in 1937 he had already produced two versions of the *Life and Lie of Franco*, a satirical cartoon strip, to be sold to raise money for a defence fund), set to work immediately on his artistic comment to the event.

The immediate response, then, was instant, but *Guernica* went through several stages of preparatory drawings. It does not constitute reportage in any sense, but is honed and polished, emblematic and symbolic, just as the bombing itself had a strong element of the symbolic. The figures which can be discerned in the final painting are not those automatically associated with war, or rather, their representation places them within a context which is domestic, human, animal, rather than within the military paraphernalia of war. In one sense, then, Picasso brings out the impact of the violence of war, on the individual man (and woman and child) in a manner analogous to that of the *Desastres*.

An initial approach to *Guernica* produces the impression of frozen chaos. Even more powerfully than Owen's painfully slow perception of the troops moving across the battlefield, bound in the shifting imagery of physical decay, Picasso depicts humans and animals transfixed in their agony, embodying the tension of the frozen scream of Munch. Placed on the far right and far left, two female figures have their heads unnaturally turned to the sky, their mouths open with – what? Inexpressible fear, agony, horror – or simply the expression of being in a situation where existence is no longer tolerable. In the centre of the painting, where the bodies of a horse and a man are entangled and jumbled, the outlines of their suffering forms variously hatched, cut through and imposed one across the other, two further figures appear on the right to contemplate them. To tidy the painting up in this way is, however, the product of contemplating it with the need to restore or impose order. The immediate impact of chaos, of force lines and shock-waves moving disturbingly in uncoordinated directions, remains, even after patterns and frames of allusion have been perceived.

Patterns of allusion there are, certainly, and their presence may pose a critical temptation which, if succumbed to, could negate the raw experience of suffering to which the spectator is invited. Hilton, for example, suggests that in this painting Picasso places in conflict two cultural modes: the pastoral (that is, the natural, Mediterranean, mythic and ahistoric), and the epic (that is, nationalist, secular, heroic, rational, precise, historical and urban).[202] The difficulty with this is, I think, the communicability of the idea of conflict when such subtleties of interpretation are required by the spectator. The stylised cultural interpretation suggested by Hilton weighs against and arguably neutralises the impact of the central visual images. By contrast, the multiple readings of the painting offered by Russell[203] reveal coexisting, overlaid patterns of calvary, bullring, labyrinth, and stage – all of which return us to the original intense human experience that is at the heart of the painting. Russell shows how the structure of the painting itself can be seen within various types of architectural framework, so that the forms of pediment, pyramid, triptych and façade are all potential containing forms, superimposed and coexistent with one another, within which the unadorned suffering of the victims is seen. When we look at detail rather than pattern of allusion to other forms we are struck by the naked communicability of what is perceptible. We may experience difficulty in tracing the outline of single human or animal forms: what emerges with no difficulty, however, is the unadorned and uncomprehending puzzlement evident in the eyes of those forms, ranging from the placid frozen stare of the bull, to the round-eyed horror of the horse, and the disjointed gaze of both the human figure on the ground and the one on the far right.

The importance and meaning of both bull and horse in the painting provide further allusive force, independent, for example, of their symbolic role within the bullfight. Both animals are evident from the earliest sketches for the painting. In one of the drawings, the bull stands looking out at the spectator, with a gesture of surprise on its face, while the horse raises its head in grotesque agony, and a fallen, disembowelled warrior is on the ground. The bull has connotations of brute strength and of the embodiment of what was thought to be traditionally Spanish, but, of course, is also, within Spanish culture, the creature of strength who is teased, outwitted, and ritually slain. Through the *Guernica* series of drawings, and the final painting, what stands out about the bull is its air of innocent surprise – whether it looks out, as in the early drawings, or whether, as later, it looks inwards, into the centre of destruction. There is no sign of the bull's aggression – and it is not clear whether the bull is cause or victim of the suffering elsewhere in the picture. The horse, meanwhile, is not just fallen manhood, but fallen humanity in all its physicality and responsiveness. Two symbols of strength are thus presented as diminished, in the bull's lack of aggressive certainty, and in the fallen horse. The two are united in their expression suggestive of a silent, frozen scream, the starkness of the vision being emphasised by the shape at the top which is reminiscent of a naked light-bulb, and thus carrying the suggestion of the harsh illumination of the torture chamber.

The examples drawn from Neruda, Vallejo and Picasso show the range within which response to the Civil War moves between the communicative and the artistic sides of the balance. On both sides there is a clear move to emotional engagement with the reader, but the basis for that engagement varies between one which is overlaid and informed by political engagement and one which is rooted in the purely human experience. In the former, exemplified in Neruda, there is, in the portrayal of the nature of conflict, a marked damping-down of the reaction of horror to the nature of conflict itself. Vallejo's poetry, while still informed by an unequivocal political commitment, communicates horror through the controlled chaos of form, the parodic and bitter use of the liturgy to shape the poems on what, as an experience, is hardly liturgical or celebratory.

In Goya's *Desastres de la guerra*, and in Owen's war poetry, an indictment of war itself provides the dominant tone (despite the move in Goya to idealise his victims of violence). The exposition of violence is unmitigated by commitment to one of the sides involved, and is reiterated in the manner in which it is relentlessly controlled and violent to the reader. Like Goya, Owen gives no alleviation to his inclusion of violence in poetry by making it overly aesthetic (as in Valle-Inclàn). Neruda and Picasso present different views of how symbolic or emblematic patterns may either detract from the impact of violence, or, as in the case of Picasso, underscore it by the sheer level of multiplicity of the symbolic and ordered readings all of which reiterate the unacceptable level of suffering. Thus, while a framework which is fundamentally ideological may provide an alleviation of the impact of violence, the use of a complex and shifting artistic framework, as exemplified by Owen and Picasso, is one which is more communicative of the bleak horrors of human violence.

The balance between art and life, control and boundary-breaking is a fine one. The examples of Goya, Owen and Picasso suggest that the impact of avant-garde art in political causes may be impaired by overt commitment to the causes espoused.

Jana Howlett

Death, war, revolution: the literature of the Russian Civil War

A few months after the establishment of a Bolshevik Government in Petrograd, Russia was plunged into a bloody civil war in which an estimated ten million citizens of the former Russian empire died. Between 1918 and 1921 the fighting, famine and disease which ravaged the country resulted in loss of human life four times greater than that sustained by Russia's armies during the First World War.[204]

Yet when the Futurist theorist Punin praised Khlebnikov's *Zangezi* (1920–22) for weaving a cloth of death, war and revolution, he was referring to a work in which the Civil War was a vague reminiscence, and the *dramatis personae* were letters of the alphabet announcing a revolution in form. It was as if the Russian avant-garde was blinded by the violence of its polemic with the past[205] to the reality of civil war violence.

During the Stalinisation of Russian society the avant-garde artists' pre-occupation with form was cited as proof of their isolation from revolutionary reality. The actual situation was of course far more complex.

Where the First World War was an event which writers could choose to avoid, the Civil War affected everybody's lives, for the horrors of the front were paralleled by the privations of civilian life. The two revolutions of 1917 had been accomplished more by word than by arms, and contemporaries were well aware that the Civil War would decide whether the Bolshevik order would stay. Responses to the event varied, but they were dictated as much by aesthetic as by political allegiances.

In 1921 the Communist Party's newspaper, *Pravda*, ran a competition for the best director of a state enterprise in which the first prize was a watch, a hat, six sets of underwear, books to the sum of 100 million roubles and a year's subscription to the newspaper.[206] Literature during the first years of the existence of the Soviet state can only be understood against the background of the extraordinary mixture of idealism and pragmatism which characterised political thinking of the period. Idealism dictated that the new ruling class should read, but pragmatism dictated that it should be supplied with underpants. The first aim was far easier to satisfy than the second, but it did pose a problem which became more acute as publishing came under the control of the state: what exactly should the proletariat read?

Three groups dominated the debate about the nature of the 'new literature': Futurists, Proletkult, and the Communist Party. For although many Futurists and Proletkultists were members of the Communist Party, they frequently found themselves in conflict with the party leadership over questions of cultural policy. All three groups shared the belief that literary activity is essential to all societies, and that Soviet society would provide the stimulus for an entirely new literature, but they disagreed on almost everything else.

The Russian Futurists had rejected the culture of the past long before the Revolution.[207] Their newspaper, *Iskusstvo Kommuny*, claimed that the right to lead belonged to the Futurists, because they had started a revolution in art a decade before 1917. In the words of Natan Altman, leader of the Communist Futurists (Komfuty): 'Only Futurist art is constructed on collectivist principles. Only Futurist art is the art of the proletariat.'[209]

The Futurist response to the challenge of creating a new art took several forms. On the one hand their emphasis on the irrational and comic attacked all the political and aesthetic certainties of the period. On the other hand they searched for new certainties.

The Futurists' reaction to the solemn earnestness of Realism, the humourless egocentricity of Symbolism and the political dogmatism of Proletkult is all too often forgotten. In 1918, the year in which the Great War ended and the Civil War started, Ilia Zdanevich devised *Janko I krul' albanskii*, a Futurist 'play'. Its main character is the fictitious counterpart of Janko Lavrin, later to become Professor of Russian at the University of Nottingham. In 1916 Lavrin had published a book full of admiration for the warlike Albanians, who 'kill each other during quarrels, because they have been insulted or because they desire blood-revenge, they kill because they want to rob, or just because they want to kill – out of love for the art of killing'.[210] Lavrin was a Slovene and in Russian the suffix 'o' of his Christian name indicated a neuter noun. This provided an excuse for the creation of parody Janko, the neuter being.

The première of *Janko I, King of Albania, a tragedy in Albanian 28,000 meters in length, performed with the participation of the Austrian Prime Minister, 10,000 fleas, Breshko-Breshkovskii and other rubbish* was an immense success, with Zdanevich supplying a free translation from the 'Albanian' and the audience taking the parts for which there were not enough actors. The play made reference to Fraser's *Golden Bough* and Apollinaire's *Le poète assassiné*, and fun of everything, especially the need for a recognisable meaning.

Zdanevich's friend, Velimir Khlebnikov, represents Futurism's search for certainties. He stated his aims in an article entitled 'The Written Language of the Earth: a System of Hieroglyphs Common to all the Nations of Our Planet' published in 1919:

> Our aim is the creation of a common written language, common to all the nations of the Sun's third planet, the creation of written signs which would be comprehensible and acceptable to all on the star inhabited by mankind. . . . Languages have betrayed their great past. Once upon a time, when words destroyed enmity and made the future transparent and calm, languages, rising up in degrees, united the peoples of the 1) cave, 2) village, 3) tribe or family, 4) state – into a single intelligent world, uniting those who exchanged the values of the mind in exchange for sounds which were the same everywhere. . . . But now . . . they have divided multilingual mankind into camps.[211]

His search for a primeval language common to all mankind which would bring universal harmony led Khlebnikov to the creation of an ever more abstract vocabulary. *Zangezi* embodies his ideas in a work which Khlebnikov described as a tale, though it is a mixture of prose, poetry and drama divided into planes instead of acts. Plane VIII opens with a speech by Zangezi, who later calls on everyone to sing the divine sounds which fall from above, such as Goum, Um, Uum, Paum:

> R, K, L and G –
> The soldiers of the alphabet
> were the *dramatis personae* of those years,
> the heroes of those days.[212]

The esoteric mysticism of Khlebnikov's *zaum* – trans-rational language – needs to be contrasted with his poems on the subject of the Civil War. These show that he turned to words which he described as *bytovye*, 'the words of everyday life', when he needed to express the horrors of Civil War reality. In October 1921 he produced a propaganda poem for a pamphlet calling upon the Russian public to aid the famine-stricken Volga region:

> You, who have rested your bellies on thick planks,
> Who have emerged, swaying, from Soviet cafeterias,
> Do you know that a whole great land
> could well become a morgue?
> I know that the skin of your ears is as thick as that of powerful buffaloes,
> and only sticks will make them feel emotion,
> But surely you will not gallop away from the *Hungry Week*
> When the talon of death hangs above the whole country?
> Cadavers large and small
> will stare at the starry sky
> While you go and get
> A large lump of bread for the night.
> You think that hunger is just a troublesome fly
> Who can be chased away,
> But you should know that there is a drought on the Volga:
> The only reason for not taking but giving.

Bring great sacks
To the collection point of 'Hungry Week'
Give away your last crust of bread
To save those who have gone grey!
The Volga was always your provider,
But now it is half-dead.

Why did Khlebnikov return to realism? As the poem was commissioned, one answer could have been need. Book production had fallen catastrophically (in 1922 the number of titles published was 90 per cent down on 1912) and royalties were minimal.[213] Writers could not rely on meagre commissions, lectures and translations for their livelihood. But with the end of private publishing the government (i.e. the Communist Party) became the only patron of the arts, and it soon became clear that the party as a whole favoured realism. But such an argument is not the whole answer, for Khlebnikov wrote other poems about the Civil War which were not commissioned and which also employ 'everyday language'. In 'The People Are Desperate', for example, Khlebnikov mixes his neologisms with images which leave no doubt of the message of the poem: that the Civil War is as destructive as any in Russia's past, and that it is driving its people into Babylonian captivity. It seems that, like his fellow-Futurist, Maiakovskii, Khlebnikov turned to a more intelligible, 'realist' language in the search for a form of expression which would do justice to that which he was trying to say.[214]

Isak Babel is perhaps the best-known chronicler of the Civil War. His work does not fit comfortably into any clear category, though his most famous work, *The Red Cavalry*, was first published in 1924 in the Futurist journal *LEF*. He started his literary career as an imitator of Maupassant and Flaubert, and, like the latter, was an obsessive stylist. In 1920 he was assigned to Marshal Budennyi, commander of the Red Cavalry, as commissar for political education. *Konarmiia* (*Red Cavalry*), his cycle of stories, has the immediacy of an eye-witness account, though it took several years to write.

The violence of Babel's narrative produces a sense of heightened clarity and an emotional state verging on hysteria. The shock comes from the resolution of the terrible prophecies carried by the descriptions which introduce his protagonists:

Fields of porphyry poppies flower around us, a midday wind plays with the yellowing rye, virginal buckwheat stems rise on the horizon, like the wall of a distant monastery. The quiet river Volyn arches. The river Volyn leaves us for the pearl mists of birch groves, it crawls into wild-flower hillocks and tangles its fingers in overgrown hops. An orange sun rolls through the sky like a decapitated head, a tender flame lights in the gorges of clouds, the banners of the sunset flutter above our heads. The smell of yesterday's blood and dead horses trickles into the evening coolness. . . .

I wake because the pregnant woman is searching my face with her fingers. 'Sir,' she says, 'you are shouting in your sleep and tossing about. I'll make you a bed in another corner, because you keep bumping into my father. . . .' She raises her thin legs from the floor, and her round belly, and she takes the blanket off the sleeping man. The dead old man lies there, his head tossed backwards. His throat has been torn out, his face has been sliced in half, blue blood lies on his beard like drops of lead.

'Sir,' says the Jewess and shakes the eiderdown, – 'the Poles were slashing at him and he begged them: kill me in the back yard in the dark, so that my daughter won't see how I die. But they did it like they wanted, – he was dying in this room and thinking about me. . . . And I want to know, – the woman said suddenly with a terrible strength, – where else on this earth will you find a father like mine?'[215]

Babel's language is full of visual references. The description of the violent curve of the old man's throat echoes the images of Goya's *Desastres de la guerra* and prefigures Picasso's *Guernica*. But for all the artifice, no suspension of disbelief is needed. The complexity of the representation strengthens the message of the narrative – violence is evil, whatever the cause.

Proletkult writers shared the idea that the Civil War was an apocalyptic event in which the old world and the new clashed in a violent life or death struggle. But where Khlebnikov and Babel saw the Civil War as opening the doors to hell, Proletkult writers greeted its violence as a necessary prelude to a new life.

Proletkult (The Union of Proletarian Cultural and Educational Organizations) was dedicated to helping 'the proletariat develop its own culture . . . which would give greater ideological independence to all forms of proletarian struggle'. According to Proletkult thinking only the proletariat could create a proletarian culture 'which will become universal with the destruction of class divisions in society'.[216] 'The proletariat must have its own class art. . .the spirit of that art is working collectivism'. . . . 'Proletarian art is a mighty weapon of class consciousness in the international proletarian revolution' and therefore only Proletkult, as a 'class-restricted workers' organisation',[217] should have the right to lead in cultural matters under the dictatorship of the proletariat. Since by 1920 Proletkult published fifteen journals[218] and claimed a membership which exceeded that of the Communist Party,[219] this was a serious challenge.

Partly because of its well-defined aims, Proletkult was far better organised than most new Soviet institutions, and Proletkult writers were the first to form a new union after the Revolution. Though Proletkult's claims challenged the leading role of the party, the organisation received support from the government until the 1920s because of its contribution to the cultural revolution – the education of Russia's largely illiterate population. The adult literacy campaign absorbed almost three-quarters of Proletkult's budget[220] and, with Proletkult's 'propaganda brigades', played a vital part in drumming up support for the Bolsheviks.

According to Proletkult, the process of educating workers to understand new art was part of the process of transforming the world into their domain. In *Proletarskaia kul'tura*, the Proletkult's chief journal, Aleksei ʿGastev called for 'a revolution in artistic techniques' and proclaimed his vision of a new art 'astounding in its declared grandeur, and negating all that is intimate and lyrical'. This idea was based on Gastev's belief that the proletariat, because it works with machines, possesses

an astounding anonymity, which allows us to classify each proletarian unit [i.e. worker] as A, B, C or 325, 075 and 0 and so on . . . in [the proletariat's] psychology massive and powerful currents travel all over the earth recognizing not millions of heads, but one universal head. In future this tendency will, almost unnoticed, make individual thought impossible.[221]

This vision of the ideal proletarian collective, later parodied by Zamiatin's *We*, is reflected in the titles of Proletkult works, dominated by the collective pronoun *We*. Vladimir Kirillov declared in his poem *We*:

> We are the indestructible terrible
> legions of Labour.
> We have conquered the open spaces
> of seas, oceans and land.
> We have lit cities by the light of
> artificial suns,
> Our proud souls burn with the fires
> of rebellion.
> . . . .
> In the name of our tomorrow we will throw
> Raphael into the flames,
> destroy museums, trample on the flowers of
> art.[222]

Aleksei Gastev, who experienced life at the Civil War front at first hand, published several poems describing the Civil War sacrifice of human life for the sake of the collective. His repetitive verse is the more shocking for being almost mawkish, in spite of its violent imagery:

> Corpses, warm, beloved . . .
> be our railway sleepers.
> Hands, make more
> Hoorah, two thousand in the train,
> Three thousand on the roof,
> What will be, will be.
> Rise.
> We move headlong over you
> Blessed sleepers.[223]

In his reliance on shock, his use of blank verse and his industrial vocabulary, Gastev attempted to find a new form, but his renunciation of poetry in favour of education may have been an admission of defeat. In 1923 Gastev founded *The League of Time* (later renamed *The League for the Scientific Organization of Labour*), whose aim was to train a more efficient labour force.[224] He perished in a labour camp, a victim of Stalin's purge of Communist Party intelligentsia.

Artem Veselyi typified the new Proletkult writer, just as his fate was to typify that of many members of his generation. He started work as a labourer at fourteen, joined the Bolsheviks at eighteen, fought in the Civil War, and after a brief period of study in a Literary Institute formed with Proletkult participation he became a writer. Like Gastev he died during the purges.

To Veselyi's heroes the violence of the Civil War is natural, like breathing. He describes the war in 'prose-poems', which are an attempt to break the restrictions of form as much as of content. In *Rivers of Fire* (1924), episodes in the life of two sailors back from war merge their two voices and the voice of the narrator, as in this passage, which describes the murder of a shopkeeper:

They walked hurriedly back from the station along familiar streets. They looked at the houses and the few surviving fences. They walked in step past the mirror windows of gluttonous shops – saliva streaming – dreamily swearing out loud:
'That's not right . . .'
'No point in arguing, capital has won'.
'Our old freedom was so much better than their new politics.'
'We had freedom, and now we have nothing but bitter slavery'
'Oh, Lord, what misery . . .'
A bitter-sweet memory of the seventeenth–eighteenth year of life, when such things came easy, rose up: cased a joint or two and got away, a month to spend without looking in the pocket.
'They should all be strangled . . .'
'Don't, Ivan . . . Words are nothing. They should have been killed while we had a gun in our hands. But now . . .
'We did not kill enough of them . . .'
. . .
Off they hurried.
For caps,
for packs,
the shop-owner shook-clicked the abacus.
'Five pounds of sausage . . .'
Misha laughed,
Ivan laughed.
'Don't bother to count, old man, we won't pay, anyway . . .
Bits of cheese in the pockets, not a sausage left of the meat – Ivan said, propitiating:
'It won't be wasted, and that's official . . .'
The owner's ears drooped.
'Comrade sailors, I, I . . .'
The abacus rolled, rattled on the floor . . .

Misha walked up to the shop owner and pulled his peaked cap over his face.
'Won't you lend us a bit of money, old man? . . . Eh?
The black mouth of the man choked on shocked mutterings.[225]

The frequent shifts of viewpoint, the inversion of word order, the use of typographic effects and punctuation to indicate shifts in the mood reflect the influence of Belyi on Russian prose. But like Gastev, Veselyi never allows form to obscure the message of the work, sharing the Proletkult approach to literature as a tool for the education of working class. The didactic purpose of Proletkult writing meant that most writers favoured prose as a medium more accessible to workers. It also meant that during the early 1920s Proletkult writers were favoured with Communist Party patronage.

Between the Proletkult and Futurist poles of the debate about the nature of new art there were many other groups representing more moderate views, such as VSP,[226] which included Symbolists, Imagists and Acmeists, and *Litfront*.[227]

Aleksandr Serafimovich, a member of the latter group, spent the Civil War on the Western Front as a correspondent of *Pravda*, and his accounts of the experience are in the style of newspaper articles enlivened by dialogue. But unlike Veselyi or Babel, Serafimovich makes no attempt to reproduce what he has seen or heard. His heroes are ideal communists, speaking a literary language to the accompaniment of the writer's commentary. His 'Lion's Brood', written in 1918, opens:

Just like the young shoots which penetrate the spring earth, thick and powerful, so too do new institutions, new people, new creators and a new workforce appear as one out of the freshly ploughed black soil of revolution.
And they do not appear, live, grow stronger and develop because they are organised above by the new institutions, creating new offices at the top, but because something stirs in the layers of the working class and peasant poor, certain fundamental changes take place which make it possible for the young shoots to grow in a responsive soil.
In front of me I see the open young face of the political commissar of the Nth brigade. A clear open forehead, wavy light hair combed back, and youth, joyful and unrestrained youth, pours from blue and happy eyes, from the youthful blush of the cheek, from the whole of the powerful figure wrapped in a tight overcoat and girdled with gun and sword belts.[228]

Serafimovich carefully excised anything unpleasant from the image of the perfect communist, providing a model for the idealised hero of the Stalinist period. But this was no more a model imposed from above than it was a response to the demands of the masses.[229] It was a model created by a writer in response to writers' calls for an art that was appropriate to Russia's new society.

The role of the Communist Party leadership in the adoption of this particular model for literature cannot be doubted. But in the first three years of the life of the Soviet state the party did not dictate what and how writers wrote. Instead the Communist Party's attempts to influence literature largely took the form of selective patronage for realist writers.

One beneficiary of this policy was the justly forgotten woman novelist, Marfa Boretskaia. Her first novel, *How they Died*, was published in Ekaterinodar, a city which finally fell to the Bolsheviks in March 1920.[230] The novel was published the same year with a large print run, and at a low price.

The reason for this is obvious from the work's clear bias. It opens with the approach of the Bolsheviks to Ekaterinodar. The besieged Whites round up the communists in the city, and the novel focuses on a Trinity of Bolsheviks. As the the strong and silent Volkov, who considers his 'weakness not a cause for shame, but regret' is led to a dignified execution, his middle-class fellow-fighter, Matushkin, asks 'why me?' and dies on his knees. The novel is full of clichéd language: 'sunken chests were convulsed with the desire for life, with the uncertain warmth of hope', but this did not prevent the growth of Boretskaia's popularity. *In the Iron Ring: Pages from the Russian Civil War*,[231] already published in Moscow, carried an introduction by Lenin's wife, Nadezhda Krupskaia, who quoted Flaubert as a fine example of 'genuine realism' and a model for the author's style. *The Anger of the People*[232] also carried an introduction by Krupskaia, who commended the work for showing 'the response of masses, rather than that which is experienced by a single, uncertain member of the intelligentsia'. By 1926 Boretskaia's work had entered the list of literature recommended for study by students in literary institutes.[233]

Zyrianov's *Earth Bathed in Blood*[234] was another beneficiary of Party sponsorship. It was printed at the Ivanovo borstal in 50,000 copies, an enormous print run at a time of paper shortages.[235] Written in a style heavily influenced by Belyi mixed with Proletkult ardour in the style of Gastev, the novel does not have a conventional division into chapters or a linear chronological development. Instead it is divided into episodes, whose temporal relationship is unclear. The descriptive passages are overloaded with adjectives, showing a mechanical understanding of the inversion of animate and inanimate attributes:

In the corner of the river Ob the steppeland is compressed, steamrolled and raised on its hackles – on the one side stands the pale blue row of Altai volcanoes, on the other the taiga, frowning with its uncombed flanks.

The steppe has no room to move. The wind has no room to move. Nowhere to let go. . . . The wind has no room to move, and neither have the people, squeezed into a corner of this black-earth land.

The plot of the novel confronts rich cossacks and poor peasants, and the 'peasant/proletarian' aspect of the novel is emphasised through use of common speech interspersed with 'lyrical asides':

But above the silence seemed full of sound and overflowing with harmony – it was the heavens radiating its hymns to the light of the moons and stars.

Again three Bolsheviks are at the centre of the novel. The novel ends with the happy union (not consecrated by marriage) of the two young heroes of the novel, a Bolshevik victory, and the words: 'Everyone was bathed in blood – their own and that of the Whites.'

Once the Bolshevik victory in the Civil War was assured the Communist Party began the process of economic and political centralisation. In 1920 the Futurists' journals closed down because of lack of funding and Proletkult lost its independence. Its educational work was transferred to a Communist Party organisation specially established for the 'political education of the masses'. These actions were taken on the direct instructions of Lenin, whose draft decree on Proletkult was adopted by the Central Committee of the Party and published in December 1920.

The text of this decree shows Lenin's ignorance, or disregard, of the differences between the many artistic movements he classified as 'leftist'. It sets the pattern for future party intervention in the arts: Proletkult was not given an automatic right of reply; artistic experiment was equated with bourgeois decadence; and the holding of aesthetic views became a political statement. Most importantly, Lenin made it clear that the party had the right to declare on all matters, including matters of form in literature.

In spite of this the debate on Soviet literature continued, encouraged by the temporary revival of private presses during the period of the New Economic Policy. But after 1924 the debate between various groups vying for the right to represent party views on literature became increasingly more violent, its vehemence reflected in the ever more military sounding names of literary groups.

The Communist Party's tolerance of plurality within literature ended with the end of plurality within the party and the defeat of the Trotsky faction within the leadership. As Cohen has pointed out, literature came to the party's attention as just one of the aspects of Stalin's policy aimed at 'a leap into socialism' after it became clear that world revolution was a long way away, and 'socialism in one country' became the slogan of the leadership.[236]

The 1925 Communist Party resolution on literature was, like the 1920 decree on the Proletkults, ostensibly a response to a call from a writers' organisation, in this case demanding the 'dictatorship of the Party in the field of literature'. The language of the resolution, written by Bukharin,[237] is far less moderate than that of Trotsky's *Literature and Revolution*, which is one of its main targets. But Bukharin still saw the Party's role as a guide, not as a dictator, because, not unlike Trotsky, he refused to simplify the relationship between art and politics.

But by 1926 'leftism' became a synonym for sabotage, and the language of the chief theorists of literature such as Rodov and Averbakh became ever more inquisitorial. After the first wave of purges within the Communist Party the way was clear for the imposition of 'socialist realism' as the 'fundamental method of Soviet fiction and literary criticism'.

It would be wrong, however, to ascribe the 'return to realism', which characterises the work of several avant-garde writers in the late 1920s, to Party pressure alone. Khlebnikov and Maiakovskii[238] were not alone in combining experiments in form with occasional recourse to a simpler, more 'realist' language for the sake of the message. In 1925 Babel wrote to Gorkii: 'I no longer feel confident about my writing. I am finding it over-elaborate and too highly-coloured.'[239] The cycle of autobiographical stories which includes 'The Story of my Pigeon-Loft' and 'First Love' was written before the imposition of a realist strait-jacket on literature, yet they are written in a style which owes a great deal to the realism of Gorkii.

Boris Pil'niak's *Naked Year* (1921) owes a debt to Belyi's *Petersburg* in the complexities of its structure, its multi-layered language and its reference to symbols. Like Belyi's description of Petersburg on the verge of revolution, Pil'niak's description of Ordynin, a city in the midst of civil war, refers constantly to Russia's Tatar past. The novel was widely acclaimed, yet by 1924 in the story 'Old House' Pil'niak turned to a more traditional, realist narrative form.

The Civil War provided the inspiration for some of the most interesting works in the history of twentieth-century Russian literature. It also showed that the violence of the Civil War could not be described adequately. For those members of the Russian avant-garde who were committed to the search for new forms it posed particularly serious problems, because ambivalence, so fundamental to avant-garde reaction against the certainties of nineteenth-century realism, seemed inappropriate in a world where everything was uncertain.

The Civil War, in which Russian had fought against Russian, was a very different phenomenon from the First World War. Because it was a war which did not face writers with a simple ethical and political choice it had a major effect on the consciousness of the literary avant-garde. The literature of the period shows that, for the Russian avant-garde, violence was not purely a violence of the imagination. But few writers could have imagined how their calls for the destruction of the past in the name of the future would come true.

The Civil War was followed by Stalin's 'accelerated class war', a civil war in all but name. Politically committed writers associated with the pre-revolutionary Bolshevik Party and Proletkult were the first to be destroyed, by the very weapons they had put in the hands of the *apparat*. Apart from Khlebnikov, who died in 1922, all the writers mentioned above found themselves the targets of party criticism at one time or another, and some paid for their commitment with their lives.

It is not surprising, perhaps, that in the face of increasing isolation from the outside world and arbitrary attacks and insecurity in their own world, many Russian writers turned to realism. But they had little in common with Socialist Realism, for theirs was not a 'return' but the conclusion of a 'search for a form of expression which was at once artistically and politically effective'.[240]

Michael Tilby

The imaginary violence of Louis-Ferdinand Céline

il faudrait fermer le monde décidément pendant deux ou trois générations au moins s'il n'y avait plus de mensonges à raconter (*Voyage au bout de la nuit*)

Langage! Parler? Parler? Parler Quoi? . . . (Mort à crédit)[241]

Between 1932 and 1941 Louis-Ferdinand Céline published two novels, a play, and four polemical pamphlets denouncing Soviet Communism, freemasonry, and what he saw as the Jewish domination of every sphere of contemporary French life. The first of his three anti-Semitic pamphlets, *Bagatelles pour un massacre* (1937), incorporated the remainder of his artistic endeavour in this period: the ballet scenarios that he had failed to get performed the previous year, wholly, he claimed, as a result of Jewish prejudice. Violence in a host of forms, physical and verbal, pervades all these writings, as it would also the author's voluminous post-war output. Although violent incidents occur in both his pre-war novels, there is a shift from an emphasis on more purely physical violence in *Voyage au bout de la nuit* (1932) to writing in *Mort à crédit* (1936) that bombards the reader with example upon example of a verbal violence of a remarkably inventive variety. Yet for all the relentless insistence on violence in Céline's fictional world, its function and purpose are by no means straightforward. As will be seen, Céline's concern was neither with documenting violence as an end in itself nor exclusively with giving vent to the animosity he undoubtedly felt towards contemporary civilisation in all its guises.

Violence is shown to be the norm both in the world in which Dr Louis-Ferdinand Destouches had grown up and in those corners of the universe to which he subsequently travelled before embarking upon a literary career under the pseudonym Céline. The young Ferdinand of *Mort à crédit* does not think to question his role as the outlet for his father's splenetic rage.[242] But in addition to the many incidental examples of violent actions and reactions in Céline's pre-war novels, violence provides the culmination, and many of the turning-points, of their sketchy plots. In *Voyage*, Robinson succeeds in murdering Madame Henrouille senior at the second attempt before meeting his own death at Madelon's hand in the taxi that is taking them away from their ill-fated visit to the fun-fair and its ominous shooting-range. With his departure from life, the novel can only peter out. In *Mort à crédit* Ferdinand leaves the parental home convinced that he has killed his father by throwing a typewriter (no lightweight portable in this, the first decade of the century) at his head.

Such violence is never denounced, at least not in conventional terms. After the incident with the typewriter, Oncle Edouard, ever protective towards his nephew, takes Ferdinand home, and, in this novel which has education as one of its secondary themes (we may note in particular the caricatural imitation of the Fourierist *phalanstère* by the eccentric Courtial des Pereires, a further father-substitute for Ferdinand), his easy-going manner of dealing with Ferdinand contrasts pointedly with that of Ferdinand's father. It had been Edouard who had come up with the adventurous idea of sending Ferdinand to an English boarding-school; he now tells him to enjoy a temporary rest, take walks and visit the cinema, the most privileged location of all in Céline's fictional universe.

Many of Céline's descriptions of violence also communicate, through their recourse to detail, a compelling fascination with the spectacle, even tinged with humour. Neither the adult Bardamu nor his youthful predecessor is a detached observer: they both participate in the violent world they describe, even if the worst examples of violence are perpetrated by others.

The way in which the several murders are presented is at odds with expected moral emphases. When Robinson first attempts to murder old Madame Henrouille but is himself mutilated by the booby-trap that he is attaching to the rabbit hutch, the reader may be forgiven for supposing that the injury was intended as retribution. Yet Céline's optic is very different. The episode is simply a further illustration of the tendency of every project to end in failure and of the universal damage that is invariably occasioned by an individual's actions, whether malevolent or well-intentioned. As for Robinson's murder by Madelon, we are not invited to see this as him receiving his due, but rather as an episode in which the representative of Society's by now thoroughly discredited and ridiculed idealism is unable to face up to the reality of the situation that Robinson portrays to her with such unemotional accuracy.

Beyond the treatment of such elements of plot, Céline's first two novels present us with a vision of humanity that, if undeniably bleak, is also entirely coherent, as well as being a development of much late-nineteenth-century pessimism. As Bardamu puts it: 'les hommes sont vaches'.[243] The Des Pereires enterprise in the Oise places its instigators 'en butte à mille menées

hostiles, sournoises, subtiles, inlassables',[244] as soon as the outside world sees
the slightest sign that it might prove successful. Madame Méhon, one of the
many shopkeepers in the Passage des Bérésinas, is merely a prominent representative of a jealousy and spite that are considered the basic character traits
of all humanity. Bardamu the doctor sees his patients as 'des égoïstes, des
pauvres, matérialistes tout rétrécis dans leurs sales projets de retraite'.[245] The
money-oriented response of the newly bereaved family which sells Bardamu a
bottle of wine during his night-time mission during the war is reminiscent of
the behaviour Maupassant had described in his stories of the Franco-Prussian
War.

Treachery is widespread (anonymous letters are a fact of life) except when
it appears in the more venial form of insincerity. The sexual favours granted
by the concierge to Bardamu and other apparently traumatised soldiers at
Professor Bestombes's wartime hospital allow her to report malingerers to
the consultant psychiatrist.

In darkest Africa Bardamu encounters an exception in the person of Alcide,
who, as his name suggests, devotes himself heroically to the cause of his niece.
Yet not only does Alcide's behaviour display some of the violence that marks
out the colonial despot, his sacrifice is seen as absurd. He is viewed above all
as a victim, misused by 'la brutalité, l'indifférence bien prouvée du monde
entier à son égard'.[246] Bardamu, appalled by the 'années de torture' that
Alcide has willingly imposed upon himself, recognises that Alcide has enough
love and devotion in him to reshape the world and is obsessed by the fact that
the world remains ignorant of Alcide's gesture. Observing that Alcide's
goodness cannot even be read in his facial expression, he concludes: 'ça serait
pourtant pas si bête s'il y avait quelque chose pour distinguer les bons des
méchants'.[247]

What is missing from all Céline's fiction is a set of beliefs that will allow
ethical distinctions to become a living force for the individual. The fact that
Bardamu can see only the physical suffering that Alcide brings upon himself
furnishes him with further evidence of the deep-seated masochism that he
considers the dominant component in our make-up. The optimism shown by
Ferdinand's mother, Clémence, in the face of the constant tribulations that
beset her is seen as evidence that if Man's lot (or, in Céline, more especially
Woman's lot) is to suffer, it is an estate to which they are perversely wedded.

The human capacity for self-punishment receives its caricatural and
doubtless racist illustration in the negro who arrives too late to receive his
fifty strokes from Lieutenant Grappa and who is reluctant to return home
without the beating that he had been promised. The cruel observation passed
on this event by Bardamu: 'Il fallut le bousculer ce masochiste hors du camp à
grands coups de pied dans les fesses. Ça lui a fait plaisir quand même mais pas
assez'[248] explains why he can describe himself as 'bien diverti par ces
multiples incidents'.

Man's sadistic urges in Céline's fictional universe are amply sufficient to satisfy the needs of his masochistic characters: the description in *Voyage* of the public delight that accompanies the tormenting of a pig by a knife-wielding butcher is matched by the scene at the beginning of *Mort à crédit* where a hiding given to Mireille in the Bois de Boulogne by the adult Ferdinand entices an audience eager to encourage him.

The adult Ferdinand begins his account of the episode with Mireille by revealing 'y a eu de la violence entre nous pour terminer nos rapports'.[249] But in many of the sexual couplings that Bardamu and Ferdinand observe, violence is an essential and lasting ingredient. The sexual act is invariably portrayed as bestial (animal, especially canine, imagery runs throughout the two novels). Thus, when Antoine is viewed in sexual congress with his employer's wife, Mme Gorloge, he is described by the young witness in the following terms: 'il était extrêmement brutal . . . ils s'agitaient comme des sauvages'.[250] It is implied that her pleasure is increased when his rough treatment of her is accompanied by verbal abuse. It is Bardamu's conclusion that women must have the temperament of 'une garce' to be able to give and receive sexual pleasure to the full. When Ferdinand instructs the young Agathe in the joys of sex, a brutal dimension is seen as an essential element in their pleasure.[251]

The American male, by contrast, cannot diminish the vigour of the good-time girl Molly in *Voyage*. Their very lack of brutality as lovers causes them to be derided by Bardamu: 'les Américains font ça comme des oiseaux',[252] he observes. The most extreme case of this association of violence and sexuality is provided by the couple in Bardamu's apartment block in Rancy who can only achieve sexual arousal after viciously beating their young daughter. This last example is recounted in the same matter-of-fact way as the descriptions of violent sexual activity that do not involve an innocent victim and no attempt is made to distinguish between the acceptable and the unacceptable.

Presiding over the whole of *Voyage* is Bardamu's experience of war: 'c'est des choses qu'on a du mal à croire avant d'aller en guerre. Mais quand on y est, tout s'explique.'[253] In particular, war convinces him that individuals are inhabited by a deep-seated urge to kill. This Céline illustrates, not in terms of Bardamu's hatred of the enemy (Bardamu confesses that he feels no antagonism towards the German soldiers), but with reference to the violent emnity he experiences towards his superiors.[254] During the war Bardamu is led to conclude: 'il existe pour le pauvre en ce monde deux grandes manières de crever, soit par l'indifférence absolue de vos semblables en temps de paix ou par la passion homicide des mêmes en la guerre venue'.[255] Yet later in the novel it emerges that this 'passion homicide' is not exclusive to war. Bardamu's *alter ego*, Robinson, becomes the incarnation of a murderous instinct spawned by his heightened sense of the absurd. What is striking is that Robinson's state is welcomed by Bardamu as an improvement.[256]

This provocative observation is further developed when Bardamu discourses on the desirability of hating as a quasi-artistic activity requiring a powerful imagination. He feels contempt for the Toulouse shop-girls whose conversations reveal that 'leur impuissance spéculative les bornait à haïr sans aucune netteté'.[257] Yet this recognition of the murderous instinct inevitably turns against the individual, who is forced to recognise in himself the object of that instinct in others.[258]

The fictional situations contrived by Céline, notably the mass invasion of Courtial des Pereires' office and subsequent pursuit, are graphic illustrations of this belief and may be seen as attempts to justify the individual's deep-seated fear of persecution, one that is responsible in particular for the paranoia that afflicts Bardamu on board the ship *Amiral Bragueton*. When Bardamu comes face to face with Robinson's 'vocation de meurtre', he marvels at just how much he has learnt as a result of following him into the night. The precise nature of the journey remains nebulous (in one of the narrator's more artistically self-conscious moments, he gives approval to Claude Lorrain's apparent contempt for the foreground in a painting and adds 'l'art exige qu'on situe l'intérêt de l'oeuvre dans les lointains, dans l'insaisissable'[259]). The uncertainty is admirably conveyed by the use of the pronoun 'ça' in the opening sentence of *Voyage*: 'Ça a débuté comme ça.'

The journey is constantly redefined, at one point being no more than the quest for 'le plus grand chagrin possible pour devenir soi-même avant de mourir'.[260] It emerges ultimately as an attempt to understand, not just the war, but the negative forces at work in the human psyche. As Bardamu and his surrogate progress further into the darkness, so the focus must inevitably be on extremes of violence and perversion. Such tendencies in man are sensed to be the product of an existential fear. Bardamu becomes aware that what is to be found at the end of the night is 'le truc qui leur fait si peur à eux tous, à tous ces salauds-là autant qu'ils sont'.[261] If he sets himself apart from others, it is precisely as a result of their lack of any desire to understand that which he is trying to comprehend.[262]

His desire to understand stems from his experience of war, which he defines characteristically as 'tout ce qu'on ne comprenait pas;'[263] he laments that most individuals lack the imagination to contemplate their own death, though others, he observes, have rather too much. It is moreover an imperative that transcends all moral considerations. Yet however much he abhors those who seek to remain ignorant of their condition, Bardamu does not appear to advocate imitation of the single-minded way in which he and Robinson pursue their journey into the night. On the contrary, he seems to recognise the desirability of the individual holding his true nature in check, however Herculean the task.[264]

Ultimately, an understanding of the brutal nature of much human behaviour has to be sought, it is implied, in the context of the omnipresence of death. It is this constant awareness of death that gives rise to an overwhelming conviction of absurdity. Perverse and unnatural behaviour becomes a way of avoiding the emptiness which Bardamu identifies at the heart of existence, proclaiming: 'dès qu'on insiste un peu, c'est le vide'.[265] In common with his younger contemporary Malraux, Céline views death as the certainty that must be uppermost in all thinking about the human condition. But his manner of evoking human mortality has little in common with the author of *La Condition humaine* and instead looks forward in its formulation to the writings of Samuel Beckett: Bardamu speaks, for example, of 'cette espèce de mort qui se fait lentement en nous, gentiment, jour à jour, lâchement devant laquelle chaque jour on s'entraîne à se défendre un peu moins que la veille'.[266] The very title of *Mort à crédit* is an ironic encapsulation of the long drawn-out process of suffering leading to death.[267] The joint existence of Ferdinand's Oncle Antoine and his wife is seen solely in terms of an encroaching death,[268] with suicide an option of which more than one character is aware. Bardamu, he declares: 'La vérité, c'est une agonie qui n'en finit pas. La vérité de ce monde c'est la mort. Il faut choisir, mourir ou mentir. Je n'ai jamais pu me tuer moi. Le mieux était donc de sortir dans la rue, ce petit suicide.'[269]

Even childbirth is not allowed to carry positive connotations: Irène des Pereires no longer exercises her skills as midwife; Mme Vitruve and her daughter want to practise as abortionists.

Bardamu's desire to comprehend the nature of human existence is matched by his determination to force an unwelcome perspective on his reader. The brutality of Céline's writing can be explained in part by his insistence on the need to be aware of death and of the futility of human endeavour in a world that does its best to remain blind to both these certainties. His two pre-war novels represent a virulent attack on the false beliefs that are held on to with such tenacity by the majority of mankind, although Bardamu, faced with a choice between death and living a lie, is unable to take his own life.

Bardamu is only too aware that 'le délire de mentir et de croire s'attrape comme la gale'.[270] It is significant that survival and success become dependent on his talents as an actor.[271] His invention of imaginary wartime exploits leads to temporary celebrity. His ability to mimic a polite and deferential language helps him avoid a lynching and his ability to interpret a number of theatrical roles ensures that he will eat. But, unlike those he denounces, he remains conscious of the distinction between such lies and the reality of his existence.

The lie which particularly attracts his venom is the widespread belief in romantic love. Such a belief, like all other idealist notions, is held to founder on its failure to take account of our corrupt and perverse nature; the over-riding attachment of modern man to materialism is seen by Bardamu as leading to the philosophy 'pas d'amour à perdre dans ce monde tant qu'il y aura cent sous'.[272] *Voyage* opens and ends with a calling into question of love. Love is immediately derided by Bardamu as 'cet infini mis à la portée des caniches'. His response to the sympathetic Molly, the most positive of which he is capable, has to stop short of love.[273] His reluctance to become emotionally involved is constant. As a boy, not only is Ferdinand similarly reluctant with regard to Gwendoline and Violette, even anodyne questions asking about his enjoyment of a film are interpreted by him as unwelcome 'questions intimes'. As usual, Robinson provides a still more extreme case of the same characteristic: the dismissive words he utters to Madelon are not so much a rejection of her as an individual as of the very ideal of romantic love on which her life is based.

According to Bardamu, man is incapable of sentiment by virtue of being 'des enclos de tripes tièdes et mal pourries'.[274] More specifically Célinian is the view: 'c'est quelque chose de toujours vrai un corps, c'est pour cela que c'est presque toujours triste et dégoûtant à regarder'.[275] No opportunity is lost to ram home the ugliness of the body's physical reality: the full range of body fluids escapes in disgusting manner from every orifice.

Céline's writing is furthermore designed to be a virulent denunciation of the *petit-bourgeois* propaganda of his upbringing, and especially patriotic rhetoric. It is to this rhetoric that Bardamu strives to become indifferent, in due course pronouncing himself 'guéri'.[276]

Among the examples of the propaganda Ferdinand and Bardamu have to learn to reject is their mother's fundamental optimism, arguably the most damaging. Bardamu recalls 'elle n'en ratait jamais une ma mère pour essayer de me faire croire que le monde était bénin et qu'elle avait bien fait de me concevoir'.[277] From his sick-bed at the beginning of *Mort à crédit*, the adult Ferdinand overhears his mother comparing him unfavourably with his father, outraged that she should omit all reference to the latter's violent behaviour. But if such pretence arouses Ferdinand's wrath, Bardamu is unable to banish his mother's values from his mind.

The desire to overturn misplaced idealism and mendacious propaganda is heightened by Bardamu the doctor's frustration at not being able to tell the full, awful truth to his patients. The frustration is allowed to erupt on several occasions. On the very first page of *Mort à crédit* medicine is described as 'cette merde'. As a medical student Bardamu torments Lola with his description of the way a cancer eats up a body. Ferdinand, faced with an importunate patient, exclaims to himself and the reader: 'Qu'il lui fonce donc son tison tout entier dans le trou du cul! Ça la redressera, la salope! Ça l'apprendra à me déranger!'[278] It is always on their impotence that Céline's fictional doctors choose to dwell. Bardamu cannot prevent young Bébert from dying, he cannot help Robinson in his final hour, acutely aware that Robinson needs 'un autre Ferdinand, bien plus grand que moi, bien sûr, pour mourir, pour l'aider à mourir plutôt, plus doucement'.[279]

The majority of the examples of the mendacious stance adopted by society are seen specifically in terms of a false rhetoric and the widespread acceptance and unthinking repetition of its tenets. It is this Robinson rejects in Madelon: 'Ça te suffit de répéter tout ce que bavent les autres. . . . Ça te suffit parce qu'ils t'ont raconté les autres qu'il y avait pas mieux que l'amour.'[280]

Ferdinand's mother practises a form of bilingualism, addressing her clients in a carefully rehearsed polite language that has the ring of hypocrisy, so far removed is it in tone from the shabby or sordid reality of the Passage des Beresinas. When she hawks her son from prospective employer to prospective employer, Ferdinand hears himself being advertised in terms that jar with his own, honest appraisal of his faults. The underlying implication is that the racy, urban slang that typifies Ferdinand's narrative is a fundamentally more honest way of expressing individual thoughts and emotions, a means of avoiding absorption by a society he despises.

A distrust of language runs through both novels. Ferdinand takes an early exception to Tante Armide's exclusive use of the imperfect subjunctive, but in due course his wariness of language becomes far more extreme. The boy learns at first hand 'toutes les vannes qu'on peut vous filer avec des paroles',[281] while Bardamu the traveller asks 'A quoi ça sert, les mots quand on est fixé? A s'engueuler et puis c'est tout.'[282]

However paradoxical it may seem in these universes created by such indefatigable wordspinners, the emphasis is on the desirability of silence. Ferdinand finds his grandmother tolerable company precisely because she is a woman of few words.[283] She takes him to the cinema where the silent films offer only music and movement. The boy's act of violence with the typewriter is aimed at stopping the flow of his father's words. Once in England, he discovers the opportunity of a land of silence. He returns claiming to have learnt just two words. Stubbornly resisting all attempts to cajole him into learning the English language, he becomes the natural companion of the mentally retarded Jonkind, whose own utterances are restricted to the refrain 'No trouble.' It is of Jonkind that he is later reminded when taking pleasure in the 'music' of his pigeons. What he appreciates in the birds is their loyalty, and it is easy to understand how this should be associated with creatures incapable of speech.

The explanation of the apparent paradox contained in this desire for silence is to be found in *Voyage*, where Bardamu reveals that the outpourings are a means of arriving as rapidly as possible at the moment when there is no more to be said.[284] The closing words of the novel are: 'qu'on n'en parle plus'.

Céline is not content to provide an assault on the false values that operate in the reader's society. His novels are also a profound exploration of the way his 'heroes' feel themselves to be victims. Adopting an image that also furnishes Céline with one of the more fantastic episodes of *Voyage*, Bardamu insists that we are 'tous assis sur une grande galère'.[285] Man is universally the victim of his existence: 'l'existence, ça vous tord et ça vous écrase la face'.[286]

The settings Bardamu encounters are invariably hostile. The Western Front and the tropical forest both fill his head with alien noises. The very vegetation in Africa is described as 'aggressive', while the New York skyline announces a city 'raide à faire peur'. The metereological conditions are invariably adverse, whether the hero is in the tropics or crossing the channel to Newhaven. The Passage des Bérésinas is, if Ferdinand is to be believed, awash with urine and excrement, which leads him to initiate an important theme in the novel with the words 'pissait qui voulait sur nous'. For in this universal hell-on-earth there is a tendency for each individual to feel that he has been singled out as a victim.[287]

The sense of being singled out as a victim cruelly mistreated by the world is inherited by both Ferdinand and Bardamu. There is much to suggest that in this sado-masochistic universe, Ferdinand welcomes this role, with which his imagination is ready to co-operate in full. When he records a rare case of approval of him (by Gustave Mandamour), he is quick to render it valueless. Thus the theme of victim, which is so crucial a component of the motivation responsible for the particular form of the fiction and its narration, is revealed to be thoroughly ambiguous. Yet it is precisely the impression of invention and exaggeration that gives this obsessive theme the ring of authenticity.

At the same time as it explores a pervasive sense of victimisation, Céline's writing in large measure charts the efficacy of a limited number of ways of attempting to escape the relentlessly dark human condition. *Voyage au bout de la nuit* is thus not merely an attempt to understand that condition, it is also an attempt to find ways of withstanding it. For a character such as Lieutenant Grappa or the Director of the Compagnie Pordurière du Petit Congo, violence itself is a means of escaping from the constant threat of 'le vide'. Bardamu describes the Director, whom he has watched ill-treat his black servants, as being 'comme délivré pour un temps par la brutalité qu'il venait de commettre'.[288] Bardamu himself, however, is more inclined to seek escape through women.

Such a tactic is paradoxical in that it is overshadowed by a response to women that is deeply antagonistic. Madelon describes Bardamau as 'un homme qu'on dirait brutal . . . avec les femmes'.[289] His affairs with both Lola (incarnation of the American dream) and Musyne turn to hatred. The collective female antagonism towards him aboard the Amiral Bragueton smacks of thwarted sexual desire, while Ferdinand's adolescence is replete with incidents of his being forced to give satisfaction to ageing female bodies. This deep-seated current of misogyny joins the theme of victimisation in that Bardamu sees men as in part sacrificed to the War by a female populace eager for a socially acceptable form of violent death.[290]

Bardamu's disgust with the human body, already noted, almost invariably highlights specifically female complaints or afflictions: the bloody complications of abortions, the effect of the tropics on the women's menstrual cycles, the removal of ovaries. It is in the female genital area that we are likely to be shown the body in its state of disfunction. As so often, Bardamu's attitude is given its most direct expression by Robinson: 'Moi, tu sais, je m'en passe des femmes . . . avec leurs beaux derrières, leurs grosses cuisses, leurs bouches en coeur et leurs ventres dans lesquels il y a toujours quelque chose qui pousse, tantôt desmômes, tantôt des maladies. . . . C'est pas avec leurs sourires qu'on le paye son terme! N'est-ce pas? Même moi dans mon gourbi, si j'en avais une de femme, j'aurais beau montrer ses fesses au propriétaire le quinze du mois ça lui ferait pas me faire une diminution!'[291]

However, certain women offer Bardamu a pure embodiment of beauty and are thus celebrated for the impression of harmony they exude. It is a quality that Ferdinand finds in Nora Merrywin. Bardamu finds it above all in the women of America. 'Quelles gracieuses souplesses cependant! Quelles délicatesses incroyables! . . . Ces blondes! Ces brunes! Et ces Titiennes!'[292]

The feminine ideal in *Voyage* is seen almost exclusively in aesthetic terms. The Slovak nurse Sophie is evoked in almost Baudelairian terms as a 'troismats d'allégresse tendre, en route pour l'Infini'.[293] Both Ferdinand and Bardamu associate their ideal female with music. Nora Merrywin delights the concealed Ferdinand with her piano-playing; when Bardamu needs to pay a compliment to the women on the *Amiral Bragueton* he describes them as 'les dames incomparablement musiciennes'.[294]

What Bardamu refers to as 'le vice des formes parfaites'[295] is in essence voyeuristic and *Mort à crédit* presents us with a host of voyeurs. Voyeurism is a means of keeping reality at a distance; for the Célinian hero, the untouchable alone has value. As such, voyeurism is a continuation of the obsession with masturbation that haunts both Ferdinand and Bardamu as well as those who regard it as their role to police the young boy.

The reference to Robinson's own obsession with his experience as an errand-boy involving the rich female customer leads to a view of masturbation as a form of private cinema and it is the cinema, not the brothel, that offers Bardamu supreme pleasure, as he moves from the poster offering 'des femmes en combinaison' to the auditorium which he describes as 'bon, doux et chaud'.[296] The inadequacy of the voyeuristic and masturbatory does not escape him. He is forced to prescribe himself 'doses' of cinema as if it were a drug.

As the name Branledore suggests, the masturbatory theme in *Voyage* is closely identified with the activity of storytelling, and it is this activity that forms the single most important form of release for the Célinian hero and the many other raconteurs in the author's two pre-war novels.[297] Truth is embroidered or entirely made up. Not that it should necessarily be assumed that the audience is unaware of the fact that what they are listening to may not be literally true. For Céline's storytellers become increasingly audacious (and therefore transparent) as they fall prey to the storyteller's spell.

The need for relief thrusts all these activities into an obsessive prominence that forms as considerable a part of Céline's project as the determination to describe and comprehend the universal human condition. They are frequently intertwined in his imagination and merge with such additional settings as fairgrounds and fun-fairs and such categories as medieval legend and the highly Célinian féerique.

In view of the close relationship between storytelling and fantasy within the fiction itself, and the close *parenté* between Céline and his fictional heroes, it is not surprising that the form of *Voyage* and *Mort à crédit* reflects many of the features exhibited by these forms of escape.

The sordid examples of domestic violence allow us to align Céline with the Naturalism of Zola, one of the few authors whose achievement he was prepared to recall in the context of his own work,[298] but the poetics of the Céline novel are very different from those of Naturalist fiction. The Naturalist concern with order and detached observation is replaced by a sense of anarchy. The Céline novel makes little effort to conceal its exploitation of artifice. The numerous proper names frequently take on a surreal appearance, at the same time exhibiting their origins in a distortion of our more familiar reality. Rather than inviting a single, unambiguous interpretation, the distortion brings into play new connotations. Bardamu's lack of reality as a character, indicated by the range of parts that he is able to assume, provides one of the themes of *Voyage*. So many of the episodes, both major and minor, simply peter out, show Bardamu as little more than a storyteller. Céline himself described the contents of his novel as 'Céline fait délirer Bardamu qui dit ce qu'il sait de Robinson.'

As is evident from Robinson's far-fetched reappearances, Céline's novels oscillate disconcertingly between 'realism' and fantasy. The characteristic movement is from a trivial everyday setting to a spectacle apocalyptic in nature and appropriate to the sense of ever-increasing disaster. Existing reality explodes, like the words in Auguste's mouth or Courtial's racing-car in the autobiographical story that he enjoys telling above all others. Episodes slowly gather momentum until they appear to lose all touch with observed reality. The inhabitants of the Kent town, for example, appear to Bardamu as fish swimming in a tank. Faced with such descriptions, the reader is frequently uncertain about the narrator's state of mind. The effect of war is such that Bardamu's head becomes 'si difficile à tranquilliser avec ses idées dedans'.[299] A tendency to hallucination is clear, but there are additional factors that play a part in controlling the vision with which the reader is presented: malaria and other forms of sickness, a capacity for vivid dreams, drunkenness, drugs (there are several hinted references in *Voyage* to cocaine). But often such clues appear only after a particular fantastic description. We frequently move from relative normality to an apparently unreal state without warning.

The separateness of 'reality' and fantasy, like the categories of sanity and madness, are called into question. As a result the apparently fantastic can illuminate the reality that forms its starting-point. Céline's idiosyncratic treatment of the war is a case in point. As Stendhal had realised a century before, no individual present at a spectacle of epic grandeur is blessed with a panoramic view. By having Bardamu make no distinction between the tragic and the petty, Céline conveys brilliantly the sheer ludicrousness of the situation and in so doing demythologises the whole concept of war on which heroic poets and conscientious objectors alike habitually base their response.

Mort à crédit, though eclipsed by *Voyage* in the estimation of most of Céline's readers and critics, may in fact be seen to represent a more radical solution to the problems of language and form that faced Céline in his innovative venture.

For all its capacity to disconcert or shock, *Voyage* is the more easily accommodated within existing notions of the genre. Bardamu's generalisations about human behaviour may partially reassure the reader that the violent vision belongs to a moralist tradition, though their often puzzlingly contradictory nature confirms Céline's avowal: 'J'ai pas d'idées, moi! aucune!'[300] and alerts us to the fact that they are part of the destabilising rhetoric that is his writing's most challenging feature. The author's unswerving commitment throughout his career to 'le passage de l'oral à travers l'écrit' is a particularly accurate pointer to his decision not to break totally with formal literary narration in *Voyage*.[301]

Céline's writing in *Mort à crédit* comes close to realising his ambition of writing as music (he claimed that Paul Morand was 'le premier de nos écrivains qui ait jazzé la langue française'[302]). At another level, his view of language constitutes recognition of the fundamental impotence of words. Words are no guarantee of anything other than their own existence. Above all, they possess neither the power to define nor the power to explain.

Céline's later pamphlets derive from his use of the diatribe in *Mort à crédit* where Auguste, reader of *La Patrie*, expresses the anti-Semitic and anti-Masonic sentiments later used in such works as *Bagatelles pour un massacre* and *Les Beaux Draps*. Their verbal excesses, rather than reflecting accurately the strength of Céline's feeling, are an example of taking a point of view to absurd lengths, as a perverse illustration of the polemicist's conviction that no one will be prepared to listen to his political line. In other words, the verbal excesses, in the pamphlets as in the novels, may be seen as marking a recognition of an inability to effect any kind of change through writing.

To conclude, the repeated emphasis in Céline's fiction on violence to the almost total exclusion of more attractive forms of human behaviour is presented in the terms of a highly ambiguous narrative language that willingly carries exaggeration to the point at which the credibility of the picture it paints is radically undermined at the literal level. It is only in such a way as this that Céline avoids what he sees as the unjustifiable self-confidence of so much realist writing.

His obvious distortion of reality is a powerful indication of the inaccessibility of that reality and of the limited value of any attempt to give it definitive representation. At the same time, it undeniably brings to the surface forces the presence of which in our make-up cannot be denied. The very fact of their power being so deep-seated inevitably entails them appearing in a almost parodic form.

Céline's writing is designed to be provocative and above all to challenge the reader's unexamined assumptions. The violent imagination of his fictional surrogates reveals the near interchangeability of hatred of others and self-hatred, of attraction and loathing within sexual desire, and of many other such contradictions that justify the view that his fictional universe illustrates a sado-masochistic principle. At the same time, it represents an attempt to understand the extent to which these surrogates, like Céline himself, are the product of a *petit-bourgeois* world whose instinct is not to question but to accept.

Behind Céline's individual self-portrayal lies the universal revelation that the creative and destructive urges in Man are terrifyingly close. Above all, Céline's claim to be regarded as an author of unique power and suggestiveness must be based on his remarkable success in developing a fictional form and language capable of exploring from within the desperate uncertainties assailing an age that had cast adrift its belief in everything.

David Midgley

The ecstasy of battle: some German perspectives on warfare between Modernism and reaction

In memory of J.P. Stern (1920–91)

> I have discovered for myself the ancient ways of men and beasts, yea the very origins of all sensory being, living on within me – living on in my writing and thinking, my loving and hating. Nietzsche, *The Gay Science*[303]

There can be few more harrowing representations of the effects of modern warfare than those by Otto Dix. The large-scale canvas *The Trench*, on which he worked from 1920 to 1923, shows the results of bombardment with explosive shells in gruesome detail. The space defined by the walls of this trench is filled with a jumble of human bodies with gaping wounds, intermingled with tattered remnants of cloth, webbing, and flesh. A solitary intact corpse rests suspended above the breastwork, supported on a frame of distorted angle-iron. Opposite it, and scarcely less macabre in its isolation and displacement, a pair of army-issue metal-framed spectacles is similarly suspended.

Dix was born in 1891, and after studying painting in Dresden for five years before the First World War, he served in a machine-gun unit from 1915 to 1918, seeing frontline action on various sections of the western front, including the Battle of the Somme (1916). His work of the early 1920s can largely be seen as a deliberate attempt to exorcise the hideous memories that others were all too keen to suppress at the time. As part of his preparation for the major canvas, he had gone to the pathology laboratory of a Berlin hospital in 1920 and drawn corpses and human entrails from the life (so to speak). And in 1924, having first perfected his etching technique, he set out to compose a series of plates that would stand worthily alongside Goya's *Desastres* – and schooled himself for the task, again, by drawing decaying corpses in the catacombs of Palermo. Items from Dix's series were reproduced for mass distribution through trade unions in connection with anti-war campaigns of the middle 1920s, and *The Trench* was presented to a wider public as the centrepiece of a pacifist travelling exhibition in 1925. Already the target of vehement denunciations in the nationalist press when it was first exhibited in Berlin in 1923, *The Trench* was destined to be pilloried as a prime example of left-wing erosion of the national will to fight in the notorious Nazi exhibition of 'decadent art' in 1937 – and appears subsequently to have been destroyed. Vituperation from the political right was matched from the outset on the left by the ardent defence of Otto Dix as a politically engaged artist. But such bland political stereotyping tends to blunt our awareness of the extraordinary power of his artistry, and also to obscure some disturbing truths about the nature of the human experience that inspired his work.

At least, that is the position of Otto Conzelmann who, in a recent book, presents the 'other side' of Dix that has been ignored by those who see only – or overwhelmingly – the dimension of social criticism in his work.[304] For as Conzelmann is able to show, Dix had greeted the outbreak of war in 1914 with an unbridled lust to experience the depths as well as the heights of human existence. His work of that time displays all the eruptive pathos of current avant-garde trends. A glowering self-portrait makes ferocious use of primary colour in the fauvist manner; an explosive mechanistic composition entitled simply *War* parallels works of the Italian Futurists at that time; and his *Self-Portrait as Mars* contrives an extraordinary balance between the stern and the euphoric, with the self-image merging darkly into a dynamic field of line and colour. His premonition of death, in *Dying Warrior* (1915), is a work of full-blown Expressionism, an ecstatic vision of a scourged and distorted human face, painted in lurid green and red, with highlights provided by beams of fiery yellow. On active service, using simpler artistic materials – chalk, pen, gouache – for obvious reasons, Dix continued to work within a visionary mode, recording impressions of bold shape and movement, with no sign of the grisly naturalistic detail that is familiar to us from his post-war works. He de-heroicises war – as he arguably already had in his earlier futuristic canvases: the self-portraits are never entirely lacking in self-irony – but he also appears to revel in the awesome power of unleashed aggression, recording it with something approaching sensual abandon, or at least a Nietzschean *amor fati*. It was *The Gay Science* that he carried in his pack, the text in which Nietzsche had expounded his insights into the material, physio-logical origins of values and ideals, and had called upon art to respond to these insights with levity, deftness, and scorn. Echoes of Nietzsche's text are to be found in Dix's notes and letters of the time. In the immediate aftermath of the Battle of the Somme he notes that war should be viewed as a 'natural occurrence' like anything else. He emphasises its biological origins when he writes that wars are fought 'because of and for the sake of the vulva'. And his (thoroughly Nietzschean) definition of the artist, fashioned amidst the carnage, is 'one who has the courage to affirm'.[306]

A curious dualism persists in Dix's post-war work. On the one hand there are the grotesque caricatures of war cripples, which were displayed in the Berlin Dada Fair of 1920, and which can scarcely be interpreted as anything other than provocatively satirical[307] (Conzelmann ignores these). And on the other hand there is an abiding fascination with the human capacity for violence, which expresses itself in the early nineteen-twenties above all in cartoon-like representations of sexual murder and mutilation, often with Dix himself portrayed as the perpetrator. His retrospective depictions of the violence of war may also fairly be said to retain a quality of sensual participation and unflinching affirmation, which provides Conzelmann with a basis on which to argue[308] that these works in turn are imbued with a reverence for war as a cosmic principle. Such a reverence arguably is apparent in the triptych *War*, on which Dix worked from 1929 to 1932, and which is indeed designed in the manner of an altar-piece. Elements of *The Trench* of 1923 have gone into the composition of the centrepiece, but in the transposition they have become imbued with something approaching iconic significance. The corpse borne aloft now appears as little more than a skeleton, and thus a more traditional emblem of death, overarching the panel's select array of horrors: a grotesquely inverted and blood-encrusted corpse riddled with (posthumous) machine-gun wounds; another slumped with gaping abdomen; an oblique charred stump drawing the eye up to the skeleton aloft; and presiding over the scene, a solitary sentry whose human features are masked beneath steel helmet and gas-mask. The left-hand panel shows us, leading into the central scene, the serried myrmidons of a heavily-equipped infantry brigade. On the right, moving towards the viewer, we have the self-image of Dix retreating from the inferno beyond. Beneath, on the predella, where we might traditionally expect a representation of the dead at rest, ashen-faced soldiers lie in a deep dugout, sleeping with the exhaustion that only the rigours of physical exposure can bring. The formal arrangement of these images absorbs them into the very tradition they might seem to parody: here is no indictment, but a monument to what the ordinary soldier had suffered and endured.

The ambiguity in Dix's depictions of war had been recognised by a contemporary art critic already in the arresting detail of *The Trench*. Ernst Kállai, writing in 1927, saw there, too, a monumentality which could not have been achieved if the artist had not been filled with a sense of the omnipotence of war. 'Dix', he concluded, 'believes in war in the same way that pious Catholics still believe in the devil.'[309] But the point that Kállai is making about the mythical potential of Dix's depiction of war is somewhat different from the construction that Conzelmann places on it. Dix's fixation on physiological exactitude – which Kállai is not alone in comparing with portrayals of martyrdom by German old masters such as Matthias Grünewald and Hans Baldung Grien – seems to reflect a kind of morbid metaphysics, which Kállai calls reactionary because it is in thrall to the horror and destruction that it so vividly depicts. He speaks of a kind of veristic *furor teutonicus* – frenzied ritual dancing of the ancient Teutonic tribes – in which the very unflinching nature of the representation makes it impossible to say whether it is done in a spirit of revulsion or of ecstatic enjoyment. An important part of Källai's argument concerns the 'mythologisation of the object', which is what makes Dix a leading representative of the New Objectivity in German art of the 1920s.[310] What Källai is voicing is the frequently heard suspicion that such a tendency is inherently regressive, precisely because the naturalistic image is ideologically indeterminate: it is the cast of mind of the interpreter that introduces the perspective of pacifist protest or of martial veneration, as the case may be.

What is striking about Conzelmann's interpretation of Dix is the extent to which what he sees in the pictures is articulated in the categories of the anti-rational strain in German Modernist writing. The two literary authors with whom he repeatedly compares Dix's attitude to war are Gottfried Benn and Ernst Jünger. In the nineteen-twenties, Benn was the foremost poetic proponent of a Nietzschean prioritisation of the aesthetic over the socio-historical, and in 1933 – notoriously – he welcomed the National Socialist movement to power as the embodiment of a new and higher biological type.[311] Jünger was the leading literary figure on the radical nationalist fringe of the Weimar Republic, and through the Stahlhelm (Steel Helmet) associa-tion of war veterans he pursued political ideals which were in many respects consonant with those of National Socialism: when he speaks of his designs for a 'new state' in the 1920s, he has in mind a model for social organisation founded in the leader-principle as he had experienced it on the field of battle in the First World War.[312] It is with Jünger's writings that we particularly need to concern ourselves here.

Born in 1895, Jünger was only nineteen when the First World War broke out. To say that he welcomed it is to say nothing remarkable: the perception of war as an opportunity to break out of a society and culture that was felt to be stagnant and stultifying is something that Jünger shared with many a young middle-class intellectual in Germany and elsewhere in Europe at that time. What is unusual about Jünger is the way that he continued to cultivate that enthusiasm for war even after the capitulation of Germany and Austria in 1918, and even after gaining protracted first-hand experience of the carnage and devastation involved. He served throughout the war as an infantry officer, and in 1920 he published a diary-style account of his experiences at the front, *Storm of Steel*, in which he sought to uphold an ideal of heroic individualism in the face of all that the random slaughter of mechanised warfare had done to undermine such an outlook. He presents the war of attrition, indeed, as a process of quasi-Darwinian selection, from which the front-line fighter emerges, tempered and vulcanised, as a new breed. Jünger's descriptions of the landscape of war unflinchingly register its objective realities, colouring them with occasional mythical references to suggest the scale and enormity of the scene, in a way which does indeed stand comparison with Dix's wartime images of eruption and devastation. The cratered area of the front is a 'hellish stamping-ground of death, encompassed at the edges by yellow flames'. It is stripped of vegetation and human dwelling-places, and lit only by 'the multi-coloured signals of destruction'. Villages gape 'like tombs laid waste', wreathed with the stench of decay, with animal carcases hanging from charred rafters, and the corpses of civilians floating in flooded cellars. And the front-line fighters themselves have the 'emptiness' of death in their eyes, and sunken faces which are 'reminiscent of the ghastly realism of old paintings of the crucifixion'.[313] But to interpret such images as betokening a glorification of war, as Conzelmann does,[314] one has to be seeing them in the perspective of what war and its horrors had come to mean for Jünger in the early 1920s, rather than Dix.

The quotations used in the previous paragraph are taken from *Battle as an Inner Experience*,[315] a programmatic treatise which Jünger published in 1922. It is here that Jünger attempts to resolve the ideological tensions between his heroic life-model and the collective experience of indiscriminate destruction in war.[316] He draws selectively on the ideas of Nietzsche and on Spengler's *The Decline of the West*, insisting repeatedly that fighting is something fundamental, something elemental in human affairs, as well as the essential means of cultural renewal. (His assertion early in the text that war is 'the father of all things' is a simplistic version of what Nietzsche has to say in *The Gay Science* about cultural achievements as the outcome of ruthless struggle.) The political thrust of his argument is directed against the liberalism of the Republic, against the Enlightenment principle of tolerance, and against any belief in a rational path of historical progress. To experience war only in a spirit of suffering and negation, he concludes, is to experience it only contingently, 'externally', and thus to endure it 'as a slave'. But in the manner in which Jünger affirms war and the courting of death, there is something which is not truly compatible with Nietzsche's vitalistic pursuit of self-fulfilment, nor with Spengler's stoicism in the face of the supposed cyclical decline of cultures. What Jünger evokes in his discussions of impending infantry attack looks much rather like a quasi-mystical vision of stepping beyond individuality, and becoming reunited with the great womb of all things. War is the embodiment of a 'powerful and incessant flux', the 'expression of an elemental force' which reduces all human works and all concepts to insignificance;[317] and in the ecstasy of battle, the fighter charges at the gates of death, seized with the desire to become merged with the cosmos 'like a wave sliding back into the sea'.[318] In this aspect of his depiction of war, Jünger evokes a behavioural pattern which the psychologist Erich Fromm calls 'ecstatic destructiveness': it is in order to overcome the existential burden of his own powerlessness and isolation that a man seeks to 'regain unity within himself and with nature' in a trance-like state of agitation, of which the *furor teutonicus* was a prime example.[319] It is therefore under-standable that Jünger's early writings have more commonly been analysed in

terms of psychopathology rather than aesthetics.[320] Moreover, the manner in
which Jünger evokes aesthetic principles in *The Battle as an Inner Experience*
– whether they be Kant's 'purposelessness', Schiller's 'play-drive', or
Nietzsche's 'intoxication' – is as arbitrary and eclectic as any other intellectual dimension of that text. And yet an apparently serious attempt has been
made, in a study by Karl Heinz Bohrer dating from 1978, to present the young
Jünger not only as the exponent of a coherent literary aesthetic, but as a
leading figure in Modernist aesthetics generally.

The German term *Moderne* can cover a variety of meanings, embracing
post-Enlightenment models for civil society generally, as well as those specific
developments in twentieth-century cultural production that literary scholars
and art historians are used to thinking of as Modernism. The world wars and
the political collapse of European nation–states into totalitarianism constitute crises of modernity in the former sense, to which the writings of Ernst
Jünger can clearly and profitably be related.[321] But as Bohrer uses the term he
really does mean the latter. His case is built on precisely the section of Jünger's
treatise from which our earlier quotations were taken: it is the section entitled
'Horror'. Horror, like fighting, puts us in touch with the most primitive level
of human responses. It is one of those emotions which, as Jünger puts it,
'erupts with elemental force, in moments of powerful shock to the system'. It
is also something which distinguishes humankind at the most basic level from
the animals, adding, as it were, a reflective dimension to the fear and terror
that they experience: Jünger dignifies horror by calling it 'the first lightning-
flash of Reason'.[322] The human capacity to take pleasure in horror is something which he naturally finds everywhere apparent in the domain of public
spectacle, from waxworks to executions. But his special interest in it derives
from the atmosphere of anticipation with which young soldiers had steeled
themselves for battle. As he insists, 'Each was driven to look the Gorgon in the
face, even if the prospect should make his heart stop beating.' Horror is the
emotional condition which lies in wait everywhere among those shell craters
and ruined villages, seizing the mind at the sight of death and decay. In a sense
it is the test which all true manly natures must undergo, the measure of what
their primal vitality can endure before it is 'released' in the act of lethal
aggression: 'they would have been lost without the surge of vital energy'.[324]

Evidence that the experience of trench warfare had profoundly determined
the way that Jünger thought about art, as well as life in general, is to be found
in the autobiographical study he published in 1929, *The Adventurous Heart*.
There he likens the sense of heightened anticipation evoked by the paintings
of Dutch old masters to the nervous tension of a sniper waiting for a human
target to appear before his sights. The secret 'essence' of a work of art is
something he expects to reveal itself suddenly, momentarily, like a pistol shot.
'Moments such as this, which alone make life worth living', he writes, 'cannot
be repeated, because what is perceived can only be perceived in this way
once.'[325] When Jünger dwells on the detail of death and suffering, it is

evidently in an attempt to recapture that unique immediacy of experience. The soldier's first encounter with a dead body is something which sees itself on the mind in the form of one or another vivid eidetic image: 'For one it is the hand driven like a claw into moss and soil, for another the bluish lips set off against the whiteness of the teeth, for a third the black crust of blood in the hair.'[326] And when he describes the aftermath of an explosion in another work, *Fire and Blood* (1925), he summons the hyperbole of literary allusion to sustain his painstaking reconstruction of momentary perceptions:

The shell-hole is like a crater filled with a thick milky cloud. A pack of shadowy figures is clambering up its steep sides. . . . From the very bottom a magical light shines forth in a glaring pink. That is the machine-gun ammunition. . . . But what is that bundle slowly writhing down there in the ruddy glow, as if it were trying to escape but is bound to the earth by some diabolical force? That mass of bodies squirming like amphibians in a boiling sea, like the damned in a Dantesque vision? . . . These are the seriously wounded . . . a hundred-voiced tumult breaking forth from a single horror.[327]

Bohrer is no doubt correct when he argues, on the strength of this and similar passages, that Jünger's works convey a sense of reality as dissolved into isolated and terrifying images. And it is no doubt also true, as he says, that these images articulate physical sensations with a directness that excludes the intervention of moral control.[328] What is disturbing about Bohrer's argument, however, is the way that he firstly separates Jünger's descriptive practice from its ideological context – he simply declines to discuss that – and secondly ennobles it by constructing a cultural lineage for it by dint of selective association. As Bohrer presents his argument, Jünger's evocations of suffering actually witnessed become assimilated to the aesthetic play on the imaginative power of terror that had been cultivated by Wilde, Poe, and Hoffmann. Bohrer places the sensory acuteness of Jünger's recollected images in a tradition which runs through Baudelaire's dandyism, Pater's aestheticism, and the symbolist iconography of the Pre-Raphaelites, as well as the more immediate heritage of Nietzsche's *Gay Science*. And he presents Jünger's preoccupation with sudden occurrences on the battlefield as an anticipation of the literary shock-techniques which were to be given prominence in the programmes of French Surrealism.

In presenting Jünger as a representative Modernist, Bohrer implicitly eliminates from the meaning of Modernism that dimension of rational self-critique and self-irony which is to be found in Baudelaire, in Wilde, in Nietzsche, and even in André Breton, and acknowledges as Modernist only a particular anti-rational strand that connects the amoral sensationalism of the nineteenth-century avant-garde to the unscrupulous political 'decisionism' of the 1920s. Conzelmann emulates him in this by assimilating the works of Otto Dix to the categories of that same anti-rational strand. And in case it should be thought that this tendency is merely a fad among contemporary

German intellectuals, it has found its way into English-language discussions of cultural Modernism in the form of a book by the Canadian historian Modris Eksteins – a book, moreover, which was received with notable sympathy on both sides of the Atlantic when it was published in 1989.[329]

The book's title is *Rites of Spring*. Spring provides Eksteins with his central image because it can appear to link Stravinsky's ballet of 1913 with a popular song of 1945, Hitler's favourite opera (*Die Meistersinger*), and the ecstatic mood in which the German and French general public greeted the outbreak of war in 1914. 'Vitalism' is the essential clue he offers to underlying cultural trends in twentieth-century Europe, because it can be found in the music of Stravinsky and Richard Strauss, the writings of Hofmannsthal and Wedekind, and the sort of theatrical hanky-panky that went on at the court of Wilhelm II. Photographs are reproduced in order to suggest links between the angular and energetically unconventional choreography of Nijinsky in *The Rite of Spring* and the post-1918 craze for the Charleston; between the protective armour worn by a look-out in the trenches and the boxed and hooded costumes of Dada cabaret dancers – as if the Dada performances in Zurich in 1917 were not themselves a calculated parody of the prevailing madness of war in surrounding Europe. When *The Decline of the West* was first published, immediately after the First World War, the Austrian Robert Musil – one of the acutest analytical minds among literary Modernists – joked that Spengler's analogical approach to historical cultures was like a zoologist grouping dogs, chairs, and fourth-degree equations under one category as 'quadrupeds' on the grounds that they all had four 'legs'.[330] The same might be said of Eksteins's approach to cultural Modernism.

All this might be dismissed as trivial if it were not for the fact that Eksteins's primary purpose is to construct a suggestive link between avant-garde art and National Socialism – and it is Ernst Jünger who emerges, again, as the presiding spirit in this enterprise. It is Jünger's vision of a 'new Europe' emerging from the intense tempo of mechanised combat that Eksteins quotes,[331] and the material in the book bears every indication of having been organised with a view to corroborating it. Germany is presented as the champion of modernity in all its aspects against the 'old order' upheld by the Western democracies. In the broad legacy of adversarial attitudes that the First World War left behind,[332] Eksteins sees the triumph of the pre-war avant-garde, because he has noticed that that was characterised by 'the idea of the Spirit at war'. And he proclaims National Socialism to be 'yet another offspring of the hybrid that has been the modernist impulse' on the grounds that, like earlier avant-garde art, it displays a combination of 'egotism' and 'technicism'. The precise relationship between the regime of National Socialism and the processes of modernisation in society with which it interacted has been the subject of much careful investigation in recent years.[333] Eksteins attempts to circumvent the difficulties of social and cultural analysis with one great biologistic explanation. In the process he blurs the distinction between the aesthetic and moral revolt of the pre-war avant-garde on the one hand, and on the other hand the murderous political 'doctrine of conflict'[334] which Hitler, amongst others, had formulated in the light of his experience of warfare, and which was to lead, under National Socialism, to the brutal suppression of the cultural avant-garde, to say nothing of those 'vitalistic' sub-cultures which are mentioned in Eksteins's review of German society at the turn of the century. (They include feminism and an incipient gay movement.)

In short, Eksteins is contributing in his turn to that counter-Enlightenment trend of our own time which so uncannily mirrors the counter-Enlightenment trend that was indisputably part of the Modernist movement itself. Bohrer, in the late 1970s, had sought to isolate the moment of horror as a fundamental motif of literary Modernism, in order to screen Jünger's aestheticising of war from ideological criticism. Conzelmann followed him in emphasising the fascination with technological destructive power, as opposed to social criticism, in the works of Otto Dix. And now Eksteins homogenises the political history of Germany into a quasi-organic image of 'her' role in leading Europe beyond the process of industrialisation and into total war. There is not room here to give more than the briefest outline of an alternative perspective on the cultural significance of the First World War in Germany, but such an alternative is to be found in the works of the novelist Arnold Zweig.[335]

Born in November 1887, Zweig was already twenty-six when the war broke out. Nietzsche had been an important element in his formative experiences, too, and by 1914 he had already established his reputation as an author of prose works imbued with a self-critical psychological awareness. Although Zweig shared in the initial enthusiasm for war, like so many young people at the time, his experience of active service between 1915 and 1918 rapidly led him to recognise the corrosive effect that war has on the slow progress of civilisation. In 1927 he published a novel which vividly illustrated the relentlessness with which the war had obliterated any finer sense for human values. *Der Streit um den Sergeanten Grischa* (*The Case of Sergeant Grischa*) centres on the fate of a Russian prisoner of war who is unjustly shot as a spy. Through the variety of characters who become involved with the case, Zweig develops his narrative, step by step, into a broad depiction of the condition of the warring (and the subjugated) nations in the third year of the war. Through the figures of lawyers, military clerks and medical staff, he highlights the dilemmas of the educated classes in the face of the injustice and sheer waste that the war has brought. He investigates the mechanisms of discipline and intimidation which demand unquestioning obedience from the ordinary soldier. And he explores the psychology of the officious and the powerful, the ideologies and mentalities upon which the very prosecution of the war is predicated. (His novel includes, for example, a sustained character analysis of the then Commander in Chief of German-occupied Eastern

Europe, Erich Ludendorff, who appears in the novel as General Schieffenzahn.)

Zweig removes heroism from the war experience by consistently showing the continuities that exist between peacetime and wartime social behaviour. The point is best illustrated from the pair of novels which followed his *Sergeant Grischa* and were published respectively in 1931 and 1935: *Junge Frau von 1914* (*Young Woman of 1914*) and *Erziehung vor Verdun* (*Education Before Verdun*). Here he tells the story of a young German intellectual, Werner Bertin, who is called up for army service in 1915, as Zweig himself had been. Bertin experiences the intoxicating fervour of the outbreak of war, and unashamedly seeks to justify it as a 'tragic' confrontation in the terms of the philosophical idealism with which his education has imbued him: he would happily give orders to fire on the Strasbourg Minster if called upon to do so. He exemplifies the appeal of Nietzsche's *Gay Science*, implicitly rather than explicitly, in his thirst for the physicality of military service – although the detached voice of the narrator helps the reader to share the irony of the mindless conditioning to which Bertin is subjected in the course of his military training. The extent to which his attitudes have become barbarised in the process is apparent from the way that he dominates and violates the fiancée with whom he has enjoyed a rich and mutually fulfilling relationship in the months preceding the war. The consequences of this act are depicted in *Junge Frau von 1914*, where the fiancée is left humiliated, pregnant, and alone to face up to the rigours of a censorious society.

It is in the sequel, *Erziehung vor Verdun*, that Bertin in turn experiences the consequences of victimisation, for himself and others. The naive intellectual – a 'Parsifal in fatigues', as he is called at one point – is brought face to face with the realities of the administration of the war, and with the opportunities that provides for petty bureaucrats to exercise the power and authority that is denied them in civilian life. And in the figure of Lieutenant Kroysing he encounters the sort of technocratic warrior that Jünger typically portrays: an officer of the pioneers who has unreservedly adopted the amoral code needed to survive in the devastated landscape and subterranean fortifications of the Verdun area. The central plot of the novel pits a vengeful Kroysing against the captain of a supply unit who has contrived to bring about the death of Kroysing's brother under enemy fire, as a way of concealing the truth about his own corrupt administrative practices. The process of disillusionment that Bertin is seen to undergo is related to his gradual recognition that on the one hand war creates conditions in which social prejudice can become converted into systematic vindictiveness, and that on the other hand military prowess is largely predicated on the unleashing of those primitive instincts and energies that Jünger prizes above all else. The effectiveness of Bertin's 'education' is in turn related to the fact that he has a predefined sense of values with which to compare what he witnesses, and to his position as a detached and reflective figure involved in the routine servicing of the war, rather than someone who sees the war only in terms of fighting. He pays just one visit to the front-line trenches, in the company of Kroysing's sappers. For him it is an exceptional escapade, but it brings its own kind of disillusionment and its own kind of self-revelation. Peeping over the breastwork to observe the artillery barrage, Bertin experiences his own moment of ecstatic participation in the destructive power unleashed around him. But in the dugout where the crack troops rest in anticipation of what will be required of them, Bertin has also made a discovery which will serve to undermine the heroic expectations that he has brought with him thus far:

The faces of the sappers, the gunners, the Saxon infantrymen almost made him feel ill. Till now they had been wreathed in fine delusions, festooned with noble titles; but no deception was possible here. . . . Here he was, squatting underground two hundred meters from the enemy, yawning with exhaustion, and registering that here, too, were men carrying out orders, that was all. The earth groaned above him, lumps fell from the walls, powdery soil rained down from between the rafters, and while the infantry calmly went on smoking their cigarettes he asked himself how he had come to see this truth. It was a truth that hurt! It took away the power to endure life. It simply could not be that the war was the same everywhere else as it was in his own company.[336]

Zweig's account does not ignore the powerful emotions, the horror and exhilaration that war can bring, but he incorporates them into a broad and differentiated depiction of how modern societies go to war. And by so incorporating them he turns warfare into a learning experience, for character and reader alike.

Tim Mathews

The machine: Dada, Vorticism and the future

Throughout the period after the Second World War, as participants in Western culture we have been threatened with a gaping divide that seems both to underpin and engulf all our attempts at defining social existence. This divide is set up by the all-too-familiar incompatibility of science and the arts. In the 1950s, with the advent of atomic energy, and the perceived advantages and threats to life associated with it, the novelist and politician C. P. Snow inaugurated the apocalyptic image of a future in which we would be divided into two cultures – the scientific and the artistic. This image became as much a part of the copper coinage of middle-class anxiety and self-awareness as the Churchillian one of Stalin's 'Iron Curtain' descending across Europe after the Second World War.[337]

What makes the image of an all-engulfing cultural divide so alarming is the implication that individuals are being denied access to certain kinds of knowledge, denied opportunities fully to analyse their own situation. It is an image which provides the Marxist analysis of capitalist economic power as resting on its systematic capacity to divide and rule with a cultural correlative. It holds a mirror up to an institutionalised compartmentalisation of our activity, which would limit our capacity to represent our participation in culture, and curtail our power to direct its course. We would then be cast in the mould of victims rather than producers of our social environment and our own involvement in it. Totalisation gives way to conflict, and a struggle for supremacy among opposing discourses is inaugurated.

Clearly the nuclear age is not the first to bring such issues to the fore. In addition, any debate about the relation of science to art involves an evaluation of the political context in which each of them functions. This kind of debate is a dominant element in French nineteenth-century aesthetic theorising. In his preface to *Feuilles d'automne*, Victor Hugo defends the eclecticism of his writing by asserting the value of producing, amidst the political upheaval of the constitutional revolt of 1830, what he calls 'disinterested verse'.[338] Théophile Gautier scorns attempts to read artistic stimulus as though it were scientific data. Both Hugo and Gautier share with Baudelaire a paradoxical, rigorously methodical commitment to promoting the imagination. Imagination is seen as the storehouse of a potential to intervene in experience as we find it, and to transform it into the material of discovery and revelation.

According to this view, the work of the imagination, the practice of art generally, cannot be assimilated to the work of social and political progress. But neither does art abandon political intercourse. This view of imagination articulates a suspicion of polarities and intellectual antagonism of any kind. In post-1789 France, and again after 1830 and the uprising of 1848, Romantic and post-Romantic artists express an increasingly intense anxiety about the discourses of scientific and political progress. The rationalism of the Enlightenment is seen to induce an impoverishment of creativity, and to seduce us into the position of willing victim in relation to economic and political pressure. Lucien Chardon de Rubempré, the hollowed-out poet-hero of Balzac's *Illusions perdues* (written between 1835 and 1843), epitomises the dynamic and amorphous qualities of such inducement as Balzac himself might have experienced it during the Restoration years and under the constitutional monarchy of the 1830s. But Balzac's own fascination with economic energy constructs a *resistance* to the erotic pull of the commodity, exposing and deconstructing Lucien's expectations of art, and the futility of Romantic self-absorption evoked by his bankrupt idealism. Balzac's aesthetic, visionary account of fascination with the commodity, of the compulsion to acquire the correct accessories, that elusive portfolio with the leading edge, weaves an image of progress spawning systems and discourses that are constricting and repetitive, though unpredictable and volatile as well. A disinterested artifice would make the thread that would lead us out of this labyrinth. Throughout the pre-Wagnerian twilight of French Romantic realism, involving not only the novels of Balzac and Flaubert, but also the poetry of Baudelaire, the idea of art is promoted for its powers to intervene in the effects of any fascination, any perversion, and to make them manifest. And no mirage is attributed with a more enticing power than the seductive pull of 'l'or et le plaisir'.[339] In immersing its practitioners as well as its consumers in the myriad facets of such phantasms, art, as an idea made flesh in an eclecticism of concomitant sensation, is itself presented as essentially progressive, though unaccountably so and with no possible application.

In a prose poem such as Baudelaire's 'Assommons les pauvres', this paradoxical locking-of-horns, involving the common values of progress with the subjective inwardness of poetry, foreshadows an increasing antagonism between the two.[340] The curtain goes up on what might seem like a dialogue of the deaf among 'fin-de-siècle' theorists and artists. Such confrontation is evident in the dramatic divergence of artistic productions during the 1880s and 1890s in Paris, facing the pseudo-scientific naturalism of Zola off against the Symbolist, allegorical fantasies of painters such as Odilon Redon and

Gustave Moreau. But rather than a clear-cut polemic or clash of aesthetic conceptions, this facing-off is more in the nature of a chaotic rivalry. The aural and visual artifices of a Verlaine or a Gauguin, manufacturing evocations of psychic mood, of spirituality and the occult, suggest a fascination with the inwardness of art and of its effects that is oddly echoed in the stylised melodrama of Zola's 'naturalistic' set-pieces. The grotesque sexual acquisitiveness oozing from male bourgeois theatre-goers transfixed by the stage début of Nana in Zola's novel of that name; the theatrical interplay of Eros and Thanatos, of fertility and perversion that shrouds the allegorical, catastrophic railway crash in *La Bête humaine* – such features suggest that the determinism of Zola's naturalist theory is an alloy made as much from a belief in the power of irrational drives as from a belief in the scientific method or in the kind of knowledge it can produce.

But in the years of dramatic industrialisation preceding the First World War, the particular interweaving of science and fiction, of the real and the imaginary characteristic of the 'belle-époque' arts appeared to the new generation of artists to be the consequence of passéist disarray, rather than a sign of any creative dynamic. A galvanised theory of creativity itself was thought to be imperative, a re-evaluation of the responsibility artists are able to assume for their own work and for the effects it produces. Machinery is dominant both as a context and as a catalyst for this fundamental re-evaluation of art.

I want to concentrate on this motif in the avant-garde art of the period. Machinery is a product of scientific enquiry, yet within the European avant-garde of the years immediately preceding the war, it is transformed into an object of aesthetic enquiry. What is at stake in such trans-formations in the operation of the machine?[341] Are the aspirations of technological advancement compatible with those of aesthetic innovation? What is the artistic gaze seeking to reveal in focusing on technological forms?

I will examine the formal elements of the artistic innovation encouraged by experiences of the machine to show the part this work with forms plays in a wide-ranging re-evaluation of the relation of art to non-art. Groups of practitioners such as the Vorticists in England and Dadaists in Zurich and Paris are products of historical and social developments featuring an oscillation between excitement and anxiety about the impact of modern machinery and its implications. What I want to concentrate on here is that sense of development absolutely disrupted, and of coherence fragmented – gloriously, irredeemably – which is a central part of the experiences and desires of the European avant-garde art in the early part of this century.

For many European artists before and during the First World War, the modern age *is* the machine age. Machinery constructs a continual challenge to accepted ideas about the purpose of art. The excitement of Marinetti and of the Italian Futurists about the emphatically manufactured, artificial quality of industrial production was taken up, from about 1909 onwards, by artists all over Europe. Artists in Paris transformed the Eiffel Tower – the engineering vision to which it testified, as well as its almost complete futility – into an emblem of technological joy at large. Vorticists in London founded the journal *Blast* in 1914 in celebration of the blast-furnaces of the industrialised Midlands and the North.[342] Even the Zurich Dadaists, while developing their own systematic scepticism into a grounding principle of human endeavour, toy with the belief that all significant expression addresses itself to the cacophony of urban chaos. Dadaist performances in the Cabaret Voltaire, inaugurated in Zurich in 1916, were immediate assaults on the senses, and thus on the expectations of their audiences. Such events, comprising yells and crashes manufactured in a variety of anti-musical ways, represented an aggressive and desperate attempt to rise to the present, and to encompass it – to smash any sense of alienation from the present, however strife-torn.

A Dada manifesto signed in Zurich by Tzara, Huelsenbeck and others in 1918 describes the Dada sound-poem as the sheer noise of urban existence, the screech of the tram-brakes, attributed with the capacity to evacuate what are perceived as defunct metaphysical accounts of human identity. 'The NOISE poems paint a picture of a tram as it is, the essence of a tram, with the fat-cat mayor's yawn, and the screech of the brakes.'[343] Philosophies of being are cast aside by the Dadaists' claim to the power to begin culture from scratch in definitive gestures of negation and affirmation:

We pull webs apart with our hands, and say yes to life that becomes more elevated through negation. Say yes – say no: the mighty hocus-pocus of Being exhilarates the nerves of the real Dadaist – who rolls over or hunts on a bicycle – half Pantagruel and half St Francis and laughs and laughs.[344]

Rabelaisian guffaws, sarcastically sanctified, are directed in the same manifesto at what the signatories regard as ideologically motivated hocus-pocus preventing us from manufacturing our own spontaneous sense of significance. What is at stake is a dramatic and wilful *tabula rasa*, a wiping-clean of all influence, of the vested interest and intellectual hegemony that had culminated in the moral catastrophe of the First World War.

Dadaists espouse urban and technological noise for its refusal to submit to any aesthetic justification. A paradoxical circularity of destruction and construction is set in motion – or is it spiked? Dadaist presentations of bits and pieces of machinery or clockwork – such as Francis Picabia's cover-design for the double number 4–5 of the revue *Dada* published in Zurich in 1919 – are theatrical obliterations of all the systems and conventions allowing any judgement, any statement whatsoever. But it is in terms of such wilful, artificial destruction of statement-making, and of the conditions which make statements possible, that Dadaists attempt a radical overhaul of the notions of sense and of making sense, of art and of artifice. 'We have to be creative.

Mankind no longer imitates, it invents . . . This is the sign of our times.'[345]
Though written in 1921, this exhortation unveils the ambition behind the
Dadaist impetus even before the War; it underlines the grandness of the
Dadaist longing to do away with influence and history, and to target them in
the cultural conventions which circumscribe meaning and make it possible.

This undermining of convention and of sense-making is as manifest in the
irony of the Dadaists' visual artefacts as it is in their paradoxical aural
attempts to negate convention and artifice altogether. This is particularly
marked in the Dadaist joke-machinery assembled by Francis Picabia and
Marcel Duchamp. These are jokes with slithery implications. What is the
status of *L'Enfant carburateur*, painted by Picabia in 1917. It now hangs in
the Guggenheim Museum in New York, a testimony to a certain fetishisation
of the early twentieth-century European 'avant-garde'. But equally, the
strategy of Dadaist 'events' in Zurich, and later in Paris in the early 1920s,
consisted in luring unsuspecting art-lovers into situations in which their
aesthetic expectations and sensibilities would be aggressed. So both in its
historical moment of production, and in terms of Western post-war perception, Picabia's picture invites us to wonder: which of the prerequisites of
art does this picture fulfil? Not the least unsettling of the ironies at play here is
that it *is* in fact possible to ask such a question looking at this eclectic, mixed
media image. For it is a question which, once asked, presupposes art-bound
answers. It is a question born only to restrict its own negating potential, and
the picture in turn seems to content itself with the instantly vapid tactics of
shock. But for all that, in fact *within* this rush from perceptions of anti-art to
the hide-bound recognition of art and back, Dadaist machine-pictures construct the terms of a probe into the making of statements and the processes
involved. They mirror a kind of imaginary, stop-start dismantling of statement-making and the categories that allow it.

The title of Picabia's picture is on the top, and included in the picture,
rather than conventionally placed underneath, so that the title's function of
designating and elucidating ceases to work efficiently. It is literally made part
of the picture, part of its functioning. But inasmuch as the picture's functioning is made literal, without recourse to metaphoric interpretation, appropriation, familiarisation, it is a functioning which collapses in bits. The
carburettor of the title has no function, it doesn't work. We see impressions of
mechanical parts whose relation to each other achieves no specifiable mechanical or technological objective. The spherical component is helpfully
labelled 'un sphère', but of course it isn't spherical, but a two-dimensional
disc plain to see. The whole thing gives me a headache or the 'migraine'
lettered in the picture. The machine doesn't build, it destroys, it un-builds, it
deconstructs at birth the machinery of myth-making – in particular myths of
a liberated future based on technological progress: 'détruire le futur' it says,
after all, along the starting-iron (or so that shape might be). Equally, the myth
of childhood innocence, the Romantic search for creativity in naivety, is

rendered momentarily inoperative by a rapid allusion to a metaphorised experience of the machine: the signifier carburettor, for an emphatic moment, supersedes the signifier 'enfant'.

Marcel Duchamp in his notorious *La Mariée*, of 1912, similarly expels an evident mainstay of the metaphoric machinery of mimesis and of its ideological support: the nude. The female form is here presented as a study in intestinal mechanics; Richard Cork writes that Duchamp's 'composition circulates around the picture-surface like the course of an alimentary canal'.[346] There is nothing aesthetically appealing about the forms presented, nor anything conventionally alluring to the male eye – although that very system of seduction, of the sexual chase and of violent male appropriativeness is overtly kept in play by Duchamp's title and the violence about which it reminisces. And yet by literally – once again – turning representation of the female form inside out, by obfuscating the distinction between the organic and the mechanical and by putting the plumbing on the outside, rather in the manner of the Centre Pompidou in Paris or the Broadgate Development in East London, Duchamp's picture effects an imaginary grinding away of the idealised female form, emblem of Humanist confidence and of the ideological, male-gendered complacency on which it might seem to rest. On the same platform as Picabia's *L'Enfant carburateur*, *La Mariée* launches its own enquiry into creativity and the values promoted by this notion. What price representation, the illusions, the images allowing command of identity and the body?

But this is a platform which can only remain suspended in so far as its collapse is anticipated and valued. Dadaist objects and performances, far from being suspended in time, intensify the effects of time. And this is not a metaphysical experience of time, but an experience of the time that forms, reforms, materialises and dematerialises our experience of cultural icons, our involvement in them, and the spectre of our identification with them. Dadaist engagement with temporality is a momentary affair, however indefinite our own fascination with it may be. It has often been noted that Duchamp's notorious *Readymades* contrive to designate any object as an art-object. In a gesture repeated at will, such contrivance dispenses with art altogether, in an indefinite set of repeated moments or immediacies. Duchamp's *Bicycle Wheel* (1913), in the aesthetic anything-goes it half-heartedly imposes, affirms that art need no longer be encountered as a privileged filter of our experience, nor need we stand quietly by while it models and remodels our experience. But this moment of awareness is as fleeting in its effects as it is violent in its manufacturing. The immediacy of its impact is the end of its autonomy. The wheel planted in the stool is not part of a machine and cannot function – or is continually ceasing to function. If all modes of discourse can be imagined to be mutually abolishing, what purchase might we have on our utterances and responses other than to imagine them silent, and to fantasise about the razing of Babel? What purchase, other than to think again for a moment about these fantasies, about the intellectual machinery through which we approach them and which supports them?

This lightning-quick oscillation from the kick-start to the false start and back functions ceaselessly, and in this way, Dada artifice maintains an essential affirmativeness. The same might be said of the Surrealist experimentation which began immediately after the First World War, the 'automatic writing' which was a development of the Dada games and whose image continued to play such an important part in the theorising of Surrealist ambition. Automatic writing, as announced by André Breton in the first *Manifeste du surréalisme* published in Paris in 1924, is thought of as an unmotivated writing, where the hand takes a sort of unmediated, pure dictation from psychic activity itself. ('Close your eyes and write' seems to be the procedure which, in practical terms, Breton is advocating, humorously and ironically.) Automatic writing is in fact wilfully *equated* by Breton in this manifesto, syntactically as well as logically, with its target, with the image of language it seeks to project: 'automatisme psychique pur'.[347] This paradoxical, Gidean interplay of the motivated and the unmotivated is a further self-aware negation of discourse, or rather of discourses in the plural, the range of which not only allows but imposes an indefinite, multiplying and slippery set of distinctions between different kinds of experience. Automatic writing, as the writer and critic Maurice Blanchot pointed out after the fact, is a violent linguistic rite, a manufacturing of a wholly imaginary sense of words, within which words themselves are uniquely moulded to a subjective, unconscious sense of self.[348] The difference between words as sound and words as image is obliterated. This Dada-inspired automatic writing seems to grant us the power to make words completely our own, and thus, in effect, to do away with them, to transcend them completely. . . . But I must return to my subject, which is the pre-1918 fascination with the mechanistic, the ludic and the violent, and the bearing this has on artists' sense of purpose in that explosive period between the 'belle époque' and the inhumanity of the First World War.

Affirmation is the founding principle, imaginatively and procedurally, of the ways of reading and encompassing the modern proposed by the Italian Futurists, and the machine is its fulcrum. Marinetti soon brought his ideas, his comrades and his publicity machine to Paris, publishing a Futurist manifesto in *Le Figaro* in 1909. In the years up to 1914, Futurism reverberated beyond Continental Europe, and attracted both the interest and the scorn of English artists such as the Vorticist Percy Wyndham Lewis and his sometime companion-at-arms Charles Nevinson.[349] In Paris, Guillaume Apollinaire bears witness to Futurist energy by opening his poem 'Zone', and the whole of the *Alcools* volume at the same time, with an expression of Futurist-type enthusiasm for the galvanising effects of modern technology and its forms. This opening is a grand dismissal of history prior to 1912, the year of the poem's composition: 'A la fin tu es las de ce monde ancien.'[350] This opening gambit of great rhetorical panache is an expression of an irredeemable frustration with existing forms of representing experience. The whole Symbolist paraphernalia of Verlaine and others, the language of introspection, of mood, of a purely poetic intimacy between the self-styled 'poète maudit' and his sympathetic reader, all this is dispensed with by Apollinaire's narrator at the outset of the poem. The Christian mythology and its aspiration to comfort us for the inadequacy of temporal existence is swept aside via glorification of the immediate, of the material and the technological. The Holy Spirit is glorified for being a champion pilot:

C'est le Christ qui monte au ciel mieux que les aviateurs.
Il détient le record du monde pour la hauteur?[351]

As far as the Paris Futurists were concerned, even the Cubist deconstruction of visual mimesis was insignificant. And yet Cubist and Futurist painters share the notion and the procedure known as simultaneity. Cubist simultaneity – whether in its earliest forms, or in its advanced abstraction, or in its so-called 'synthetic' mode – involves a manipulation of shapes and planes so as to explore the illusion that a multiplicity of points of view has access to the two-dimensional surface of the painting. In *Les Peintres cubistes* of 1913, Apollinaire refers to the practice as 'imiter les plans pour représenter les volumes'.[352] Cubist art seeks to exploit the flatness of the painted surface, but it does so not only, or even predominantly, so as to suggest everything that is *not* flat. It is even more a relishing of the flat surface, and of the expressive and textural possibilities that are opened out in this way. Cubist practice abandons the fictions of perspective, the fiction that looking repeatedly at represented objects arranged in relation to a point on the horizon would fully explore our understanding of perception and our relation to the world.

For the Futurists, the Cubist obsession with the surface exhibited its own futility, its lack of involvement with technology and culture; the questions it asked seemed purely artistic ones. For Marinetti, the painter Boccioni and others, it is not merely art that is at stake, but identity itself, the ways in which we construct its power to embrace the open-ended spectrum of information and sensation. Futurist simultaneity is an urgent one grounded on an excited response to speed: 'Nous déclarons que la splendeur du monde s'est enrichie d'une beauté nouvelle: la vitesse', writes Marinetti in the 1909 Manifesto.[353] Speed is the new beauty, along with the violence of industrial explosions, and ultimately, the anti-aesthetic formlessness of shrapnel.

Surrealist automatic writing and the theory of the 'convulsive', endlessly admixing image that develops from it, are a response to Freudian notions of the unconscious. 'La beauté sera CONVULSIVE ou ne sera pas.'[354] While such concerns are lacking in Futurism, what the post-war Surrealists share with the pre-war Futurists and Dadaists is the desire to break the frame of art itself, to dissolve the definition and the limits of aesthetic response. By altering our response to aesthetic artefacts, by opening them out to the perceptible forms of scientific progress, Marinetti claims to open the way to integration rather than fragmentation, and to a power to encompass experience rather than be alienated by it. Umberto Apollonio translates: 'the single man must communicate with every people on earth. He must feel himself to be the axis, judge and motor of the explored and unexplored infinite. Vast increase in a sense of humanity and a momentary and urgent need to establish relations with all mankind'.[355] Marinetti uncompromisingly promotes a vision of language able to function independently of any specific context, and having the power to communicate regardless of any cultural or sociological distinction.

Let us take Marinetti at his word and imagine that disregard (a refusal to look at) difference need not construct dominance or the censorship of the many by the one. Boccioni's *States of Mind: The Farewells of 1911* might then exemplify the social optimism invested by Futurists in the power of the male artist to model and remodel cultural experience imaginatively. Intertextually, the picture asserts its supremacy over a previous chapter in the ballet of the Parisian 'modern': Monet's Impressionist accounts of La Gare St Lazare in Paris, of his viewers' involvement in this urban icon on the perceptual level, as well as the subjective and intimate one. In Boccioni's picture, it is again the experience of the train station that is addressed, the farewells of the title are platform ones. But the sensual, material qualities of the social and cultural relation are presented with a renewed formal emphasis on dynamism, on its capacity to make nothing of any disintegration in our sense of self and of others. The swirling steam-clouds of Monet's St Lazare nostalgically allow the uniqueness of perception to melt into an invasion at the hands of the diversity and the pluralism of the city, but allow the reverse as well. This perpetual return to the intimate and the private is erased, Boccioni seems to suggest, by his own swirling forms which involve in one another evocations of human shapes to the left of the picture, electricity pylons above, and a cityscape to the right, the whole construction being dominated by an artifice or a veil of centrifugal mobility. And at the vortex appears the number 6943, as though painted on the profile of that iconic machine signifying progress and travel, the steam-engine itself. This naively anti-illusionist number presents itself differently from the numbers and letters that are included in what came to be known as 'synthetic' Cubist paintings and collages: there, the practice is an anxious one, serving to explore the diversity of elements that make up our sense of context and complicating our capacity to interpret it. But here, the anti-figurative figuration of number and machine offers a self-extending common language, a democratic sign and the sign of a democracy dissolving the discourses which permit it and limit it. The picture makes an immediate appeal to the viewer, in the sense that it puts down its marker against mediation and makes a bold plea for a culture that is readable and open to an indefinite and extensive embrace.

But what if we refuse to take Futurist boldness at its word? What if we refuse to participate in any textual seduction at the hands of Boccioni's pre-war pictures or Severini's, and see only a grotesque overvaluation of the image, of its power to absorb experience and to offer it up for consumption? I would like now to explore the paths of a critical approach to the pre-war cult of the modern, of the machine and of the ludic violence it offers. I will try and do so by turning to the response to such prospects suggested by the work of the Vorticist group of artists in England during the same period. I am indebted for much of what I shall have to say to Richard Cork's seminal and fascinating volumes on Vorticism – *Vorticism and Abstract art in the First Machine Age* – to which much of the rest of this chapter is a kind of modest tribute.

The concerns of the Vorticist artists in London might seem at first glance to reflect those of the Futurists in Paris. The dominant image of the modern era is emphatically technological in both cases. Lewis named the journal which he founded in 1914 in celebration of the blast furnaces of the British industrial heartland. The title *Blast* also functions as a pun, an invocation to blast all complacency and indolence.

The manifestos Lewis published in his revues express what might sound like a Futurist commitment to dismantling the restrictions of any point of view, context, or system of thought. One manifesto, included in *Blast* no. 1, 1914, opens with these assertions:

1. Beyond Action and Reaction, we would establish ourselves.
2. We start from opposite statements of a chosen world. Set up a violent structure of adolescent clearness between two extremes.
3. We discharge ourselves on both sides.
4. We fight first on one side, then on the other, but always for the SAME cause, which is neither side or both sides and ours.[356]

The valorisation of violence as a weapon against cultural complacency; a disgust with binary antagonism as a mainstay of intellectual infertility and alienation: these are some of the sentiments which Lewis's polemic shares with the Futurist one and the Dadaist one as well. The composition itself of this and almost all of Lewis's other Vorticist manifestos is made up of rectilinear geometric typography, in an attempt to give words an immediate impact, and to prevent that impact from being diffused in the reflective and interpretative process of reading. The Italian Futurist Carrà, with his *Words-in-freedom* published in the Futurist journal *Lacerba* in 1914, and Marinetti in his 'Turkish Captive Balloon' from *Zang Tumb Tuum* (1914), were making similar experiments with what we might now call 'concrete' typography. Apollinaire engages in his own semi-parodic way with this kind of typographic procedure in 'L'Antitradition futuriste' (1913).[357]

Richard Cork shows that Lewis was particularly stimulated by the work of the Italian Futurist painter Ballà, and especially by the series of his pictures entitled *Vortex*. These were never exhibited in London, but it seems clear that Lewis had contemplated reproductions of these pictures at some length. He writes in *Blast*, no.1 that 'if "dynamic" considerations intoxicate Balla and make him produce significant patterns (as they do), all is well. But Balla is not a "Futurist" in the Automobilist sense. He is a rather violent and geometric sort of Expressionist.' In the *Vortex* of *c*. 1913, Balla's curved planes suggest simultaneously concentration and decentralisation, focus and exorbitance. The picture seeks to give form to the very response that it strives to provoke: the sense of a vortex, a sense of energy concentrated but also all-embracing. In *formal* terms, rather than the mimetic ones of Boccioni's *States of Mind: The Farewells*, Balla's picture combines concentration, simultaneity and aggression.

But this attempt to do violence to our response to images by involving us explicitly in the process of reading forms is essentially uncharacteristic of Futurist productions. Lewis is reacting to this in accusing the Futurist aesthetic of Automobilism – an instance of naive, non-interventive idolisation of the industrial product, and of the cultural status quo at large. The pursuit of instantaneous impact and of immediacy in Futurist imagery has the effect of pre-empting and silencing the process of interpretation. This is evident in the verbal as well as the visual forms which Futurist practitioners developed. Marinetti asserts that language as a whole, and not only visual imagery in particular, should trigger an expanded sense of human capabilities. Apollonio translates in this way: 'the poet's imagination must weave together distant things *with no connecting strings*, by means of essential *free* words. . . . By imagination without strings, I mean the absolute freedom of images or analogies, expressed with unhampered words, with no connecting strings and with no punctuation.'[360]

Marinetti's notion of an 'essential free word' is exemplified by the number 6943 figured on the side of Boccioni's 'dynamic' steam-engine cab which I discussed earlier: this sign is constructed so as to signify without reference, and to multiply and concentrate simultaneously the contexts in which it is decipherable. With his notion of analogy, Marinetti is seeking space for the fantasy of an indefinite connecting and merging of contexts, systems of thought and response. The related Futurist notions of dynamism and of analogy articulate a naively democratic, narcissistic effort to explode the frame of reference, to encompass experience in its totality and to draw it in.

This idea of the totalising capacity of human consciousness to envisage situations differently and to build new ones is fundamentally inconsistent with that of other self-aware avant-garde practitioners of the period. The galvanising effect of Futurist emphasis on machinery and simultaneity casts a veil of seductive appeal over its imaginary project of a new beginning. But the tatters are quickly reabsorbed in that sense of history and of the relativity of any artefact, of any sign – a set of sensations which Futurism, ultimately, leaves undisturbed. Apollinaire's own 'words-in-freedom', for example, the ideograms that were ultimately included in *Calligrammes* (1918), engage quite differently with the project of exploring and extending the scope of the readable and the decipherable. In 'Lettre-Océan', first published in 1913, reading the words, or bits of fragmented message, and reading the imaged figurations which they form of the Eiffel Tower – that Parisian emblem of a New World – cannot happen simultaneously. The one excludes the other, though each is in a continually shifting, vibrating relation to the other. The textualisation of the Eiffel Tower, its fragmentation in the reading of 'Lettre-Océan' and in the poem's network of unaccountably interlocking contexts, involves the reader in a re-examination of his/her subjective identification with dominant cultural emblems. How do we construct our relation to the measureless diversity of material and perception that is instantly and obscurely processed by our mentality? Of what value are the systems we appeal to or imagine – verbal, visual, cultural, ideological – in fashioning an identity out of our psycho-physiological responses to that indefinite range of stimuli which threatens to invade any sense of identity, and to brush aside any ego? And, on the other hand, what is the value of any resistance to this razing of an overestimated subjectivity?[361]

Such are the implications of a critical, formalist involvement with the experience of modernist simultaneity, as opposed to a Futurist idealisation of those same forms. A sense of anxiety and of an alienated subjectivity, on one level, also drives the work of Lewis and other Vorticists. The signal of this, as well as the effect, is to put interpretation and intervention in gear as a driving principle of the manipulation of form. Very much in the Baudelairean tradition, Lewis remarks in *Blast*, that 'intrinsic beauty is in the Interpreter and the Seer, not in the object or content', and that 'it is always the POSSIBILITIES in the object, the IMAGINATION, as we say, in the spectator, that matters. Nature itself is of no importance.'[362] This imagination, this capacity to analyse 'modern' experience rather than simply consuming it, involves a confrontation with the environment – the raw material of perception and of art - as potentially eluding the purchase on it we seek to construct. The Vorticist formal response to the mechanistic and to the urban is constricting as opposed to expansive, it construes alienation as opposed to complacency. Its aggression is critical and defensive, rather than anarchistic and impressionistic.

Richard Cork highlights this discriminating constriction by contrasting Boccioni's *States of Mind: The Farewells*, which I discussed earlier, with Frederick Etchells's *Hyde Park* of 1915. Some of Etchells's etchings appear in *Blast* no. 1. 'Where Vorticism used the machine as a basis for the construction of a brutal world,' writes Cork, 'Futurism simply regarded it as one more means of celebrating its own exalted feelings.'[363] Apollinaire ultimately comes to isolate emphatically the incoherence of this passive, non-interventive celebration in a brief account of the paradoxically descriptive, naively representational approach to art he attributes to Marinetti: 'Les mots en liberté de Marinetti amènenent un renouvellement de la description, et à ce titre ils ont de l'importance, ils amènent également un retour offensif de la description et ainsi ils sont didactiques et antilyriques.'[364]

And following on from Cork's comment, one could add that Etchells's *Hyde Park* functions as a *re*construction of industrial brutality, that it moulds itself to a fragmentation of the body and of the subject within a heightened sense of the social and cultural moment. This is re-presentation which distorts inhumanly, but refutes the illusion of impregnable critical distance, finding forms instead for an intermeshed involvement *in* that inhumanity. Cork shows the ways in which Etchells has modelled his style on the engineering drawings in the mechanical manuals of the time, emphasising the effect this has of 'levelling' the human figures who cross the bridge over the Serpentine – flattening out the differences between them as well as between them and the park. The equating of figuring the body with figuring the machine further embeds the making of artistic images in the marketing of the body and of the sensibilities. In this way, image-making is actively involved in a desperate and defensive battle for autonomy – psychic, cultural, economic – where there is none to be found or maintained. How different from Boccioni's swirling, expansive, idealised integration of human and urban morphology. *Hyde Park, States of Mind: The Farewells*, and Cubist treatments of the human form all share in a dethroning of the male and female body from its structural position of dominance in pictures and in theories of making pictures. Wyndham Lewis proclaims: 'THE ACTUAL HUMAN BODY BECOMES OF LESS IMPORTANCE EVERY DAY.'[365] The Humanist, gendered apportioning to the mind and the body of powers to compose and attract is violently flattened in a reconstitution of the two-dimensional in the image, and of its own power to reconstruct and deconstruct. But in Futurist technological iconography, the two-dimensional is erased, it dynamically dissolves any sense of dimension and of its potency. The violence of Cubist de-formations of the body engages more affirmatively and more desperately with its aesthetic and cultural targets, which are inevitably part of the psycho-cultural *given*, and as such are modifiable only from *within*. Picasso's self-consciously inaugural *Les Demoiselles d'Avignon* of 1907 engages with the semiology of perception by levelling perspective, with sexual politics by setting itself in a brothel, and with cultural politics by invoking the masks of Oceanic figures and rites. But the magnificence itself of this broad stage casts a veil of obscurity over the performers and our efforts to interpret them. These are figures in search of context, of culture and even of sexuality, and we are implicated in this fertile limbo as we look. But limbo it is; we may be able to lay it to rest, or we may be engulfed by it. Can a formalist examination of the violence with which dominant structures are sourcelessly enshrined in our consciousness be securely distinguished from a confirmation of this violence? To what extent does critical detachment involve a testimony to the oppressor? At another extreme of Cubist formal evocation of experiential depth, the breathtaking devastation of Picasso's *Guernica* (1936) is both an illustration of the effects of Francoist violence and massacre, *and* an imaginary incarnation of Francoist desire. Picasso entitles a sketch for the work *The Dream and the Lie of Franco* – and not only the body, but also icons of Spanish culture itself (bulls, picadors' horses . . .), in all the subjectivity of the ways in which it might be sensed, are implicated in this orgy of horror.

What power do we have, and should we accord ourselves, to bury our sense of the past and to dominate the present? Such a question might be a way of formulating the high stakes of abstract, avant-garde, *textual* involvement with the modern and with the machine. Cubist and Vorticist artists are not playing for the same high stakes as the ones of the Spanish Civil War. But the bloodbath of the First World War is imminent. How are we to interpret the erasing of the human form and of sexual difference in these works? The power of the individual ego to keep itself intact and to control stimulus by keeping it at bay, is uprooted in the same procedural gestures. In Vorticist stylisation, the denial of the human form is executed in a heightening of the flat surface of the image, and in a constricting paring down of the visual elements involved. Lewis's *Portrait of an Englishwoman* of 1914 is a response to the female form in terms of a suggestion of industrial shapes, and in particular those of girders; it is a denial of female humanity and sexuality. Approaching the picture as a kind of twisted profile, girders figure the Englishwoman's hair, eyebrows and eyes, another figures the bottom line of her nose. In a different configuration, the facial outlines are absorbed in a suggestion of the iron skeleton of a building stretching upwards. . . .

But there is a constructive impetus behind this very male denial of the female. Cork emphasises this by stressing the different implications that emerge from this picture when it is set beside the organic and mechanical tubes Duchamp uses in *La Mariée* in his attempt formally to digest and excrete male-constructed mythologies of the female body.[366] The stylised abstraction of Lewis's picture acquires a coherence all its own: it attributes to artist and viewer the imaginary power to manipulate their involvement in the urban here and now. The uniformity of the style acts as a signal and proof of this power. The aggressively dominant parallel bars articulate a capacity to impose form on experience. And yet in the same moment, this stylisation articulates an imprisonment within the industrial, depersonalised shapes it seeks to transform, and which now threaten once again to obliterate the human form and the human ego. Such anxiety is itself signalled in the male artist's obliteration of gender difference in the nominally female subject of his portrait.

The nature of the involvement with machinery which the picture projects is thus ambivalent and unresolved. It is an involvement which offers the imaginary prospect of an indefinite capacity to construct and reconstruct; it proffers the equally imaginary fear of invasion of the subject from the outside. This spectre of invasion suggests that the relationship developed in the picture to

industrial forms is one of paranoia. In his paper 'On Narcissism: an Introduction' of 1914, Freud describes paranoia in terms of the way our moral
conscience develops in relation to the voice of our parents, to which are added
'the voices of the innumerable and indefinable host of all other people in our
environment'.[367] In Freudian terms, paranoia results from psychic construc-
tions of intense power attributed to the critical gaze coming at us from society
at large. In the case of Lewis's picture, these voices take on the forms of
industry and mechanisation, which invade the space of the artist's work,
dehumanise and unsex the female body.

At the same time, the picture could be described as *paranoiac–critical* –
even though Salvador Dalì was to coin the term to describe his work with
dream and dream-imagery of the late 1920s and 1930s. There is no
encouragement to link Surrealism and Vorticism historically. There is no
explicit involvement with oneiric experience in Lewis's painting, just as there
is none in Futurist art. Indeed Wyndham Lewis asserts in *Blast* 'to dream is
the same thing as to lie: anybody but an invalid or a canaille feels the
discomfort and repugnance of something not clean in it'.[368] But what makes
the term appropriate here is Dalì's attempt to develop the illusion of an
imagery that would perfectly match dream-imagery, that would be indistinguishable from the memories available to us of the dream experience – and
to affirm interpretative and critical import in *that*.[369] In a painting such as
Soft Construction with Boiled Beans: Premonition of War of 1936, Dalì
mimes on the level of fantasy – terrified? perverse? – imagined shapes of war
and torture; and it is in that balletic, self-aware *inability* to break free from its
own terms, its own obsessions and terrors, that the painting seeks out an
interventive space.

Lewis's *Portrait of an Englishwoman* is paranoiac in that it allows nothing
in its space but invasion by impersonal, industrial forms. It is critical in that it
asserts its power to manipulate the urban forms in which that very alienation
is cast. As we attempt to make sense of the abstract design of the work, our
involvement in our own technological present is given shape and called to
question. As Vorticist abstraction develops, the elements in a sense of
alienation are transformed into the component parts of a creative act. But
once again, what if the textual bringing-together of the paranoiac and the
critical resulted in the dissolution of any distinction between the two? Or if
critical defensiveness assumed the forms of aggression and the desire to
dominate? Lewis's *The Workshop* (1910–15), which hangs in the Tate
Gallery, is a further abstract combination of analytical and alienating
elements. The title affirms the value of the craftsman as opposed to the
Romantic 'genius'. Once again, urban morphology proliferates: ladders,
scaffolding, window-frames, façades, are all made into the raw material, the
medium itself of stylistic invention. And this invention is of the most
aggressively resistant and resisting kind. There is nothing in it of the conventional appeal to the viewer's eye; it refutes aesthetic satisfaction. It projects a

style that frustrates stylistic appeal. Sections in the picture disintegrate. Suggestions of three- and two-dimensionality alternate without ever creating any continual counterpoint. Instead, a series of blockages and impasses is developed. At the same time, the impact of the colour is magnetic, as though seeking to fascinate with its own magnificence, and as though the violent contrasts it sets up could bear witness to the picture's independence from the industrial raw material it treats. And yet perhaps the assertive violence of this independence might trouble, dominate, alienate. Where is the way in for the viewer? Is the picture not giving form to pride taken in the construction of an impenetrable, impermeable, static network of imaged *potential*, that remains invulnerable not only to the urban real it manhandles in the abstract, but also to any input, any change or movement that would come from the participating gaze of the viewer?

In 'On Narcissism' Freud argues that there is a masochistic pleasure to be derived from paranoid delusions – precisely the pleasure of being watched, but exclusively so, in ways which suppress any sense of others also being watched, and in ways which imprison and immobilise the intrusive gazer. Here, paranoia merges with megalomania.[370] Paranoia and the reign of Narcissism it thus proclaims are signals of the notorious Freudian pleasure principle, constantly and desperately re-accommodating itself to the reality principle and to the 'exigencies of society', and 'beyond' which there is the equally desperate drive to put an end to these irredeemable cuts and breaches made in the psychic surface of the ego.[371] Each person's readings of this existential narrative will inevitably shape his or her own acceptance of it, of the Freudian account of the ways in which we imagine, grapple with and ward off the presence of others, and of the ways in which we construct our relation to death. I offer neither any deconstruction of Freudian theory, nor any 'application' of it to Lewis's image-making. But I have alluded to it as a way of alerting my reader and myself to the high stakes that are being played for in avant-garde practices of dehumanising the body. Such practice pulls apart egoistic illusions of supremacy and immortality – or does it confirm them? 'Profondeurs de la matière qui est le commencement des moyens.'[372] Here, Apollinaire, striving for an optimistic art that would enmesh alienation with creativity, suggests that the continued contemplation by an artist of his or her own means and methods allows the beginnings of an opening-out to the reality of our material being – and perhaps even to a relishing of it and of all its ego-dissolving textures and dangers. Once again, only each viewer can decide where she or he will look to find humanity in this art. Will it be in the self-removing abstraction of Lewis's *Workshop*, or of his *Red Duet* (1914)?[373] In the *perpetuum mobile* of Dadaist self-critical, stop-go conceptualisation? Or perhaps in the savouring and the cherishing of diversity and the *viscous* – what Apollinaire speaks of as 'la vérité des objets' – exhibited in Cubist collage as well as in the collage work of Kurt Schwitters.[374] Perhaps the brief episode of avant-garde formal and imaginary investment in machinery raises the curtain once again on the undecidable conflict of influence and the novel, the interminable race between successive generations in which each seeks and inevitably fails to be the last in the ground. 'On ne peut pas transporter avec soi le cadavre de son père', writes Apollinaire. But the very next sentence reads: 'Mais nos pieds ne se détachent qu'en vain du sol qui contient les morts.'[375] On the mobility of our response to this paradox of a creativity simultaneously redeemed and doomed for banishing, for murdering the past hinges the fate of avant-garde art and of the violence which it demands the right to espouse. Will it free us by constructing plural, open-ended readings of our situation and our identity? Or will it entrap us in Fascistic mirages of impregnability and dominance? If there is no escaping the violence of the ways in which our psychic and cultural condition is imposed, then perhaps, as Roland Barthes argued in the 1970s it is up to us to find forms of expression which *de-compose*. Alienation might dissolve in reading images and discourses as so many scenes of a continual new beginning, or of a fertile opening-out to the fragility and mortality of our own sense of self.[376]

Naomi Segal

Who whom? Violence, politics and the aesthetic

The violent muse: the title brings a shudder of incongruity. Muses stand with eyes downcast, the body proffered somewhere around the navel, mindless, organless, giving. An inspiration at the price of being fast-frozen. No, if she darts, glances or even wriggles violently, she is no muse.[377]

Men want muses that behave. 'I do not see the . . . hidden in the forest' murmur sixteen Surrealists, all male of course, with their ties nicely fastened and eyelids buttoned.[378] In the centre, the nude is the bleep that substitutes for a vocable unspoken and unnecessary. Of course she is hidden, in her own body's forest, and of course she is unseen. Thus a muse.

But what does 'violence' mean? Who whom? In this brief essay, I want to argue that violence is essentially both bodily and political and to debate the sexuality of the given and received blow. The issue here is a celebration of violence typical of the avant-garde, crucially masculine and aesthetic precisely as it evades the body, the other and their implicit politics.

On the television news the word 'violence' is generally used of a subordinate group acting up. Does the ANC advocate violence, or does it not? Amnesty International defines as prisoners of conscience 'men and women detained anywhere for their beliefs, colour, sex, ethnic origin, language or religion, provided that they have neither used nor advocated violence'.[379] We know exactly what they mean. I do not wish here to go into the complex question of the ethics of revolutionary violence, merely to observe that as a term it is normally invoked, with a certain incongruity, only of the weaker against the stronger. We know of course (with or without Foucault) that the institutionalised force of a state machine that incarcerates, 'disappears' (a verb which has gained an interesting grammatical elasticity in its political usage: the *desaparecidos* are not so much the subject as the object of their disappearance, so that by popular connotation the participle has become transitive) and tortures is committing a far more significant and consistent violence than the striker that throws a brick or the revolutionary a petrol-bomb – but the term is used more readily of the latter, and this begins to link up to the implied politics of the avant-garde artists, fancying themselves in rebellion against a jaded and faceless power-structure. If the torturer is somehow not 'violent', then violence suggests a kind of heat, energy, a more nearly body-to-body encounter (here the beginning of erotics), above all force perceived as graceless, out of place. Thus if the police are arraigned with acting violently, it is because we perceive them as having become (perhaps momentarily) bodies rather than uniforms, overstepping the line this once – or else because they belong to other regimes than the symbolic order under which we, however reluctantly, live. The torturer who acts cold, seeks information, hides any attendant pleasure and employs machinery is not violent in this everyday usage. But if violence is force out of place, it must be chaotic – how then can it be aesthetic?

'Beauty will be CONVULSIVE', writes Breton after his text has seen, deplored and ignored the incarceration of Nadja, 'or will not be at all.'[380] Too right it/she will not be at all. She is no longer, at the point where beauty becomes convulsive, violent after the special model of the not-quite-physical erotics of avant-garde rhetoric.

If violence belongs to the heat of action and peculiarly is used for the action of the underling rather than the overlord, how is it that we know violence is always inflicted upon a weaker? Easily: the blow could barely fall if it were not that the victim were smaller and frailer, much less continue into a drawn-out act. There is, then, a paradox. Violent people attack not the institutions and machinery of a system for which they are the repressed chaotic, since abstracts cannot bleed and the symbolic (the fathers) are what they are by being abstract. If the rebel attacks the patriarchy in a more immediate way, it is the silly old man at a crossroads, the absurdity of Oedipus's murder of Laius consisting precisely in that he turns out to have dealt a blow to a whole mythic structure while swatting a cranky fly. That is why the body-blow is always against an other who can be hit (violence against objects is strictly not 'violence' at all: violence must properly be felt) – the child, the animal, the woman.

No one can hit the fathers: they are the abstraction and institution of power. We can go instead for what they have, seeking to destroy in its idols the property-owning of a class whose true invisible ownership is of power. Or we, in a kind of flailing they can easily co-opt, turn against something that is more theirs than we are, thus ours too, our subordinates, the cur, the brat, the slag: the mother. If violence must be against sentient material, it is ultimately performed in the secret name of a greater slavery, inflicted upon the object of common exchange or ownership, and for this reason I suggest that violence is always by men (is, rather, an act in the masculine position), by young men (for a posture of rebellion gives it its glamour, but Oedipus is not the breaker of the oedipal-patriarchal system, he is its crux) and against women (for the material is the maternal, and every figure of slavery is feminised).

I used the pronoun 'we' in the foregoing paragraph with some distaste, for none of us is always or exclusively in the morally safer place of the potential victim; and a certain taking of the 'we' position is inevitable in imagining violence. Whoever is violent is 'we' – not 'I' of course, for the violent one is in or substitutes for a group (hence his strength; and even drink can pluralise), nor quite 'he' or 'she' because it is a masculine position that is being taken up, not a gender-stance, though it may be a sexual standpoint too.

How is violence masculine? Not just in the virility mystique we will all readily recognise, though it is this mystique that I shall go on to examine. Violence is masculine in two ultimately contradictory senses: in its use of a strength that must try to be graceless, for the graceful is too aesthetically quieted, not chaotic enough for the rebel's gesture; and because of its quintessential place in the subject-position. Violence is always a subject–object encounter, that is clear; but the more it is perceived as the subject's place, the transcendent subject in free flight or aggression, the less we see of the object, until there is no trace of the receiver of violence and her slavery, the more it becomes simultaneously and self-productively masculine and aesthetic. (And then comes the risk of grace and then the loss of energy; this is what we shall see in our authors.)

Let me offer three examples of this aestheticising of violence, two from everyday life, the third from nineteenth-century literature. First, an otherwise nice-natured little boy holds out anything longer than it is wide, shouts 'kill, kill, kill!' or the more universal 'peeeow! peeeow!' and annoys all the family – but he does not actually hit out. Thus his play, sometimes more earnestly irritable, is here simply aesthetic, and hurts no one, perhaps because the others are all bigger than him and he has no safe opportunity to be violent. This gestural violence is a small, male art-work, full of ideological menace but without immediate danger. The second example is more obviously bracketed into the aesthetic. A children's entertainer brings out his modelling balloons and reliably every time stretches the balloon out and lets it snap against his fingers. His 'Ow!!' and the children's delighted laughter is the high spot of the afternoon to one little girl; asked why, she explains: 'because we knew it wasn't real'. Here the pain delights because it is confected, predictable and above all not painful. Violence, self-directed this time so that the children are simply voyeurs, is aesthetic when it does not hurt anyone, turning instead into enjoyment.

My third example seeks a key antecedent of the modernist mystique of violence in Baudelaire. In this poem he presents an idyll to be found in a number of Romantic poets:

Elevation
Up above the ponds, up above the valleys
The mountains, the woods, the clouds and the seas
Up beyond the sun, up beyond the ether
And beyond the confines of the starry spheres,
My spirit, you move with agility

And, like a good swimmer swooning in the wave,
You joyfully forge through the immense depth
With an ineffable and masculine delight.
Take off, fly far from the morbid miasma,
Go to be purified in the higher air
And drink, like a pure divine liquor,
The clear fire that fills the limpid realms of space.
Behind the cares and the endless griefs
That load down with weights this foggy existence,
Happy is he that with a vigorous wing
Can leap and fly towards the bright serene fields.
He whose thoughts are like the morning larks
That take off soaring freely to the skies,
– Who hovers over life and can read without strain
The language of flowers and of silent things!

Baudelaire's whole aesthetics of pleasure rests on a dialectic of incarceration (spleen, boredom, the enclosure of rooms, heads, cities) and free flight, which departs from the fog of material things but relies on that very physical starting-point (despised love, buzzing cityscape, oppressed imagination) to set off the soaring of fantasy and flow of words. But 'Eléva-tion' is a special and especially erotic case, for it encapsulates (right at the start of the text) the central paradox of this pleasure. In every other line – 'Au-dessus . . . par delà . . . tu sillonnes . . . envole-toi . . . va . . . et bois . . . derrière . . . s'élancer . . . prennent un libre essor' – movement is marked, with a powerful onomatopoeic rhythm (readers brought up in British schools will start humming 'Faster than fairies, faster than witches . . .') and a repetitious vocabulary of 'take-off'. But where does he go? Nowhere it seems, having (like the poor old codger of pornographic fantasy) to keep on starting and precipitating himself again; the idyll is one of sheer zooming, movement not just *from* but *off*, yet never movement to. It is clearly a component of this complex fantasy that the phallic transcendence carries a risk of castration. 'Taking off' is its own pun. The earth then (or any form of consummation/arrival) would be the dangerous feminine from which potency might not re-emerge. At the other end of the book, the poet avows that 'the only real travellers are those who leave /For leaving's sake',[382] showing again that pleasure is never in arrival. The text ends in the uncoiled spring of a suicide just about to be imagined – for 'to die', as Barrie reminds us, 'will be an awfully big adventure'.[383] 'Charles Baudelaire' and Peter Pan can, of course, never grow up into real men or people, essentially because the fantasies of zooming must be immaterial to give such excitement. And hence their suicidal pretence.

Perhaps this aesthetic violence is always a play at self-destruction, an auto-erotic masochism that toys childishly and safely with a never-tried landing. But 'Elévation' does not entirely end in this frantic idyll: at the close it offers what is surely a clear politics of the necessary other. The poet has got nowhere also because, like the albatross, his final wish is not to go away but to hover over. Hovering over that humanity defined as miasmic because irredeemably material, he can of course read – flowers (of evil?) and things that, exactly like the muse, never answer back.

'It was her eyes: she was staring at me; so I hit her.' Violence, perceived as rebellion, proffered as correction, is really the response to the 'dumb insolence' of the more enslaved than yourself. Muteness, a shrinking taken to invite pursuit, these are the extreme gestures of the beaten dog, child, slave or wife, to whom of course language is never properly given. Baudelaire's flying and hovering implicitly carry an idea of swooping, a predatory closure that is never enacted. In order to come down on deck, the albatross has to be captured; then his weakness (read: genius) is the object of cruel mockery. Thus the Romantic poet carries his predatoriness up on high where he can look down, but never swoops – and never really zooms.

Baudelaire is not alone. Hugo's *Les Contemplations* is a veritable aviary of beating wings – swans, doves and butterflies in sweeter moments, eagles and whole flights 'of white birds at dawn and black ones in the dark' as the tone rises.[384] In him too, flight, rebellion and knowledge are tied together: the aim of the 'winged thinker' is to 'rob God'[385] – but does he? Never; rather, he does a great deal of hovering, leaning down, reading and contemplating the book of nature. The Oedipal–Promethean gesture is overt in its sufficiency; but the leaning remains a solution it is essential not to admit. For leaning is a form of erotic interruption. Below the poet must be a maternal/material object (flowers, mountains, the world: in a word, the mother's body) upon whom his violent excitement forbears to act.

Bird-poets abound in the poetry of the modern period, mostly out of their element. Swans in particular invite the irony of the urbane – but while Baudelaire's bird paddles painfully in the Paris dust and Mallarmé's hovers between ice and air, Rilke's stops looking clownish as soon as it sets feathers on water. High places, towers and masculine ambition are the novelistic equivalent, and from Elijah to Superman is a fairly straight line.

Most sexy of all is another bird, Leconte de Lisles's doughty predator in 'Le Sommeil du condor'.[386] The poem begins, exactly like Baudelaire's, with a repetition of 'up beyond', and presents a map-like panorama of great complex shapes and features, above which this 'vast Bird, filled with a gloomy indolence' floats in the air 'like a spectre, alone', gazing at America from which slowly night unfurls, putting everything to sleep. When the darkness arrives:

> He groans out his pleasure, shakes his plumage,
> Erects his muscular, hairless neck,
> He rises up, whipping the acrid snow of the Andes,
> With a harsh cry soars to where the wind cannot reach,

And, far from the black globe, far from the living star,
Sleeps in the icy air, his great wings outstretched.

Again, the extreme erotic effect of this poem comes from the idyll of tension unappeased: this bird can sleep on the wing, so utterly does 'he' combine erectile power with pure serenity. Nothing so small as an outlet is envisaged; instead the world has diminished to a round dark thing, still material and living but no longer consumable prey: he is above.

This excursus suggests an antecedent for a key aspect of avant-garde aesthetic violence: the rebel is more exactly a predator but a predator who prefers to hover, leaving the endpoint of the energies, a violent con-summation, to be imagined by the more material, less infinitely patient reader. (Thus are readers always Bovarys, always women, natural victims of writers who 'lean' – victims not of their violence but their knowledge, for he who hovers is not Prometheus but God, 'everywhere present and nowhere visible'.)[387]

We come full circle. The 'ineffable and masculine delight' that begins as free flight ends in the pose of a Flaubertian deity, no longer contemplating but controlling – as it were coldly, facelessly and apparently only for the sake of information. It may be that in authorship, however disavowed, there is never much escape from the paternal position to which the oedipal son sues to attain. Precisely the *deus absconditus* is the most institutional authority (all post-monotheistic authority residing in the invisibility of command) and we have seen how simply Romantic passion stopped in mid-air. At this point, surprisingly perhaps, we rediscover grace – precision, harmony, the *mot juste* applied with irony to the representation of the unpalatable. No more violence, only distaste.

If these are the pre-Modernist antecedents of our avant-garde authors, what of the latter? Among the eleven aims of the first Futurist Manifesto published in *Le Figaro* on 20 February 1909 are 'the love of danger, the habit of energy and fearlessness . . . courage, audacity and revolt . . . aggressive movement, a feverish insomnia, the gymnast's stride, the somersault leap, the slap and the punch'.[388] All intransitives, though the link between the fearless, the stride and the slap does not need to be drawn. Marinetti introduces 'a new beauty: the beauty of speed. . . . We want to hymn the man holding the wheel, whose ideal starter-rod traverses the earth, hurled upon the circuit of its orbit. The man remains at the wheel, observe, not driving off for there is nowhere to go to, and not leaping but hurling.' The text continues:

6. The poet must spend himself with heat, brilliance and generosity, to enlarge the passionate fervour of primordial elements.
7. There is no beauty now but in struggle. No masterpiece without aggression. Poetry must be a violent assault on unknown forces, to summon them to lie down before man.
8. We are on the extreme promontory of the centuries! . . . What is the use of

looking behind us, now that we have to smash down the mysterious gate-posts of the impossible? Time and Space died yesterday. We are already living in the absolute, for we have already created eternal omnipresent speed.

9.   We wish to glorify war – the world's only hygiene – militarism, patriotism, the destructive gesture of the anarchists, beautiful ideas that kill, and contempt for women.

10.   We wish to demolish museums and libraries, fight against moralism, feminism and all other forms of opportunistic and utilitarian cowardice.

In abstract terms, Marinetti throws together aesthetics, politics and mysticism in an inclusive rhetoric of the battle, demolition, aggression and contempt. All, of course, nicely turned in phrases as harmonious as they are loud-mouthed, and presentably numbered. It is not only obvious that the imagery belongs to male sexuality but also that it has no precise goal. The gateposts of the impossible, the wild forces of the primordial and the absolute are surely both with them and against them; solely contrasted are the dull and 'soft' figures of a past – dead art, moral structures and women. How will the battering-ram fare against them? Unnecessarily.

The real object of this prodigal aggression is familiarly feminine: old art (in the figure of the Victory of Samothrace, disparagingly contrasted with a 'roaring automobile') is a sort of grandmother no longer to be respected when 'Sagesse' the straitjacket is cast off. More explicitly:

Admiring an old picture is like pouring our sensibility into a funerary urn instead of hurling it far off, in violent spasms of creative action. Are you going to waste your best powers in a useless admiration of the past from which you can only emerge exhausted, diminished, trampled underfoot?

Elsewhere in Futurist rhetoric, the loathing of the feminine and its identification with a despised cultural past becomes more explicit and at once more vicious. In 'Il discorso di Roma' (1913) Giovanni Papini writes of Rome, battened on by tourists, as a syphilitic old whore, and in the war-time polemic 'Amiamo la guerra' (1914) fantasises street-corner butchery while jeering at the weeping mammas who should have known what to expect when they enjoyed engendering the sons they now blub over. Hacking away in imagination, he was as appalled as anyone when the real carnage occurred.[390]

The past is old sex from which the hero can only emerge unmanned. New sex is the 'convulsive' orgasm but, familiarly, it is nowhere, in no one and for no one, not even for the self. This is a peculiar kind of Narcissism, utterly without caressiveness because it is always about departures, leapings and stridings, never about pleasure or consummation, even perverse. This is still a kind of hovering above, gesturing violence and making noises like the little boy with his water pistol.

For this rhetoric, with all its speediness, goes too far and not far enough – and I want here to gather together my scattered distinction between the chaotic and the graceful as the point where violence ends in the aesthetic.

What Marinetti is proposing is a masculine beauty very close to grace. The hurling arm, the machine gliding on its circuit, are precisely not violent (indeed as the lance as phallic symbol shows, they are both gestural and classical) and in proportion as they aestheticise the masculine, they eschew action. The natural end of this logic, conclusion of the Romantic bird-imagery, is the bomber-plane. In 'The Battle of Tripoli' (1912) Marinetti describes the pilot's pleasure in hovering above the land he is, without needing to dirty or almost move his hands, pitting with bombs. In the novel *The Steel Alcove* (1921), he takes the image a stage further, writing with extraordinary prescience of

phantom-aeroplanes laden with bombs and without pilots, remote-controlled by a 'shepherd' aeroplane. Phantom-planes without pilots which will explode with their bombs, which can also be guided from the ground by an electric control-panel. We will have aerial torpedoes. One day we will have electric war.[391]

If the hovering aeroplane is the modernist version of the Romantic image of flight, Saint-Exupéry is its voice. His barely human Rivière is the paternal shepherd keeping the young men aloft, the feminine is always on the ground (behind, before or in an oasis of refuelling) and, as the almost bathetic task of carrying the mail hints, the motive of this flying is close to the hovering myth after all. Who cares where they zoom to, it can only be to some uncomprehending bed; true erotics belongs to the silent body on high: 'once again, in flight, the pilot felt neither vertigo nor intoxication, but the mysterious labour of a living flesh'.[392]

Real violence is always serious. I return to the knowledge that blood must, however explained, be spilt. So where is the pain and destruction here, among the eagles, lances and sky-pilots? Why, after all in the muse and her very stillness. What is unknowable is, again, always feminine – a despicable, destructible world one stage beyond Yonville, in which boredom can no longer even be represented (in Eliot's *The Waste Land*, where destructiveness is anything but violent, we see the extreme point of a repulsion too fastidious even to represent its object). The unknowable above which, strenuously wishing to rob God of that knowledge, these poets lean but do not swoop, is the bodily existence of the woman at whom, after all, it is directed. And this confected energy is the aggression which finds it vulgar to descend. She is pure material alterity. She is the 'whom' that the intransitive verb has repressed.

Marinetti invented some peculiar recipes but he did not burn any museums. Breton and his friends fired on no crowds. What it is not is mind-changing, world-transforming stuff. Ah yes, maybe worlds can only be changed in that gasp between erection and entry but if so, what hope for the material into which, for pleasure or pain, this energy never reaches? Knowing, indeed, that it wishes us ill but cannot reach out a hand even to signal its arrival? Wipes us out rather, by the silence of the intransitive.

When the blow falls, it can only be as pornography or fascism, those supremely institutional violences that cannot go without uniform. Until then, it is pure ballet.

Notes

1 Baudrillard, *In the Shadow*.
2 The term is here used in its Lacanian sense.
3 *Canti squadristi della vigilia*, quoted in Grimaldi and Bozzetti, *Farinacci*, p. 20.
4 Sarfatti, *Dux*, p. 250.
5 Rigotti, 'Il medico-chirurgo', pp. 501, 504.
6 See *Understanding Sexual Violence*, p. 103.
7 Soffici, *Opere* p. 115.
8 Sarfatti, *Dux*, pp. 248–50.
9 Quoted in Woolf, 'Italy', p. 41.
10 Soffici, 'Intorno'; cf. *Battaglia*, p. 96.
11 The core of Sorel's best-known work first appeared as articles in the Rome
   periodical *Il Divenire Sociale*, collected in 1906 in *Lo sciopero generale e la
   violenza*. This volume, with further articles from *Le Mouvement Socialiste* and
   Sorel's dedicatory letter to Daniel Halévy, was published in Paris in 1908 as
   Réflexions sur la violence. The latter was then used for an Italian translation
   published in 1909 with Croce's introduction.
12 On Gramsci's relations with Sorel, see 'The Communist Party', pp. 225–9;
   Badaloni, *Il marxismo di Gramsci*, pp. 147–60; *A Gramsci Reader*, pp. 407–8.
13 Sorel, *Lo sciopero*, p. 60.
14 Sorel, *Lo sciopero*, p. 102.
15 *The Anarchists*, p. 192.
16 Sorel, *Lo sciopero*, p. 41.
17 Sorel, *Lo sciopero*, p. 52.
18 Sorel, *Lo sciopero*, p. 63.
19 Marinetti, 'Che cosa è il futurismo?', p. 35.
20 Papini, 'Amiamo la guerra', pp. 274–5.N
21 See Fussell's list of English 'war diction' in *The Great War and Modern Memory*,
   pp. 21–3. He notes that as late as 1918 it was possible for men who had actually
   fought to sustain the old rhetoric.
22 Marinetti, 'Manifesto tecnico', p. 50.
23 Marinetti, 'Bataille, Poids + Odeur', p. 567.
24 Marinetti, *La battaglia*, p. 48.
25 Marinetti, *Guerra sola*, p. 131. On the significance of flying in relation to

violence, see Naomi Segal's chapter in the present volume.

26 Marinetti, *Taccuini 1915–1921*, pp. 415–16.
27 Marinetti, *Taccuini 1915–1921*, p. 415.
28 Marinetti, *Taccuini 1915–1921*, p. 431.
29 Liebknecht, *Militarism and Anti-Militarism*, p.21.
30 Luxemburg, *The Junius Pamphlet: The Crisis in German Social Democracy*, London, n.d., p. 20.
31 Theweleit, *Male Fantasies*, p. 173.
32 Theweleit, *Male Fantasies*, p. 430.
33 Theweleit, *Male Fantasies*, p. xv.
34 Reich, *The Mass Psychology of Fascism*, p. 118.
35 Hitler, *Mein Kampf*, p. 53.
36 Hitler, *Mein Kampf*, p. 277.
37 Cited from Mayer, *Why did the Heavens*, p. 309.
38 Mayer, *Why did the Heavens*, p. 432.
39 Mayer, *Why did the Heavens*, p. 390.
40 Cited from Lifton, 'Medicalized killing', p. 15.
41 Lifton, 'Medicalized killing', p. 14.
42 Mayer, *Why did the Heavens*, pp. 382–3.
43 Lifton, 'Medicalized killing', pp. 17–19.
44 Compare, for example, Coudenhove-Kalergi, *The Totalitarian State*.
45 For a critique of such 'instinctivist' explanations of human aggression see Fromm, *The Anatomy of Human Destructiveness*.
46 See 'Politics as a Vocation'.
47 J-F. Lyotard and J-L. Thébaud, *Just Gaming*, trans. by W. Godzich, Manchester, 1985, p. 10.
48 Lyotard, 'Defining the Postmodern', p. 99.
49 Brecht, *Gesammelte Werke* (hereafter *GW*), vol. 17, p. 948.
50 *GW*, vol. 17, p. 947.
51 There are five versions of *Baal*, written between 1918 and 1955, plus a fragment (see Brecht, *Baal*).
52 Brecht, *Baal*, pp. 173–4.
53 Knopf, *Brecht-Handbuch*, p. 16.
54 Brecht, *Baal*, p. 95.
55 Brecht, *Baal*, p. 105.
56 *GW*, vol. 1, p. 4. All references are to the last version of the play, published in 1955.
57 *GW*, vol. 1, p. 4.
58 *GW*, vol. 1, p. 67.
59 *GW*, vol. 1, p. 64.
60 J. Knopf, *Brecht-Handbuch*, p. 18.
61 *GW*, vol. 1, p. 53; *CP*, vol. 1, pp. 47, 48. The translation of this and subsequent passages from Brecht's plays are cited from Brecht, *Collected Plays* (hereafter *CP*).
62 *GW*, vol. 1, pp. 42–3.
63 *GW*, vol. 1, p. 11.
64 Deleuze and Guattari, 'Rhizome'.
65 Deleuze and Guattari, *Anti-Oedipus*, p. 271.

66 Deleuze and Guattari, *Kafka*, p. 78.
67 *GW*, vol. 1, p. 4.
68 *GW*, vol. 1, pp. 60–61; *CP*, vol. 1, pp. 54–5.
69 *GW*, vol. 1, p. 126.
70 *GW*, vol. 15, p. 67; *CP*, vol. 1, p. 434.
71 *GW*, vol. 17, pp. 96–72.
72 *GW*, vol. 17, pp. 98–9.
73 *GW*, vol. 1, p. 138; *CP*, vol. 1, p. 129.
74 Lacan, *Écrits*, p. 20.
75 *GW*, vol. 1, p. 186.
76 *GW*, vol. 1, p. 130; *CP*, vol. 1, p. 122.
77 *GW*, vol. 1, p. 128; *CP*, vol. 1, pp. 119–20.
78 *GW*, vol. 1, p. 193; *CP*, vol. 1, p. 178.
79 Lewis, *The Art of Being Ruled*, p. 119.
80 Sorel, *Reflections*, p. 19.
81 Sorel, *Reflections*, p. 212.
82 Sorel, *Reflections*, p. 66.
83 Portis, *Georges Sorel*, p. 89. See also his discussion of the break-up of French workers' organisations by 'capillary' action: 'the coalescence of organised political parties was characterised by an effort to dissimulate material interests under ideological aspects', p. 93.
84 Sorel, *Reflections*, p. 131.
85 Sorel, *Reflections*, p. 31.
86 Talmon, 'The Legacy', p. 57.
87 Introduction to a reissue of the Hulme translation of *Reflections*, p. 14.
88 See Mazgaj, *The Action Française*.
89 Lewis, *Rude Assignment*, p. 39.
90 *Blast* No. 1 was published in 1914, *Blast* No. 2 in 1915. I quote from the easily available reprints issued by the Black Sparrow Press in 1981.
91 See Meyers, *The Enemy*.
92 Sorel, *Reflections*, p. 49. See also Vernon, *Commitment and Change*, p. 56, for comments on this 'economic' model of change.
93 Campbell, *The Enemy Opposite*, p. 33.
94 *The Egoist*, 15 June 1914, p. 233.
95 Cork, *Vorticism*, p. 255.
96 Cork, *Vorticism*, p. 262.
97 Pound, *Gaudier-Brzeska*, p. 92.
98 'Our Vortex', *Blast*, No. 1, p. 148.
99 Cork, *Vorticism*, p. 250.
100 Hulme, *Speculations*, p. 104.
101 Stuart Hughes, *Consciousness and Society*, p. 169.
102 Sorel, *Réflexions*, p. 287.
103 Reuleaux, *The Kinematics*, p. 241.
104 See Worringer, *Abstraction and Empathy*.
105 Reuleaux, *The Kinematics*, p. 243.
106 Wees, *Vorticism*, p. 176.
107 *Blast* No. 1, p. 133.
108 *Blast* No. 1, pp. 34–5.

109 *Blast* No. 1, p. 61.
110 *Blast* No. 1, p. 55.
111 I am indebted to Levenson's *The Genealogy of Modernism*, Chapter 5.
112 Lewis, *Time and Western Man*, p. 6.
113 Jameson, *Fables of Aggression*.
114 'Afterword' in Lewis, *The Art of Being Ruled*, p. 439.
115 Lewis, *The Art of Being Ruled*, p. 119.
116 See *Aesthetics and Politics*, p. 12.
117 Cited from Kreuzer, *Die Bohème*, p. 343.
118 *Expressionismus*, p. 294.
119 Willett, *Expressionism*, p. 102.
120 *Expressionismus*, pp. 304–5.
121 Willett, *Expressionism*, p. 111.
122 Kolinsky, *Engagierter Expressionismus*, 1970.
123 Bridgwater, *The German Poets*, p. 16.
124 Bridgwater, *The German Poets*, p. 15; *Expressionismus*, pp. 294–5.
125 Goering's *Seeschlacht*, p. 58.
126 Toller, *Die Wandlung*, p. 21.
127 Toller, *Die Wandlung*, p. 67.
128 *GW*, vol. 15, p. 44.
129 Sokel, *The Writer*, p. 183.
130 *Aesthetics and Politics*, pp. 9–59.
131 *Aesthetics and Politics*, p. 23.
132 *Aesthetics and Politics*, p. 22–3.
133 Paul Nash to Margaret Nash, 4 April 1917, quoted in Nash, *Outline*, p. 193.
134 According to Ruth Clark, reported by Andrew Causey, *Paul Nash*, p. 67.
135 Paul Nash to Margaret Nash, wrongly dated 7 March but probably mid-May 1917, quoted in Nash, *Outline*, p. 187.
136 Paul Nash to Margaret Nash, 6 April 1917, Nash, *Outline*, p. 194.
137 Paul Nash to Margaret Nash, end of March 1917, Nash, *Outline*, p. 191.
138 Nash told Edward Marsh, in a letter of 7 July 1917, that he had just met Nevinson (see Andrew Causey in Nash, *Outline*, p. 73).
139 Campbell Dodgson to C. F. Masterman, 18 October 1917, Imperial War Museum, Nash file.
140 Quoted by Taylor, *The First World War*, p. 194.
141 Paul Nash, letter in Imperial War Museum Nash file, quoted in Paul Nash, *Through The Fire*, n.p.
142 Paul Nash to C. F. Masterman, 16 November 1917, Imperial War Museum Nash file.
143 Paul Nash to Margaret Nash, mid-November 1917, quoted in Nash, *Outline*, pp. 210–11.
144 Paul Nash to C. F. Masterman, 22 November 1917, quoted by Bertram, *Paul Nash*, p. 95.
145 *Column on the March* was reproduced as the colour frontispiece in Nevinson's *Modern War Paintings*, London 1917, a publication that Nash was bound to have seen.
146 Paul Nash to Gordon Bottomley, 16 July 1918, published in *Poet and Painter, Being the Correspondence between Gordon Bottomley and Paul Nash,*

1910–1946, p. 98.

147 Nash, *Outline*, p. 216.

148 King, *Interior Landscapes*, p. 85.

149 Blake, *Tiriel*, pp. 156–7.

150 Blake, 'Milton: Book The Second', in *Tiriel*, p. 431. As Andrew Causey points out in Nash, *Outline*, p. 77, Nash painted a picture with the Blake-like title *Defence of Albion* in the Second World War.

151 Paul Nash to Gordon Bottomley, 1 August 1912, in Abbott and Bertram (eds), *Poet and Painter*, p. 42.

152 A. N. Lee to Alred Yockney, 2 May 1918, Imperial War Museum Nash file.

153 Montague and Salis (Jan Gordon), *British Artists at the Front*, vol. 3.

154 Francis Stopford to John Buchan, 16 August 1917, Imperial War Museum Nash file.

155 All references to the work of Maiakovskii are taken from *Sobranie sochinenii v 13 tomakh*, hereafter *VM*.

156 All references to the work of Khlebnikov are taken from *Sobranie sochinenii*, (hereafter *VK*) and *Tvoreniia*, (hereafter *T*).

157 Cf. David Forgacs's chapter in the present volume.

158 'Civilian shrapnel', *VM*, vol. 1, p. 304.

159 'To Those Who Take Up the Paintbrush', *VM*, vol. 1, p. 308.

160 'Civilian Shrapnel', *VM*, vol. 1, p. 309.

161 'Poets on Landmines', *VM*, vol. 1, p. 306.

162 'War and Language', *VM*, vol. 1, p. 328.

163 'War and Language', *VM*, vol. 1, p. 325.

164 'Battles 1915–1917: A New Teaching About War', *VK*, vol. 3, p. 413–34.

165 'Wonderful Nonsense', *VM*, vol. 1, p. 92.

166 'War is Declared', *VM*, vol. 1, pp. 64–5.

167 'The Funeral Pyre', *T*, 94.

168 'Where, like the hair of a girl', *T*, 104.

169 'War in a Mousetrap', *T*, 456.

170 Barooshian, *Russian Cubo-Futurism*, p. 110.

171 Vs. Ivanov, *Moskovskii golos*, 2 December 1914, p. 4.

172 Briusov, 'Posledniaia Voina', p. 83.

173 Markov, *Russian Futurism*, p. 286.

174 'War and the Universe', *VM*, vol. 1, p. 229.

175 'Cloud in Trousers', *VM*, vol. 1, pp. 173–196.

176 'War and the Universe', *VM*, vol. 1, pp. 211   212.

177 'War in a Mousetrap', *T*, p. 456.

178 'War in a Mousetrap', *T*, p. 455.

179 'War in a Mousetrap', *T*, pp. 461–62.

180 'War in a Mousetrap', *T*, p. 463.

181 'War in a Mousetrap', *T*, p. 465.

182 'War in a Mousetrap', *T*, p. 458.

183 'War in a Mousetrap', *T*, p. 457.

184 'War in a Mousetrap', *T*, p. 458.

185 *VK*, vol. 5, pp. 258–9.

186 'War and the Universe', *VM*, vol. 1, p. 225.

187 'Ballad about a King and a Bedbug', in V. Maiakovskii, *Stikhotvoreniia i p'esy*,

pp. 73–4.
188 '150,000,000', *VM*, vol. 2, pp. 113–66.
189 'Life', *T*, 112.
190 ' "E-e! Y-ym!" – All in a Sweat', *T*, p. 135.
191 'Night search', *T*, pp. 317–30.
192 Aseev, 'The Sense of the New', p. 3.
193 Lopez Vazquez, *Los Caprichos*.
194 Klingender, *Goya*, pp. 152–3; Glendinning, *Goya*, p. 95.
195 Valle-Inclán, *Obras completas* (hereafter OC), vol. 2, pp. 629–67.
196 OC, vol. 2, p. 643.
197 OC, vol. 2, p. 660.
198 Neruda, *España en el corazón*, pp. 64–6.
199 Vallejo, *Obras completas*, p. 341.
200 *The Poems of Wilfred Owen*, pp. 59–60.
201 See Sheppard, 'German Expressionist Poetry', pp. 387–8.
202 Hilton, *Picasso*, pp. 244–5.
203 Russell, *Picasso's Guernica*.
204 Maudsley, *The Russian Civil War*, p. 287.
205 *Literaturnye manifesty*, vol. 1.
206 *Epokha gazetnoi strokoi*, p. 65.
207 See Katherine Hodgson's chapter in the present volume.
208 *Literaturnye manifesty*, vol. 1.
209 Cited from *Bolshevik Visions*, pp. 400–1.
210 Lavrin, *V strane vechnoi voiny*, cited from *RLA*.
211 *T*, pp. 619–23.
212 *T*, 1.
213 Brooks, 'The Breakdown', p. 157.
214 Cf. Nadine Gordimer's explanation for the return to realism in 'The Essential Gesture'.
215 Babel, *Izbrannoe*, pp. 5–6.
216 *Bolshevik Visions*, pp. 62–6.
217 *Bolshevik Visions*, pp. 344, 399.
218 IRSl, p. 626.
219 Williams, *Artists in Revolution*, p. 56.
220 *Bolshevik Visions*, pp. 340–3.
221 *Proletarskaia kul'tura*, Nos. 9–10 (1919), pp. 44–5.
222 *Proletarskie pisateli*, p. 318.
223 Gastev, *Poeziia*, p. 205.
224 Stites, *Revolutionary Dreams*, pp. 152–7.
225 *Zhivaia voda*, pp. 96–7.
226 The All-Soviet Union of Poets, founded 1918.
227 'The Literary Front', founded in 1920 in association with Narkompros.
228 'L'vinyi vyvodok', *Okrylennye vremenem*, pp. 94–104.
229 Cf. Clark, *The Soviet Novel*; Ermolaev, 'Rozhdenie'; Brown, *Russian Literature*.
230 Boretskaia, *Kak oni umirali*.
231 Boretskaia, *V zheleznom kruge*.
232 Boretskaia, *Gnev narodnyi*.
233 Vitman, *Vosem' let*, p. 317.

234 Zyrianov, *Krovianaia zemlia.*
235 Brooks, 'The Breakdown', p. 157.
236 Cohen, *Bukharin,* p. 204.
237 Cohen, *Bukharin,* p. 186.
238 See above, p. 91.
239 *Literaturnoe nasledstvo,* vol. 70, p. 38.
240 Gordimer, 'The Essential Gesture'.
241 All references to *Mort à crédit*) (hereafter *MC*) and *Voyage au bout de la nuit* (hereafter *V*) are to Volume 1 of the Pléiade edition of Céline's *Collected Works,* Paris, 1981.
242 *MC,* pp. 560–70. Although there is much to suggest that Ferdinand in *MC* and Ferdinand Bardamu in *V* are the same character, the question of the continuity between them is not entirely straightforward. Hence the clear distinction between the former as 'Ferdinand' and the latter as 'Bardamu' maintained here.
243 *V,* p. 25.
244 *MC* p. 1011.
245 *V,* p. 334.
246 *V,* p. 511.
247 *V,* p. 160.
248 *V,* p. 155.
249 *MC,* p. 520.
250 *MC,* p. 676.
251 *MC,* p. 1003.
252 *V,* p. 288.
253 *V,* p. 37.
254 *V,* p. 23–4.
255 *V,* p. 82.
256 *V,* p. 308.
257 *V,* p. 383.
258 *V,* p. 306.
259 *V,* p. 80.
260 *V,* p. 236.
261 *V,* p. 220.
262 *V,* p. 235.
263 *V,* p. 12.
264 *V,* p. 418.
265 *V,* p. 289.
266 *V,* p. 373.
267 *MC,* p. 568.
268 *MC,* p. 557.
269 *V,* p. 200.
270 *V,* p. 54.
271 *V,* p. 90.
272 *V,* p. 40.
273 *V,* p. 228.
274 *V,* p. 337.
275 *V,* p. 272.
276 *V,* p. 50.

277 V, p. 172.
278 MC, p. 514.
279 V, p. 496.
280 V, p. 439.
281 MC, p. 724.
282 V, p. 296.
283 MC, p. 560.
284 V, p. 327.
285 V, p. .
286 V, p. 216.
287 MC, p. 626, 775, 643, 541.
288 V, p. 95.
289 V, p. 409.
290 V, pp. 95–6.
291 V, p. 314.
292 V, p. 194.
293 V, p. 473.
294 V, pp. 120–1.
295 V, p. 220.
296 V, p. 201.
297 V, p. 352.
298 Céline, 'Hommage', pp. 22–4.
299 V, p. 59.
300 Céline, *Entretiens*, p. 19.
301 See Godard's Introduction to V, p. X and fn. 1.
302 Hindus, *Céline*, p. 143.
303 Nietzsche, *Werke in drei Bänden*, vol. II, p. 73.
304 Conzelmann, *Der andere Dix*. For general accounts of Dix's works in English, see Löffler, *Otto Dix*; Karcher, *Dix*.
305 Cf. Conzelmann, *Der andere Dix*, pp. 121f, 182.
306 Conzelmann, *Der andere Dix*, pp. 130–3.
307 Willett, *The New Sobriety*, pp. 52–4.
308 Conzelmann, *Der andere Dix*, pp. 142f–67ff.
309 Källai, 'Ďmonie und Satire' (quoted in Conzelmann, *Der andere Dix*, p. 143).
310 See Eberle, 'Otto Dix', pp. 452–4.
311 See E. Timms, 'Treason of the intellectuals?'; H. Ridley, 'Irrationalism, Art and Violence'.
312 For a precise account of Jünger's ideological development in the 1920s, see M üller, *Der Krieg*.
313 Quotations are taken from Jünger, *Sämtliche Werke* (hereafter *SW*). The wording of the passages quoted has been verified as consistent with early editions of the texts in question.
314 Conzelmann, *Der andere Dix*, p. 121.
315 *SW*, vol. VII, pp. 21–3.
316 Müller, *Der Krieg*, p. 235f.
317 *SW*, vol. VII, pp. 100, 103.
318 *SW*, vol. VII, p. 54.
319 Fromm, *The Anatomy*, p. 274f.

320 See Stern, *Ernst Jünger; von Krockow, Die Entscheidung; Barnouw, Weimar Intellectuals*, pp. 194–230.
321 Herf, *Reactionary Modernism*.
322 *SW*, vol. VII, p. 18.
323 *SW*, vol. VII, p. 19.
324 *SW*, vol. VII, p. 22.
325 *SW*, vol. IX, p. 60f.
326 *SW*, vol. VII, p. 20.
327 *SW*, vol. I, p. 473.
328 Bohrer, *Die Ästhetik*, pp. 140–3.
329 Eksteins, *Rites of Spring*; cf. Michael Howard in *The Times Literary Supplement*, 9 February 1990, p. 138.
330 Musil, 'Geist und Erfahrung', 1042–3.
331 Eksteins, *Rites of Spring*, p. 144.
332 See Fussell, *The Great War*, pp. 75–113.
333 For the most recent findings, see *Nationalsozialismus und Modernisierung*, 1991.
334 Eksteins, *Rites of Spring*, pp. 80, 303, 314.
335 For an introduction to Zweig see Midgley, *Arnold Zweig*; for an interpretation of *Erziehung vor Verdun* see Müller, *'Militanter Pazifismus'*.
336 Zweig, *Erziehung vor Verdun*, p. 245.
337 Snow, *The Two Cultures*. The piece was originally given as the Rede Lecture in 1959. It covers a wide range of issues, predominantly that of equality between the rich nations of the West and the poor nations of the developing world. The work quickly acquired notoriety. Although it was read by some as an attack on literature and by others as a hymn of praise to everything scientific, it is primarily a call for an education which would reconcile the intellectual demands of the sciences with those of the humanities.
338 Hugo, *Les Feuilles d'automne*, p. 184.
339 Balzac, *La Fille aux yeux d'or*, pp. 165, 176.
340 Baudelaire, 'Assommons les pauvres', in *Petits pòmes en prose*, no. XLIX.
341 I am borrowing the word-play 'trans-formations' from Lyotard, *Les TRANS-formateurs DUchamp*.
342 'Blast' also suggests a hygienic gale blowing from the north. The emblematic representation of the vortex which appears in the first pages of *Blast* is simultaneously a figuration of a storm-cone with the apex up: a signal used by coastguards to represent strong winds from the north.
343 Dada, p. 28.
344 Dada, p. 29.
345 Huidobro, *Epoque de création*, in *Dada*, p. 31.
346 Cork, *Vorticism*, vol. 2, p. 331.
347 Breton, *Manifestes du surréalisme*, p. 37.
348 Blanchot, 'Réflexions sur le surréalisme'.
349 Marinetti and Nevinson, 'Vital English Art'.
350 Apollinaire, 'Zone', in *Alcools*, p. 39.
351 Apollinaire, 'Zone', in *Alcools*, p. 40.
352 Apollinaire, *Les Peintres cubistes*, p. 77.
353 Marinetti, 'Le Futurisme'. The manifesto is also included in Marinetti, *Le*

Futurisme, pp. 141–54; *Futurism*, p. 6; *Futurist Manifestos*, pp. 19–24.

354 Breton, *Nadja*, p. 187.

355 *Futurist Manifestos*, 97.

356 *Blast*, no. 1, 1914, p. 30.

357 See *Futurism*, pp. 94, 99, 164. 'L'Antitradition futuriste' was originally published in *Lacerba*, September 1913. Reprinted in Apollinaire, *Oeuvres complètes*, vol. 3, p. 876.

358 Cork, *Vorticism*, vol. 1, pp. 255–6.

359 *Blast*, no. 1, p. 144.

360 *Futurist Manifestos*, pp. 98–9.

361 Apollinaire, *Calligrammes, poems of peace and war*. For an extended discussion of some of Apollinaire's ideograms see Mathews, *Reading Apollinaire. Theories of Poetic Language*, Chapters 2 and 3.

362 'Long Live the Vortex', *Blast*, no. 1, p. 7; 'A Review of Contemporary Art', *Blast*, no. 2, p. 45. See also ' "Life is the Important Thing!" ', *Blast*, no. 1, pp. 129–31.

363 Cork, *Vorticism*, vol. 2, p. 327.

364 Apollinaire, *Oeuvres complètes*, vol. 3, p. 884.

365 *Blast*, no. 1, p. 141.

366 Cork, *Vorticism*, vol. 2, p. 331.

367 Freud, 'On Narcissism', p. 90.

368 *Blast*, no. 1, p. 134.

369 For a further account of the response to Dalì's 'paranoiac-critical' procedure from other Surrealists, see Breton, 'Le Cas Dalì'.

370 Freud, 'On Narcissism', pp. 79–80.

371 Freud, 'Beyond the Pleasure Principle', pp. 275–335.

372 Delaunay, *Du Cubisme à l'art abstrait*, p. 115.

373 Cork, *Vorticism*, vol. 2, p. 337.

374 Apollinaire, *Les Peintres cubistes*, p. 76.

375 Apollinaire, *Les Peintres cubistes*, p. 55. For an extended account of Apollinaire's poetic thinking on 'avant-garde' art see Mathews, *Reading Apollinaire*, pp. 19–41.

376 'Pour détruire, en somme, il faut pouvoir *sauter*. Mais sauter où? dans quel langage? ... Tandis qu'en décomposant, j'accepte d'accompagner cette décomposition, de me décomposer moi-même, au fur et à mesure: je dérape, m'accroche et entraîne' (Barthes, *Roland Barthes*, p. 68).

377 Unless otherwise indicated, all italics, ellipses and translations are the author's.

378 An illustration from *La Révolution surréaliste* 12, it is reproduced as Figure 7 in *Visions and Blueprints*.

379 From Amnesty International's *Urgent Action Scheme* booklet, London, n.d.

380 André Breton, *Nadja*, p. 190.

381 Baudelaire, *Oeuvres complètes*, p. 46.

382 Baudelaire, *Oeuvres complètes*, p. 123.

383 Barrie, *Peter Pan*, p. 87.

384 Hugo, *Les Contemplations*, p. 462.

385 Hugo, *Les Contemplations*, p. 338–9.

386 Leconte de Lisle, *Poèmes barbares*, p. 171.

387 Flaubert, *Correspondance II*, p. 204.

388 I quote from a facsimile of the Figaro text. The Lausanne edition of the work is

full of typographical inaccuracies and, most significantly, omits the words 'le féminisme' from item 10.

389 The ellipsis is Marinetti's.
390 Cf. David Forgacs's chapter in this volume.
391 Marinetti, *L'Alcova di acciaio*, p. 121.
392 Saint-Exupéry, *Vol de Nuit*, p. 23.

Bibliography

Aesthetics and Politics: Ernst Bloch, Georg Lukács, Bertolt Brecht, Walter Benjamin, Theodor Adorno (London, 1977)

The Anarchists (2nd edn, London, 1979)

Apollinaire, G. *Alcools*, ed. G. Rees (London, 1975)

    Calligrammes, poems of peace and war, trans. A. Hyde Greet and S. I. Lockerbie (Berkeley and London, 1980)

    Oeuvres complètes, 4 vols (Paris, 1965)

    Les Peintres cubistes. Méditations esthétiques (Paris, 1980)

Aseev, N., 'The Sense of the New', *Literatura i iskusstvo* (3 April 1943), p. 3

Babel, I. *Izbrannoe* (Kiev, 1989)

Badaloni, N. *Il marxismo di Gramsci. Dal mito alla ricomposizione politica* (Turin, 1975)

Ballestrini, N. *The Unseen* (London, 1990)

Balzac, H. *La Fille aux yeux d'or*, in *La Duchesse de Langeais*, suivi de *La Fille aux yeux d'or* (Paris, 1958)

Barnouw, D. *Weimar Intellectuals and the Threat of Modernity* (Bloomington and Indianapolis, 1988)

Barooshian, V. D. *Russian Cubo-Futurism 1910–1930: A Study in Avant-Gardism* (Paris and The Hague, 1974)

Barrie, J. M. *Peter Pan and Wendy* (London, 1988)

Barthes, R. *Roland Barthes* (Paris, 1975)

Baudelaire, C. *Petits poèmes en prose (le spleen de Paris)* (Paris, 1987)

    Oeuvres complètes, (Paris, 1968)

Baudrillard, J. *In the Shadow of the Silent Majorities* (New York, 1983)

Bernstein, C. 'Performance as News' in *Performance in Postmodern Culture* (Madison, Wisconsin, 1977)

Bertram, A. *Paul Nash. The Portrait of an Artist* (London, 1955)

Blake, W. 'Tiriel', William Blake. *Complete Poetry and Prose*, ed. G. Keynes (London, 1939)

Blanchot, M. 'Réflexions sur le surréalisme', in *La Part du feu* (Paris, 1949)

Bohrer, K. H. *Die Ästhetik des Schreckens. Die pessimistische Romantik und Ernst Jüngers Frühwerk* (Munich, 1978)

Bolshevik Visions: First Phase of the Cultural Revolution in Soviet Russia, ed. W. G. Rosenberg (Ann Arbor, 1984)

Gnev narodnyi (Moscow, 1924)

Boretskaia, M. *Kak oni umirali* (Ekaterinodar, 1920)

V zheleznom kruge. Stranichki grazhdanskoi voiny v Rossii (Moscow–Leningrad, 1924)

Brecht, B. *Collected Plays* (CP), vols 1 –, trans. J. Willet and R. Mannheim, (London, 1970)

Gesammelte Werke (GW), 20 vols (Frankfurt, 1967–82)

Breton, A. 'Le Cas Dalì', in *Le Surréalisme et la peinture* (New York, 1945), pp. 144–7, and in *Surrealism and Painting*, trans. S. Watson Taylor (London, 1972), pp. 130–5

Nadja (Paris, 1964)

Bridgwater, P. *The German Poets of the First World War* (London and Sydney, 1985)

Briusov, V. 'Posledniaia Voina', *Voina v russkoi lirike* (Petrograd, 1915)

Brooks, J. 'The Breakdown of Production and Distribution of Printed Material, 1917 – 1927', *Bolshevik Culture: Experiment and Order in the Russian Revolution*, eds. A. Gleason and R. Stites (Bloomington, 1985), pp. 151–74

Brown, E. J. *Russian Literature since the Revolution* (Harvard, 1982)

Campbell, S. E.*The Enemy Opposite: the Outlaw Criticism of Wyndham Lewis* (Ohio, 1988)

Causey, A. *Paul Nash* (Oxford, 1980)

Céline, L.-F. *Collected Works* (Paris, 1981)

Entretiens avec le professeur Y (Paris, 1955)

'Hommage à Zola', in *Louis-Ferdinand Céline* (Paris, 1972)

'Interview avec Merry Bromberger', *Cahiers Céline*, I, 1976

Clark, K. *The Soviet Novel: History as Ritual* (Oklahoma, 1981)

Cohen, S. F. *Bukharin and the Bolshevik Revolution* (New York, 1971)

Conzelmann, O. *Der andere Dix. Sein Bild vom Menschen und vom Krieg* (Stuttgart, 1983)

Cork, R. *Vorticism and Abstract Art in the First Machine Age*, 2 vols (London, 1976)

Coudenhove-Kalergi, R. *The Totalitarian State Against Man* (London, 1938)

Dada, eine literarische Dokumentation, ed. R. Huelsenbeck (Hamburg, 1964)

Delaunay, R. *Du Cubisme à l'art abstrait* (Paris, 1957)

Eberle, M. 'Otto Dix and "Neue Sachlichkeit" ', in *German Art in the 20th Century. Painting and Sculpture 1905–1985*, ed. C. M. Joachimedes, N. Rosenthal and W. Schmied (London, 1985), pp. 452–4

Eksteins, M. *Rites of Spring. The Great War and the Birth of the Modern Age* (London, 1989)

Epokha gazetnoi strokoi. Pravda 1917–1967 (Moscow, 1968)

Ermolaev, G. 'Rozhdenie sotsialisticheskogo realizma', *Sintaksis* (1965) pp. 295–313

Expressionismus. Manifeste und Dokumente zur deutschen Literatur, 1910–1920 ed. T. Anz and M. Stark (Stuttgart, 1982)

Fitzpatrick, S. *The Commissariat of the Enlightenment. Soviet Organization of Education and the Arts under Lunacharsky* (Cambridge, 1970)

Flaubert, G. *Correspondance II*, ed. J. Bruneau (Paris, 1980)

Freud, S. 'Beyond the Pleasure Principle', in *Freud* (Harmondsworth, 1984)
   'On Narcissism: an Introduction', in *Freud* (Harmondsworth, 1984)
Fromm, E. *The Anatomy of Human Destructiveness* (Harmondsworth, 1982)
Fussell, P. *The Great War and Modern Memory* (Oxford, 1975)
Futurism, ed. C. Tisdall and A. Bozzolla (London, 1977)
Futurist Manifestos, ed. U. Apollonio (London, 1973)
Gastev, A. *Poeziia rabochego udara* (Moscow, 1918)
Glendinning, N. *Goya and his Critics* (New Haven and London, 1977)
Goering, R. *Seeschlacht. Tragödie* (Stuttgart, 1972)
Gorlov, N. *Russkii futurism* (Moscow, 1924)
Gordimer, N. 'The Essential Gesture: Writers and Responsibility', *Granta*, 15 (1985), pp. 135–1
A Gramsci Reader, ed. David Forgacs (London, 1988)
Grimaldi, U. A. & Bozzetti, G. *Farinacci. Il più fascista* (Milan, 1972)
Herf, J. *Reactionary Modernism. Technology, Culture and Politics in Weimar and the Third Reich* (Cambridge, 1984)
Hilton, T. *Picasso* (London, 1976)
Hindus, M. *Céline tel que je l'ai vu* (Paris, 1969)
Hitler, A. *Mein Kampf*, trans R. Manheim (London, 1974)
Hugo, V. *Les Contemplations* (Paris, 1969)
   Les Orientales, Les Feuilles d'automne (Paris, 1964)
Hulme, T. E. *Speculations: Essays on Humanism and the Philosophy of Art*, ed. H. Read (1st edn London, 1924; reprinted 1987)
Istoriia russkoi sovetskoi literatury (IRSL), 4 vols (Moscow, 1967)
Ivanov, V. *Moskovskii golos*, 2 December (1914)
Jameson, F. *Fables of Aggression: Wyndham Lewis, the Modernist as Fascist* (Berkeley, Los Angeles and London, 1979)
Johansson, K. *Aleksej Gastev. Proletarian Bard of the Machine Age* (Stockholm, 1983)
Jünger, E. *Sämtliche Werke (SW)* (Stuttgart, 1978–)
Källai, E. 'Dèmonie und Satire', *Das Kunstblatt*, XI (1927–28), pp. 97–9
Karcher, E. *Dix* (Cologne, 1988)
Khlebnikov, V. *Sobranie sochinenii (VK)*, 4 vols Munich, (1968–72)
   Tvoreniia (S), Moscow, 1986
King, J. *Interior Landscapes. A Life of Paul Nash* (London, 1987)
Klingender, F. W. *Goya in the Democratic Tradition* (London, 1968)
Kolinsky, E. *Engagierter Expressionismus. Politik und Literatur zwischen Weltkrieg und Weimarer Republik* (Stuttgart, 1970)
Kreuzer, H. *Die Bohème. Analyse und Dokumentation der intellektuellen Subkultur vom 19. Jahrhundert bis zur Gegenwart* (Stuttgart, 1971)
Leconte de Lisle, C.-M.-R., *Poèmes barbares* (Paris, 1985)
Levenson, M. *The Genealogy of Modernism. A Study of English Literary Doctrine, 1908–1922* (Cambridge, 1984)
Lewis, W. *The Art of Being Ruled*, ed. Reed Way Dasenbrook (Santa Rosa, 1989)
   'The Physics of the Not-self', in Wyndham Lewis, *Collected Poems and Plays*, ed. Alan Munton (Manchester, 1979), pp. 193–204
   Rude Assigment, ed. T. Foshay (Santa Rosa, 1984)
   Time and Western Man (London, 1927)
Liebknecht, K. *Militarism and Anti-Militarism*, trans. G. Lock (Cambridge, 1973)

Lifton, R. J. 'Medicalized killing in Auschwitz', *Psychoanalytic Reflections on the Holocaust: Selected Essays*, ed. S. A. Luel and P. Marcus (New York, 1984)

Literaturnye manifesty ot simvolizma k oktiabriu, ed. N. L. Brodskii, vol. 1 (Moscow, 1929)

Löffler, F. *Otto Dix. Life and Work* (New York and London, 1982)

Lopez Vazquez, J. M. B. *Los Caprichos de Goya y su significado* (Santiago de Compostela, 1982)

Luxemburg, R. *The Junius Pamphlet: The Crisis in German Social Democracy* (London, n.d.)

Lyotard, J.-F. *Les TRANSformateurs DUchamp* (Paris, 1977)

Maiakovskii, V. *Sobranie sochinenii v 13 tomakh* (*SS*), (Moscow, 1955)

Stikhotvoreniia i p'esy (Leningrad, 1983)

Marinetti, F. T. *L'Alcova di acciaio* (Milan, 1985)

La battaglia di Tripoli (26 ottobre 1911) (Milan, 1912)

'Bataille, Poids + Odeur', *Poesia italiana del Novecento*, ed. E. Sanguineti (2nd edn, Turin, 1971)

'Che cosa è il futurismo?' in *F. T. Marinetti futurista: inediti, pagine disperse, documenti e antologia critica* (Naples, 1977)

'Le Futurisme', *Le Figaro* 20 February, 1909.

Le Futurisme (Paris, 1911)

Le Futurisme (Lausanne, 1980)

Guerra sola igiene del mondo (Milan, 1915)

'Manifesto tecnico della letteratura futurista', *Sintesi del futurismo. Storia e documenti*, ed. L. Scrivo (Rome, 1968)

Taccuini 1915–1921, ed. A. Bertoni (Bologna, 1987)

Marinetti T.-F. and Nevinson, C. 'Vital English Art. Futurist Manifesto', *The Observer* 7 June 1914

Markov, V. *Russian Futurism: A History* (London, 1969)

Mathews, T. *Reading Apollinaire. Theories of Poetic Language* (Manchester, 1987)

Maudsley, E. *The Russian Civil War* (London, 1989)

Mayer, A. J. *Why did the Heavens not Darken? The 'Final Solution' in History* (London, 1990)

Mazgaj, P. *The Action Français and Revolutionary Syndicalism* (Chapel Hill, 1979)

Meyers, J. *The Enemy: A Biography of Wyndham Lewis* (London, 1980)

Midgley, D. R. *Arnold Zweig. Eine Einführung in Werk und Leben* (Frankfurt, 1987)

Milne, D. 'Nostalgia', *Edinburgh Review* (1992)

Montague, C. E. and Salis, J. *British Artists at the Front*, vol. 3 (London, 1918)

Müller, H.-H. *Der Krieg und der Schriftsteller* (Stuttgart, 1986)

'Militanter Pazifismus. Eine Interpretationsskizze zu Arnold Zweigs Roman Erziehung vor Verdun', *Weimarer Beiträge*, vol. 36:12 (1990), pp. 1894–1914

Musil, R. 'Geist und Erfahrung. Anmerkungen für Leser, welche dem Untergang des Abendlandes entronnen sind', in *Gesammelte Werke* (Reinbek, 1978), vol. 8, pp. 1042–59.

Nash, P. *Outline: An Autobiography and Other Writings* (London, 1949)

Through The Fire: Paintings, Drawings and Graphic Work from the First World War (London, 1988)

Nationalsozialismus und Modernisierung, ed. M. Prinz and R. Zitelmann (Darmstadt, 1991)

Neruda, P. *España en el corazón: Himno a las glorias del pueblo en guerra (1936–7)*, *Tercera residencia 1935–1945* (Buenos Aires, 1970)

Nietzsche, F. *Werke in drei Bänden*, ed. K. Schlechta (Munich, 1977)

Oliver, D. 'The Diagram Poems', in *Kind* (Lewes, 1987)

Owen, W. *The Poems of Wilfred Owen*, ed. E. Blunden (London, 1964)

Papini, G.'Amiamo la guerra', *Lacerba*, II:20 (1914)

Perloff, M. *The Futurist Moment: Avant-garde, Avant guerre and the Language of Rupture* (Chicago and London, 1986)

Poet and Painter, Being the Correspondence between Gordon Bottomley and Paul Nash, 1910–1946, ed. C. C. Abbott and A. Bertram (London, 1955)

Portis, L. *Georges Sorel* (London, 1980)

Pound, E. *Gaudier-Brzeska: A Memoir* (1st edn London, 1916; reprinted 1960)

Proletarskie pisateli, ed. S. Rodov (Moscow, 1925)

Read, C. *Religion and Revolution in Russia, 1900-1912* (London, 1979)

Reich, W. *The Mass Psychology of Fascism* (Harmondsworth, 1975)

Reuleaux, F. *The Kinematics of Machinery. Outline of a Theory on Machines*, trans. A. B. W. Kennedy (London, 1876)

Ridley, H. 'Irrationalism, Art and Violence: Ernst Jünger and Gottfried Benn', in *Weimar Germany: Writers and Politics*, ed. A. Bance (Edinburgh, 1982), pp. 26–37

Rigotti, F. 'Il medico-chirurgo dello Stato nel linguaggio metaforico di Mussolini', in *Cultura e società negli anni del fascismo* (Milan, 1987)

Russell, F. D. *Picasso's Guernica: the Labyrinth of Narrative Vision* (London, 1980)

Russkii literaturnyi avangard: Materialy i issledovaniia (RLA), ed. M. Marzaduri, D. Rizzi, M. Evzlin (Trento, 1990)

Saint-Exupéry, A. de *Vol de Nuit* (Paris, 1931)

Sarfatti, M. *Dux* (Milan, 1928)

Serge, V. *Memoirs of a Revolutionary* (London, 1963)

Sheppard, R. 'German Expressionist Poetry', in *Modernism*, ed. R. Bradbury and G. Macfarlane (Harmondsworth, 1976)

Sheridan, C. *Russian Portraits* (London, 1922)

Snow, C. P. *The Two Cultures and Scientific Revolution* (Cambridge, 1959)

Soffici, A. *Opere*, vol. II (Florence, 1959)
  Battaglia fra due vittorie (Florence, 1922)
  'Intorno a una carogna', *Il Popolo d'Italia* 13 May 1921

Sokel, W. *The Writer in Extremis* (Stanford, 1959)

Sorel, F. *Lo sciopero generale e la violenza* (Rome, 1906)
  Réflexions sur la violence (Paris, 1908)
  Reflections on Violence, trans. T. E. Hulme (London, 1916)

Stern, J. P. *Ernst Jünger* (Cambridge, 1953)

Stites, R. *Revolutionary Dreams. Utopian Vision and Experimental Life in the Russian Revolution* (Oxford 1989)

Stuart Hughes, H. *Consciousness and Society* (Brighton, 1979)

Talmon, J. C. 'The Legacy of Georges Sorel' *Encounter*, XXXIV:2 (1970)

Taylor, A. J. P. *The First World War. An Illustrated History* (Harmondsworth, 1982)

Theweleit, K. *Male Fantasies, I: Women, Floods, Bodies, History*, trans. S. Conway *et al.* (Cambridge, 1987)

Timms, E. 'Treason of the intellectuals? Benda, Benn and Brecht', in *Visions and*

Blueprints. Avant-garde culture and radical politics in early twentieth-century Europe, ed. E. Timms and P. Collier, (Manchester, 1988), pp. 18–32

Toller, E. *Die Wandlung. Das Ringen eines Menschen* (Potsdam, 1920)

Understanding Sexual Violence: A Study of Convicted Rapists (Boston, 1990)

Valle-Inclàn, R. del *Obras Completas* (OC) (Madrid, 1954)

Vallejo, C. *Obras Completas* (Lima, 1974)

Vernon, R. *Commitment and Change: Georges Sorel and the Idea of Revolution* (Toronto, 1978)

Visions and Blueprints, ed. E. Timms and P. Collier (Manchester, 1988)

Vitman, A. M. et al. *Vosem' let russkoi khudozhestvennoi literatury (1917–1925)* (Moscow and Leningrad, 1926)

von Krockow, C. *Die Entscheidung. Eine Untersuchung über Ernst Jünger, Carl Schmitt, Martin Heidegger* (Frankfurt a.M., 1990)

Weber, M. 'Politics as a Vocation' in *From Max Weber: Essays in Sociology*, eds H. H. Gerth and C. Wright Mills (London, 1970)

Wees, W. C. *Vorticism and the English Avant-Garde* (Manchester, 1972)

Willett, J. *Expressionism* (London, 1970)

Willett, J. *The New Sobriety. Art and Politics in the Weimar Period 1917–1933* (London, 1978)

Williams, G. (ed) *Proletarian Order: Antonio Gramsci, Factory Councils and the Origins of Communism in Italy, 1911–1921* (London, 1975)

Williams, R. *Artists in Revolution. Portraits of the Russian Avant-Garde 1905–1925* (London, 1977)

Woolf, S. 'Italy', *Fascism in Europe*, ed. S. Woolf (London and New York, 1981)

Worringer, W. *Abstraction and Empathy: A Contribution to the Psychology of Style*, trans. M. Bullock (London, 1953)

Zhivaia voda: Sovetskie rasskazy dvatsatykh godov (Moscow, 1986)

Zweig, A. *Erziehung vor Verdun* (Amsterdam, 1935)

Zyrianov, N. *Krovianaia zemlia* (Moscow and Leningrad, 1925)

Index

symbol, 14, 35, 53, 74, 148

Thanatos, 126
Theweleit, K., 15–17, 151, 166
Tikhonov, N., 75–6
Tocqueville, A., de 10
Toller, E., 46–9, 53–4, 153, 166
Trakl, G., 49–52
Tzara, T., 52

Valle-Inclán, R., del 3, 80–2, 87, 155, 166
Vallejo, C., 82–3, 87, 155, 166
Verdun, 46, 121–3, 160, 165, 166
Verlaine, P., 24, 126, 131
Veselyi, A., 94, 96
Voloshin, M., 70
von Killinger, M., 15

Vorticism, 2, 34, 37–41, 57, 129–30, 133–5, 137–9, 153, 160, 162, 166

Wadsworth, E., 41
Weber, M., 20, 166
Weimar, 116, 118, 161, 163, 165–6
Werfel, F., 47
Western Front, 12, 56–7, 63, 107, 113
Wilde, O., 119

Ypres 56–7, 64

Zamiatin, E., 93
Zaum 90
Zdanevich, I., 89
Zola, E., 110, 125–6, 162
Zyrianov, N., 96, 156, 166